Revolutionary Parks

Revolutionary Parks

Conservation, Social Justice, and Mexico's National Parks,
1910–1940

Emily Wakild

THE UNIVERSITY OF ARIZONA PRESS   TUCSON

The University of Arizona Press
© 2011 The Arizona Board of Regents

www.uapress.arizona.edu

Library of Congress Cataloging-in-Publication Data
Wakild, Emily, 1977–
    Revolutionary parks : conservation, social justice, and Mexico's national parks,
1910–1940 / Emily Wakild.
        p. cm. — (Latin American landscapes)
    Includes bibliographical references and index.
    ISBN 978-0-8165-2957-5 (hard cover : alk. paper) 1. National parks and reserves—
Mexico—History—20th century. 2. Nature conservation—Mexico—History—20th
century. 3. Landscape protection—Mexico—History—20th century. 4. Cultural
property—Protection—Mexico—History—20th century. 5. Social justice—Mexico—
History—20th century. 6. Mexico—Politics and government—1910–1946. 7.
Environmental policy—Mexico—History—20th century. 8. Mexico—Environmental
conditions. 9. Mexico—Cultural policy. 10. Mexico—Social policy. I. Title.
    SB484.M4W35 2011
    333.78'30972—dc22

                                                                                    2011010724

Publication of this book is made possible in part by grants from the Publication Fund of
the Office of the Dean of Wake Forest College and the Department of History of Wake
Forest University.

Manufactured in the United States of America on acid-free, archival-quality paper and
processed chlorine free.

16   15   14   13   12   11   6   5   4   3   2   1

For Eric

Contents

Illustrations

Acknowledgments

This book grows out of my enduring fascination with Mexico, a country whose people and landscapes never cease to amaze and delight. Over the course of researching and writing I have received assistance and inspiration from numerous individuals and institutions. A generous Fulbright-Hays Dissertation Research Grant in 2005–2006 afforded me ample research time in Mexico after the Hewlitt Foundation, Tinker Foundation, University of Arizona Department of History, Center for Latin American Studies, and Social and Behavioral Sciences Research Initiative funded my first forays into the archives. Institutional and financial support from Wake Forest University, especially generous support from the Department of History, two awards from the William H. Archie Fund for the Arts and Humanities, and a grant from the Dean of Wake Forest College's Publication Fund, helped with the transformation of the dissertation into this book. A National Endowment for the Humanities Summer Stipend gave timely financial assistance.

Throughout my research I spent less time in actual parks than inside buildings where I relied on the tireless work of librarians and archivists from a wide array of repositories in Mexico City. I thank the Archivo General de la Nación, the Archivo Histórico del Agua, the archives of the Secretaría de Educación Pública, and the Archivo Histórico del INAH for access to their collections. Ramón Arturo Nava Moctezuma and the Archivo General del Registro Agrario Nacional deserve special recognition for generous copies of dozens of maps, plans, and documents. I also spent many hours at the Biblioteca Miguel Lerdo de Tejada and the

Hemeroteca of the Universidad Nacional Autónoma de México in Mexico City. The professional staff at the Fundación ICA and the INAH Fototeca Nacional permitted me to investigate, analyze, and reproduce their fantastic photographs. Outside of Mexico City I made use of several archival gems. I am indebted to Marcela Tostado Gutiérrez and Floriberta Martínez Hernández at the Museo Exconvento Tepoztlán for stimulating conversation and indispensable materials in their fabulous library. Carlos Urraca Varela in the Instituto Estatal de Documentación de Morelos provided crucial information on Morelos forest history. In Amecameca, Doña Rosalia Aguirre Espinoza and Raúl Sánchez Pineda staff an exceptional archive. In the United States, the Oscar Lewis Papers at the University of Illinois–Urbana Champaign provided a treasure trove of information on Tepoztlán. I must also mention the staff at the Z. Smith Reynolds Library at Wake Forest University who admirably fulfilled scores of interlibrary loan requests as I completed the manuscript. Nicole Diaz and especially Emma Lawlor helped with essential tasks related to the visitor logs.

Many teachers, mentors, and colleagues have given of their time and shared their wisdom. My initial interest in history came from Bill Smaldone and Jenny Jopp who lit the fire and fanned the flames. At the University of Arizona I benefited from exceptional educators who shaped my thinking about Latin American and environmental history, including Diana Liverman, Margaret Wilder, Martha Few, Jadwiga Pieper Mooney, David Ortiz, Richard Eaton, Alan Weisman, and especially Katherine Morrissey, Doug Weiner, Kevin Gosner, B. J. Barickman, and Bill Beezley who each provided valuable advice on the genesis and various stages of the dissertation. I hope they each see their own positive influence in my work. Lively conversations with fellow graduate students greatly stimulated my thinking, and I thank them for their patience and impatience with my ideas.

This project would have never begun without the unflappable confidence of my dissertation advisor Bill Beezley, who patiently guided me with his incisive critique, characteristic good humor, and persistent openhanded pleading of "C'mon, Emily!" The initial ideas would have rapidly fallen flat without the perceptive guidance of Chris Boyer, who generously shared sources, notes, books, transportation, meals, perspective, and enthusiasm with me at critical junctures. I am similarly indebted to an extraordinary cadre of Latin American environmental historians who graciously invited me into their community and have nourished my spirit and my work with their insights and open-mindedness; they include but are not limited to Myrna Santiago, Chris Boyer, Rick López, Cynthia Radding, Lise Sedrez, John Soluri, Mark Carey, Sterling Evans, Lane

Simonian, Alejandro Tortolero Villaseñor, Shawn Miller, Richard Tucker, Nik Robinson, Tom Rogers, and Mikael Wolfe. Conversations with Guillermo Palacios, Nelly García Robles, Jack Corbett, Bill French, Charlie McGraw, Brian Price, Michelle Berry, Aurea Toxqui, María Muñoz, Elena Albarrán, Amanda López, Amie Kiddle, Steve Neufeld, Jeff Banister, Robbie Weiss, Louise Walker, Ben Fulwider, and others have shaped my thinking on Mexico. I was honored by the invitation to contribute to this book series and delighted when the terrific editorial work of Patti Hartmann and Kristen Buckles made it a reality. I eagerly await the next volumes.

Many people expended considerable effort reading parts of the manuscript or discussing it with me. Members of the Wake Forest History Department gave important critiques of chapter three and Sterling Evans read early versions of chapter four and showed much interest in the entire project. Michelle Berry offered attentive criticism paired with relentless championing from start to finish. Chris Boyer commented extensively on the entire manuscript, including multiple versions of the first and last chapters, and he graceful steered me away from several catastrophes. Monique O'Connell and Stavroula Glezakos read nearly all of it in weekly installments, and their good judgment refined the book and motivated the writer. Miles Silman contributed many of the best ideas in the conclusion, and it doubtless would have been better still had I listened to more of them. I also benefited tremendously from two anonymous University of Arizona Press readers whose outstanding suggestions improved the book's arguments and presentation.

The obvious secret to academic writing is having a supportive family, and here I have been fortunate. Geoff and Debbie Middaugh nurtured my insatiable hunger for knowledge at a tender age and convinced me that anything was possible. They've offered resolute backing and vital "sabbaticals" ever since. Chuck and Susie Wakild enabled my curiosity with relentless affection and true interest. More than anyone, credit for this book's inspiration and completion goes to Eric, who introduced me to my first Mexican national parks nearly a decade ago. I am grateful for his brilliance, encouragement, and love.

Revolutionary Parks

Introduction

Creating a Common Cultural Patrimony
of Nature

This book tells the story of the unlikely creation of forty national parks in Mexico during the latter stages of the first social revolution of the twentieth century (1910–1940). Mostly within one or two hours of Mexico City, the parks largely protected pine, oak, and fir forests that overlapped with long-standing peasant communities in the highland volcanic plateau. By 1940, national parks encompassed more than 827,000 hectares in fourteen states and Mexico led the world in the number of national parks.[1] Rarely have tropical or postcolonial countries had the ability or the ambition to protect nature on a national scale. Why did Mexico? This book seeks to answer that question.

In short, Mexico's national parks were an outgrowth of revolutionary affinities for both rational science and social justice. For a brief span of time, roughly 1935–1940, Mexicans tried to blend nature protection and environmental justice in a way that rarely happened afterward or elsewhere. Formally trained foresters and experts established parks in places they deemed most critical to restoring the forests around the nation's capital, protecting watersheds for agriculture, and preserving nationally symbolic landforms. At the same time, rural people continued to inhabit these landscapes and use them for a range of activities from growing crops to producing charcoal. Because the revolution embraced the promise of "land to the man who works it," pushing these residents off the land or completely restricting their activities was politically untenable. Sympathy for rural people tempered the plans of scientific conservationists, but a concern for the rapidly degrading environment allowed the defenders of the natural

1

world to enter forcefully into national policies. This fine balance between recognizing the morally valuable, if not always economically profitable, work of rural people and designing a revolutionary state that respected ecological limits proved a radical episode of governmental foresight.

In and around the territory that came to hold these parks, Mexico's national history had unfolded, its buoyant economy reemerged, and the largest populations of citizens lived their lives. As the map of park distribution shows, reformers created so many parks in the physical center of the country that they could hardly be displayed on a map including the entire country. Like a bull's-eye, Mexico City radiated political and economic power outward in addition to boasting the most densely settled population. Parks emerged in this epicenter where more citizens could use them. Visitor logs show that by 1938 more than 50,000 people visited the parks each year, and these visitors included union members, picnicking families, and foreign travelers.[2] Because of the parks' connection to domestic policy, tourists routinely proposed their own suggestions for the

Mexican national parks, ca. 1942. Note the inset at top right of Federal District and the state of Mexico.

parks, from adding playground equipment to building cabins, but a growing number of scientifically trained and politically connected administrators had their own sense of what the parks should accomplish.

As experts like foresters came to hold positions of power within the government, they routinely promoted arguments that intertwined the scientific worth, natural beauty, and national glory found in areas they deemed worthy of national park status. They wanted to protect and bring attention to "one of the few countries on the globe extraordinarily endowed by Nature and hosting the richest and most varied of flora and fauna due to the inter-tropical geographical location and the outstanding mountains that top the Altiplano or Great Central Plateau at an elevation higher than 4,000 or even 5,000 meters."[3] This rugged topography created enormous natural diversity and affirmed the agenda of park planners to "protect the true marvels of nature that cannot be observed in other Nations."[4]

But science did not guide reforms alone: government officials developed national parks within a plan for social reform in a pattern that today might be called sustainability.[5] Recently, scholars have argued that the resilience of Mexico's diverse ecosystems derives from the "persistence of a complex mosaic of past and present traditional land uses" that provided a more sustainable approach to conservation than simply reserving land.[6] The values that supported this mosaic emerged in national conservation strategies of the 1930s. Rather than segregate nature to distant rural landscapes and culture to the domain of cities, parks formed a special part of the far-reaching tapestry of development designed to harness nature's bounty and elevate humanity to its highest potential.

This tapestry, which reached its fullest form under President Lázaro Cárdenas (1934–1940), captured a harmonious vision (despite the chaotic reality) of a landscape configured to draw out productivity from all of the population to benefit rural families and the national economy. Because the revolutionary government had to be responsive to its citizens' demands, changes brought legislation that helped punctuate the countryside with producers' cooperatives, campesino unions, and rural schools. Reformers resurrected and reformulated pre-Columbian patterns of land tenure, especially the community property holdings known as *ejidos*, and neatly stitched these reconfigured land reform plots across the country. Pastures for livestock surrounded ejidos and intermittent irrigation works moistened arid landscapes. Protected reserves of forests laced the edges of these designs, providing a layer of stability for the irrigation projects and helping to regulate the climate. Laborers hewed lumber, families gathered firewood, and nurseries produced saplings for reforestation. A small village in the center of the tapestry, with a school, a museum, and a road, elegantly embedded the residents inside this natural productivity. And the most delicate areas with distinctive features unique to the community or to broader national history were embroidered with the name "national park." Parks formed sanctuaries complementing economic plans for increasing production while simultaneously furthering the political goals of keeping rural people rooted in the land.

Why and how the revolutionary government was able to consider nature conservation a political priority worthy of action (with an annual budget of nearly four million pesos) forms the central inquiry of this study.[7] The unique circumstances that coalesced in Mexico during the mid-1930s fostered notions of environmental protection and helped redefine the meaning of national parks. In particular, the government borrowed from a foreign template that excluded local residents and reformulated it to fit their own society's intention to quicken the pace of inclusion. To understand this process, historians must ask what citizens thought about these parks and how they came to use them. A brief window of opportunity— after civil war dissipated and before world war broke out—allowed federal officials and local residents to construct dozens of national parks with discernable characteristics. The parks represented a common cultural patrimony of nature constructed to confirm the connections between social stability, economic productivity, and landscape conservation.[8] This ethic, designed by federal foresters but contested and shaped by local residents, upheld the centrality of common property to national welfare, promoted a shared national revolutionary culture, articulated the responsibility of government to protect the public inheritance, and raised popular respect and concern for natural spaces. The result delicately balanced national parks like pearls across the country's core.

National parks today are one piece of a sophisticated portfolio of protected natural areas distinguishable in categories ranging from natural monuments to wilderness areas.[9] But no such globally recognized distinctions existed in the 1930s.[10] It is striking that Mexican politicians, scientists, and citizens did not create a cluster of city or state parks or even management reserves. They self-consciously created *national parks* as cultural products, political statements, and environmental gestures. While it might be easy to look at Mexico's early national parks today and say they better fit the definition of state parks or extractive reserves, to these revolutionary citizens they were emphatically national parks.

A chronological account of institutional decisions and individual actions would obscure, rather than illuminate, the unique features of these parks because park creation occurred rapidly with no progression toward a singular goal. Indeed, the declaration of parks produced different results in different places, each of which had strong similarities and important distinctions. To draw out these features this study examines four parks that best illustrate the intersection of five interlocking themes—science, education, productivity, property, and tradition—that were essential to the revolution and to arguments for conservation. This selective, case-based history strives to capture both national trends and local specificity while offering broader lessons about conservation in unexpected places. Namely, it shows that compromises can be forged between economic development and environmental protection when careful concessions and restrictions are enforced on both. Before turning to these themes, this introduction considers global histories of national parks and Mexico's revolutionary context.

A Comparable Concept

National parks have long held a certain cachet in popular and scholarly circles. As one of dozens of nature protection areas designed to steward ecological systems and increase appreciation for nature, parks are also overtly political symbols of state power. In the past 100 years, parks have gone from rare sites to common features. As Mark Dowie notes, "From 1900 to 1950, about six hundred official protected areas were created worldwide. By 1960 there were almost a thousand. Today there are at least one-hundred-and-ten thousand, with more being added every month."[11] In the past four decades the total area of worldwide nature protection has enlarged from an area the size of the United Kingdom to one the size of South America![12] With over a century of formal protections, much is known about the history of conservation, but major regions and decades are missing that change the larger picture. In historical literature on national parks, two interpretations explaining their origins generally hold sway: democratic traditions and the colonial roots. The Mexican case adds a sui generis model that is revolutionary in many ways.

Scholars by and large recognize the formulation of the national park concept to mean an oasis of wild and pristine nature created originally in the United States as the frontier closed and conservationist thinking rose in popularity among elite and urban easterners. Most histories of the national park idea generally date the concept to the gazetting of Yosemite in 1864 or the founding of Yellowstone National Park in 1872. The U.S.

government separated parks from urban areas, sited them in areas remote from large populations, and used them to provide proof that although the United States lacked the cultural heritage of Europe that stretched to antiquity, it held natural monuments that could stand in for man-made achievements. In addition to the classic works of John Muir, scholars have treated national parks as examples of U.S. exceptionality, signs of democratic innovation, and evidence of a profound commitment to elevating the worthiness of wilderness.[13] In this view, national parks as outstanding sites of beauty stood apart from ordinary resources available for exploitation. The foresight to conserve such places in perpetuity similarly marked an exceptional act. Subsequently, conservation has been viewed as a privilege only available for people who no longer rely on their position in the natural world to provide them with daily sustenance. Only by leaving the land did people realize its inherent value.[14] In this way, national parks became products of affluent culture and attributes of civilized and modern societies that advocates assumed would become universal as development spread worldwide.[15]

Other scholars have carefully challenged the idea that national parks spread democratic and modern ideals. These scholars claim that parks proved another way to deepen colonial relationships and exclude native peoples' access to crucial resources, from forests and pastures to hunting grounds.[16] Much of the criticism of parks has come out of studies of wildlife conservation in southern and eastern Africa, although scholars have also reinterpreted the creation of emblematic parks like Yellowstone and Yosemite.[17] In the United States, these scholars have shown government officials forcibly removed the Blackfeet and Miwok peoples from inside park boundaries or restricted their resource use within the park. In Tanzania and South Africa, racialized policies of exclusion provided large animals more rights than local inhabitants. These scholars point out that the park ideal overlooks the breadth of opinions and actions on behalf of the poor, who at times have a much greater stake in the preservation of nature because of their more intimate relationship to it, and who sometimes have created the conditions that maintain the natural features of such inherent value.[18] Such criticisms portray parks as tools of dispossession wielded capriciously by imperial actors to deprive locals of their customary livelihoods.

Missing from this debate are insights from modern Latin America where formal colonial rule had dissipated and native peoples insisted on a role in democratic governance by staging revolutions. Several histories of Latin American conservation do exist, including studies of Brazilian parks that expand understandings of the intellectual roots of conservation in the hemisphere.[19] For Mexico, Lane Simonian has written a masterful consideration of Mexican conservation ideas that chronicles environmental activities from the botanical gardens of the Aztecs to the antipollution campaigns of the 1980s.[20] Other authors offer useful critiques of human-caused environmental destruction.[21] Unfortunately, these do little to put events in the early twentieth century into the context of global park movements. In particular, studies of conservation leave out the relationship between revolutionary social change and nature protection, a relationship foundational to creating an atmosphere in which politicians were willing and able to create parks.

This absence of park histories is particularly striking for a region where the relationship between users and defenders of natural areas is acutely intertwined. In the latter part of the twentieth century, fishermen, rubber tappers, and inventors in Latin American countries engaged their own governments and the appeal of international audiences to impart a pragmatic agenda for natural resource use and protection. On the plains of eastern Colombia, a remarkable group of individuals worked during the 1970s to develop an ecologically sustainable community, and in the same period Costa Ricans established their country as a "green republic."[22] In Bolivia, fishermen at Lake Titicaca sought out government assistance in some matters but strove to keep control of their territories and resources in others.[23] Since 1988, official reserves for rubber tappers in the Amazon have been promoted by local people and their allies as spaces necessary for securing the integrity of the rain forest and tappers' livelihoods with minimal governmental intervention.[24] These examples demonstrate that even before the 1992 Brundtland Commission Report popularized the term *sustainable development*, which became a catchphrase for incorporating native peoples and environmental concerns into development programs, ordinary people made it clear that they would not be ignored.[25]

The inclusion of long-standing residents into park planning has been explained as a recent phenomenon brought about in tandem with U.S. environmentalism that spread awareness about rain forest depletion and biodiversity loss.[26] This narrative credits environmental awareness with the rise of environmental movements in the United States in the 1970s and makes wealthy, white, urban actors the protagonists of "saving the planet." In fact, recognizing how Mexican revolutionaries insisted that their social programs had an environmental face alters these exclusively foreign interpretations. The Mexican version of environmentalism that ascended earlier should be seen as part of a domestic genesis of ideas promoting conscientious and careful management of natural resources. The willingness of government officials to make hard choices, such as to limit extractive uses in certain areas or to deny infrastructure projects, speaks directly to current dilemmas facing parks. The rapidity with which such commitments were abandoned also conveys critical warnings. To understand these ideas, the impetus for revolutionary reform merits consideration.

A Revolutionary Context

The Mexican revolution began as an effort to end the rule of Porfirio Díaz (1876–1911), which had opened the country to immense inflows of British and North American culture and capital. In this period, elites redesigned the capital city in European styles and allowed ownership of the economy, from factories to farms, to fall into foreign hands. The initial attempts to overthrow Díaz came from those who saw his rule infringing on political liberties such as free elections, but the rebel groups quickly escalated to include various factions of rural and urban people who saw themselves as either imbued with native tradition or thoroughly endowed with modern persuasions, or somewhere in between. They were able to depose the dictator by 1911, but the widely ranging aspirations of these social groups led to an intense civil war, one without an obvious resolution. The Constitution of 1917 encapsulated the varied political aims of the revolutionaries and promised that all Mexicans would benefit from access to land, education, and unionization, as well as fair elections. Such promises hardly masked the tensions and disunity among revolutionary leaders and the peasant and proletariat masses. Yet the Constitution afforded the first guarantee that lower-class peoples would be extended the rights and benefits of citizenship in the society to be built after the fighting.[27]

Although violence continued into the 1920s, important steps were taken to stabilize the political system, including the creation of a national party, the National Revolutionary Party (PNR).[28] In 1933, the PNR published a Six-Year Plan articulating concrete goals that matched up with the promises in the Constitution of 1917, and the populace overwhelmingly elected Cárdenas with this plan as a platform for his presidency. He has long been credited with following through on these social goals, which included labor codes and secular public education, as well as the nationalization of oil resources and the redistribution of millions of hectares of land to rural dwellers. While the material gains were impressive, Cárdenas's deepest legacy proved his acuity for formally inscribing the political interactions between social groups and the state.[29] Peasants and workers joined organizations, such as the Mexican Labor Confederation (CTM) or the National Peasant Confederation (CNC), that structured demands and concessions through membership. These arrangements had the secondary effect of helping to organize state efforts to recover from the global economic crisis of the 1930s by facilitating the turn toward import-substituting industrialization and the protection of domestic industries.[30] In this way, the state as constructed by supporters of Cárdenas, or Cardenistas, reached into the daily lives of peoples who had been left behind during Díaz's quest to modernize Mexico along European lines.

Importantly, this process of social reform involved repackaging the popular understanding of the revolution as a unified, and unifying, historical event. Historians have noted how this gendered process created heroes out of martyred leaders and showcased a "myth" of the revolution.[31] The public face of the revolution came to be "performed" by party members and politicians as well as by ordinary citizens in commemorations, annual festivals, and monuments. A refurbished revolutionary story highlighted unity over divisiveness and the core constituency of this new myth was the group of rural people who came to have the political identity of *campesinos*.[32] Campesinos received a contradictory focus as idyllic representations of the benevolence of the revolutionary cause and as receptacles for modernizing reforms that might turn them into productive, industrious citizens. For policy makers, the rural landscape provided an entry point into campesinos' lives. Repurposed forests and mountainous spaces entered into the pantheon of national heroes as embodiments of this contradiction between revering the rural and aspiring for the modern. Inspired in part by national park and conservation movements in the United States, Mexican modernizers no longer strove for a facade of European civilization—they could look to the natural world around them to find unique sites of reverence.

The land, in all of its heterogeneity, became a focal point for federal reforms because of its economic potential and historic importance. Slogans of "Mexico for Mexicans" and "Land and Liberty" encapsulated the popular leanings and nationalist sentiments of the revolution, and they also underscore the role of natural resources. Like schools and labor unions, Cárdenas and his policy makers nationalized the natural world in the 1930s. State intrusion into campesino life mediated through access to land carried material rights and benefits, yet it often meant giving way to condescending outsiders. As a cadre of bureaucrats rose to fill the ranks of the burgeoning state, the distance between those who received state-based benefits and those who administered them mirrored the class distinctions and cultural differences revolutionary promises aimed to ameliorate. Federal scientists, engineers, and other "experts" were sent out to demarcate land reform parcels, to allocate irrigation works, and to decide park boundaries. How (and if) these officials obtained the appropriate information to make such decisions became a highly contested matter in villages across the country, and many disgruntled villagers readily articulated their complaints. That they felt compelled to speak out and located a forum to do so was itself an important feature of these reforms. While such grievances levied charges against particular officials, rural recipients often identified with and applauded the initial state growth geared toward benefiting them and at times they hesitated to dismiss the reforms aimed at their own inclusion, despite deep conflicts with their practitioners. In the political sphere, conflicts over resource allocations were publicly minimized by bureaucrats who published commitments to the revolutionary program and the Six-Year Plan.[33] Despite the flaws, the fact that officials heard villagers' demands at all marked a new chapter in public resource management.

But how could a nation emerging from devastating violence and immersed in a radical social revolution afford to spend time declaring national parks? Nature figured into these radical plans because Cárdenas and other leaders believed that every Mexican had a stake in the environment. Cardenistas predicated their governance on the federal control of land, water, forests, and minerals, and they configured laws to both use and conserve them while increasing numbers of citizens saw natural resources as vital to national well-being. Parks were not whimsical oases for wealthy urbanites—they became tangible representations of how revolutionaries nationalized their natural territory. Understandably, historians have paid attention to the social realms of revolution—labor demands, socialist education, political formation, economic empowerment. Yet in each of these processes, revolutionaries themselves paid specific attention to nature and natural resources. Usefully termed "social landscaping," this vision of state-guided development reliant on natural resources and revolutionary politics sought to expand rural production with the simultaneous aims of social reform.[34] As a result, as much as the bureaucratic machine put in place during the Cárdenas era oversaw people, it also oversaw and regulated the natural world.

One place where national parks seem to have contradicted other reforms is in the realm of land reform. The land reform program has a reputation as the most successful in Latin America, and certainly in terms of acreage redistributed, it stands out with over eighteen million hectares of land distributed to nearly 800,000 rural families.[35] Surprisingly then, historical literature on agrarian reform overlooks forests and parks that extend land tenure debates beyond agriculture. This literature's primary concerns involved peasant interests and related debates about the political orientation of the revolution.[36] There remains more to learn about how land reform rehabilitated ideas of the commons, contributed to a national patrimony, or recognized variations among natural ecologies. Certain authors address the varying quality of ejido lands and the perennial issue of water access, yet in these studies the acquisition of production inputs (i.e., seeds, tools, credit) dominate. In a parallel strand of scholarship, works of environmental history have flourished in recent years helping to explain the environment as a complex facet of these changes, one that informed people's understandings of the revolution in different ways.[37] The environmental side of land reform deserves its own study, but national parks provide a view of a lesser-known, and in many ways complimentary, vision of federal resource control.

Importantly, just as land reform anchored campesinos to the land, the Cardenista vision for the parks did not involve evicting resident campesinos or extinguishing economic activity altogether. Instead, this administration, equipped with a new federal entity created in 1935, the Departamento Forestal y de Caza y Pesca (Department of Forestry, Fish, and Game; hereafter, the Forestry Department), sought to incorporate an extractive resource economy and a landscape of parks into the developing state. The Forestry Department employees promoted a vision that saw nature everywhere— not as a separate, uninhabited wilderness removed by distance and time from the modern trappings of society. Rather than slivers of nature fixed in time or refuges designed to dispossess traditional inhabitants, national parks became part of daily life as dynamic, contested, and inhabited sites with multiple patrons. Mexican national parks earned their status because of the intermingling of nature and society, not their apparent separation.

Despite their inclusion in such sweeping plans, citizens did not agree on what the parks meant. They conferred a tangled significance onto these spaces that allowed parks to fit into the nationalistic agenda of reformers while still meeting the immediate needs of regular citizens. Parks opened up roles for individuals, especially giving foresters a sense of importance and a project to save their country's environmental integrity. Some individuals, such as the nation's principal forester Miguel Ángel de Quevedo, guided park creation on a practical level, whereas other famous personalities, such as the artist Dr. Atl, displayed spectacular enthusiasm for the parks. The individuals and groups connected to the parks came from a spectrum of the population and reveal the inescapable resonance of park creation. Campesinos, foresters, or politicians as groups were neither unified nor homogenous collectivities, but the political atmosphere gave them each a voice and an arena to contest each others' visions. Federal officials planned programs of inclusion, from summer camps to museum displays that conveyed their belief in the appropriate ways to manage parks. Nearby residents benefited from park creation programs that revitalized dwindling forests, provided employment, and increased amenities like roads, but they objected when parks threatened to encroach on customary practices.

Rural inhabitants proved a crucial component of the national parks and were integrated into management plans as much as the mountains and the trees. Rural people provided political legitimacy for federal environmental policy as the revolution's authenticity became hitched to the plight of the poor. They were comrades and compatriots who had earned a right to recognition, although state experts remained skeptical of their capacity for unsupervised control over lands. In maneuvering among the varied constituencies park officials created an umbrella of federal authority over economic activities and used solidarity rather than exclusion to buttress increasing state power. The revolution provided a political opening for ambitious reformers to enact environmental policies and reclaim national spaces.

When citizens fashioned, visited, used, and discussed the parks they revealed the role the environment played in nation-building. Revolutionary idealism limited the ability of government scientists to exclude country people from federal plans and simultaneously provided a legal framework for campesinos to legitimately claim natural resources for their own management. Park plans and social policy coincided in this revolutionary context to provide a safety net for residents who might otherwise have been evicted. Parks did not represent zones of dispossession; they became highly contested areas where Mexicans, from bureaucrats to campesinos, spoke their opinions about national resource control. At the same time, foresters placed concrete limits on the extractive power of residents, although reformers' hesitation to use the military for enforcement made them unable to prevent charcoal fabrication in the parks, for example. Fraught with conflict, the revolutionary process of nationalizing natural resources catalyzed environmental policy at an unexpected, yet logical, moment.

But, the moment proved fleeting. Despite the surge to the forefront of global conservation and the creation of forty parks by 1940, Mexican conservation slowed to a trickle shortly thereafter. Only nine additional parks were added in the years between 1940 and 1976 as national development programs focused on industrialization at any cost. By the late 1970s, the desire for conservation areas once again took hold in governmental circles in response to changes in international science paradigms that elevated the value of tropical nature and species diversity. In the final decades of the century, protected natural areas surged in Mexico but were largely designated as biosphere reserves and areas for the protection of flora and fauna.[38] Unlike the earlier national parks, these spaces protected lands distant from the capital and landscapes seen as exotic and rare, not magnificent and nearby.[39] These later developments reveal the uniqueness of the early national parks that tied conservation to radical social reforms. This truncated arc of conservation helps explain the absence of a reputation for conservation in Mexico today but the chronological story does not alone provide insight into the historical reasons for establishing parks. Conservation surfaced initially connected to themes of social justice and rural development but then dropped out of political favor for decades only to reemerge detached from its social roots. This trajectory moved Mexican conservation from the forefront of global initiatives to a distant relic, despite the fact that what revolutionaries created provides an intellectual heir to many of today's protected areas and most compelling conservation strategies.

This study probes the intersection of environmentalism and justice, adding fresh insight into interpretations of environmentalism and moving the environmental justice framework beyond urban and industrial examples. It makes the methodological innovation of considering bodies of literature on environmental conservation and revolutionary change interdependently to understand a type of revolutionary environmentalism. The actions and policies of Mexican park promoters in the 1930s share similarities with recurring models in global park literature, but in many ways they transcend the bifurcation of government and citizen because of the revolution's orientation. Peasants, politicians, and practitioners put into place parks that linked environmental policy to their nation and their revolution. In doing so, they expressed vibrant, radical opinions about the importance of national parks in a just, equitable, and peaceful society. Rather than a point of exclusion, parks served to unite people by giving priority to the one thing everyone had in common—a life shaped by the resources of nature. This did not result from the benevolence of elite scientists or their compassion for the plight of poor residents. Compromises on resource use came about through the actions of local peoples demanding their rights and articulating their custodianship abilities. Because of the social revolution, campesinos had the authority to make demands of their own. Although they rarely conceded outright, government officials could not ignore such demands because that would mark them as traitors in their own revolution.

Instead of using the U.S. wilderness ideal to shape their parks, Mexicans promoted a concept of human integration with nature. They recognized that landscapes could be harmed or damaged in various ways—such as the clear-cutting of much of the land around the basin of Mexico City, which led to intense erosion and flooding in the capital—but they believed firmly in the resiliency of nature and their own ability to reforest critical areas. They saw the detrimental effects of mistletoe and of clearing too many forests for agriculture. However, the lack of an *idea* of wilderness meant they never protected *actual* wilderness and let such wild places fade away. The animal-less, quiet woods are hollow approximations of the nature that once sheltered the capital and that these parks still exist has not been nearly enough to conserve healthy natural processes into the present.[40]

The record of inclusion also shows that campesinos, local peoples, and indigenous communities did not defend their resources out of an innate affinity for and knowledge of the wild world. They never lived as proto-typical "noble savages" stuck in a pre-Columbian era.[41] Instead, when they defended their environment they did so for modern, rational reasons, among them, a socioeconomic status that mandated laboring directly with nature, prior exclusion that had once placed them outside mainstream channels of citizenship, and a lived experience of tradition and innovation that continually revised their understanding of how natural cycles and systems worked. In other words, rural people thought about their environment because it formed part of their lives. Neither static symbols representing wildness nor irreverent transgressors, rural communities shaped their nation's relationship with the natural world. Few, if any, hoped to leave nature untouched, but thousands thought about the generations that would follow them and hoped to conserve the benefits of thick forests and healthy waters for recreation, agriculture, and daily life. This meant the nature these parks created was explicitly for people, not for nature alone.

A Common Cultural Patrimony of Nature

By 1940, Mexicans could boast more national parks than any other country in the world.[42] More important, Mexican officials had constructed a new model of conservation tempered by the quest for matching rural development with scientific know-how. Mexico's park model can be seen as a precursor to contemporary ideas of sustainability because it constructed

Iztaccíhuatl from the north, with Popocatépetl in the background, ca. 1940.

a compelling and inclusive vision for the interdependence of social and environmental policy. The unlikely story of Mexican park creation should lead us to rethink the reach of the Mexican revolution and the insularity of polarized debates over global conservation. Lessons from the era of revolutionary environmentalism demonstrate the symmetry between sustaining social justice along with protecting nature and the precarious risks involved with balancing both.

In this way, the history of how Mexicans used parks to construct a common cultural patrimony of nature contributes to the understanding of several major ideological issues. First, in park creation both federal officials and their revolutionary brethren used access to the natural world to promote their own visions of the future. Revolutionary bureaucrats and planners wove a web of authority and stability through education campaigns, public festivals, tourist displays, and summer camps. They also unified disparate people through a revised legal apparatus. The Constitution of 1917 provided a starting point for any federal policy and carried the corollary benefit of affording campesinos political influence. Additional federal laws, like the 1926 Forestry Law and the Six-Year Plan of 1934–1940, stated a coherent national agenda for managing forests and provided a means for implementing the Constitution. While nationalistic plans appeared from upper levels of the federal government, campesinos' demands reordered political agendas as they also could draw on the Constitution to assert communal claims to land management.

Second, establishing federal authority over natural resources triggered a fierce debate over the commons, that is, community-owned land. The lengthy Spanish colonial structure of land tenure recognized and relied on indigenous common properties in fields, woods, and pastures. Liberal reforms in the nineteenth century attempted to eradicate these in favor of individual landownership, although how precisely this unfolded remains ambiguous.[43] Widely reduced by the eve of the revolution, communal property did not disappear, and many residents who lost their holdings clung to the memory of these lands. With the revolution, associations of campesinos reasserted their collective rights and reclaimed the duties that came alongside them. At the same time, new common property emerged in park form. To foresters, parks created a public good, a commons available for the enjoyment of all citizens and their families. For some campesinos, long-standing traditions of small-scale extraction resulted in the superior condition of park areas. In their view, local customs provided more accurate guidelines for fair use and such issues were not easily resolved. In contrast to the absence of democratic participation before the revolutionary era, attention to inclusive governance in the 1930s flourished on many fronts ranging from land reform to expressions of indigenous cultural inheritance. Rather than confrontational, scientific experts' plans acceded to pluralistic aims of justice.

Third, park creation fit into the widespread process of cultural incorporation that followed revolutionary fighting. Led by intellectuals and artists like José Vasconcelos, Manuel Gamio, and Diego Rivera, national reconciliation called for the integration of the nation's indigenous past into notions of nationalism. Certain national parks emphasized pre-Columbian civilizations by highlighting relics of their sophistication, including the ancient pyramid in El Tepozteco National Park (chap. 5). This nationalist message repudiated political strongmen and memorialized heroic revolutionary figures while maintaining that the country had the natural and cultural wealth for a prosperous future. For example, park planners did not name a national park after Hernán Cortés, the Spanish conquistador but instead honored La Malinche (chap. 3), the Indian translator woman who assisted him. Along these lines, Benito Juárez, the first indigenous president of Mexico who served five terms between 1858 and 1872, had

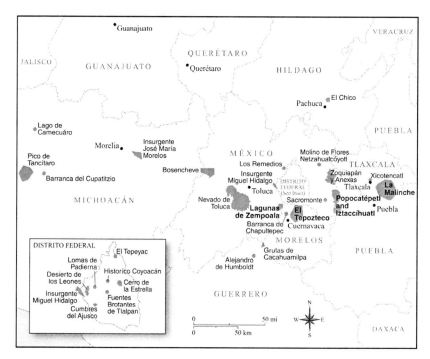

National Parks in the Valley of Mexico, ca. 1940.

a national park named in his honor near his birthplace in Oaxaca. Art and literature came to the service of the revolutionary agenda and creating parks out of the idyllic natural world also aimed to bring rural people into the national story. Through community schools, public murals, radio programs, indigenous congresses, racial theories, and even national parks, intellectuals promoted the idea of an ethnically diverse, but unified, citizenry. Revolutionary environmentalism embraced the vision that sanctuaries adjacent to the seat of power promoted coexistence.

Reformers created the parks rapidly while juggling multiple opportunities and obstacles. To explore the tension between difference and sameness, this book addresses five overlapping and intertwined themes—science, education, productivity, property, and tradition—that informed each park in specific ways in different social, environmental, and human contexts. The themes shaped the creation of four national parks that, more than the other thirty-six, collectively provide an explanation for why Mexicans were willing and able to promote conservation in the 1930s. Before turning to these cases, the subsequent chapter addresses the roots of conservation by giving attention to the development of forestry and the mounting awareness of the central valley's degradation. This intellectual and scientific background provides a broader picture of the forces that contributed to formative park ideas.

The book then turns to individual parks. Chapter 2 examines Lagunas de Zempoala National Park to address how social changes found a place in the parks through educational campaigns, tourist experiences, foreign exchanges, and national festivals. The forested lakes lured visitors because they provided an alternative rural landscape—lakes, not agricultural land—where tourists could learn modern ways to enjoy nature. These recreational and leisure activities promoted the authority of the federal government by legitimating national control over the forested landscape, but this popular park also met the needs of various local constituencies.

Chapters 3 and 4 take up issues central to the revolutionary reforms: rural productivity and property rights. Chapter 3 examines the dense alpine pine and fir forests around the snow-capped volcanoes Popocatépetl and Iztaccíhuatl that became Cárdenas's first national park and the sixth largest in size. The volcanoes had long been recognizable landscape features guiding travelers and enticing explorers, and the forests boasted a range of wood-based productive industries, from paper manufacturing to firewood collection. This park helps explain how revolutionaries harnessed economic and aesthetic resources to promote cautious development, personal stoicism, and holistic nationalism. The fourth chapter, a study of La Malinche National Park, examines an isolated volcano with a degraded forest and highly contested land tenure situation. The chapter delves into the ways a reconfigured property regime exacerbated the overlap between village lands and a federally managed national park. The process whereby foresters extended federal property and confronted local protests demonstrates how residents used legal and political channels to assert their claims to the commons into unfolding environmental policies. This contested process was further complicated by the spread of mistletoe through the forest, which compromised the health of the parklands. The buildup of scientific arguments and competing productive enterprises climaxed in a fight over property that fractured communities and undermined the set of justifications for the park's existence.

Chapter 5 turns to the cultural aspects of creating national patrimony by considering El Tepozteco National Park. This park included an entire municipality with eight communities and their farmlands and forests as well as a dramatic rocky ridgeline with a pre-Columbian pyramid. In the 1920s, the village of Tepoztlán earned international fame as the site of a study by the American anthropologist Robert Redfield, who used it as a model "village in transition" and opened the door for scores of subsequent researchers. These accounts confirm that residents of this well-studied municipality discussed and debated the proper uses of their forest lands for years before the president declared the area a park. When he did, the sacred spaces of ancient societies (a pyramid) merged with the historic space of the Catholic Church (a convent) and formed a new shrine to the revolutionary government (a national park).

The conclusion evaluates the ambitious agenda of park creation in the context of twentieth-century development. Although the tapestry of national parks made conservation radical in the 1930s, it grew rapidly threadbare as national priorities shifted toward industrialization and urban migrants encroached on compromises made to protect the parks. The final chapter explores the reasons for less enthusiastic park policy from the 1940s onward and the deleterious effects of national and global shifts in conservation priorities. Rather than a stage of modernization, a monument to democracy, a site of resistance, or a minor deviation in revolutionary bravado, national parks were tangible places that promoted the nearby forest as a world for rediscovery and national reflection. Mexico's national parks embodied a promise to incorporate all people into a national system of governance and to provide stability through federal resource control. These parks today exist degraded, but they have not disappeared altogether. Thus they provide a fortuitous warning and enduring symbol of how revolutionaries turned an agenda for social change into tangible environmental policy. Before revolutionaries could articulate such an agenda, they turned to rational science to explain the deforestation they saw unfolding around them.

CHAPTER ONE

Science

Elite Societies, Revolutionary Conservation, and National Park Development

Reminiscing aloud to a room full of scientists on the evening of November 5, 1923, Felipe Ruiz Velasco described what had once been abundant forests and springs between his home state of Morelos and Mexico City, just to the north. Ruiz Velasco began with a description of the well-known route from the nation's capital to the city of Cuernavaca, traversed for centuries through "treacherous yet radiant woods" by people from the countryside seeking markets in the city and urban dwellers seeking escape from the tempestuous rainy season. The sexagenarian called on the audience to think back to transport before highways and railroads, when "nervous mules and able drivers carefully navigated the mountains and canyons" and where "towering trees perfumed the healthy air" as birds raced through the canopies.[1] He warned that this privileged area, one always linked with the vibrancy of the nation's core, now faced an alarming and desperate situation.

Over the last decades of the nineteenth century, Ruiz Velasco explained, large portions of the central temperate forests had been completely leveled, with dire repercussions for the residents.[2] The rains stopped coming, and springs dried up. People abandoned their cultivations for lack of water, their livestock disappeared, health and general tranquility faltered, and mortality increased for those who relied on forests for their livelihoods. "For three hundred years," he claimed, "these woods had vibrated with life as communal lands were used by villagers who themselves had been ignored and overlooked in the nation's history."[3] The frenzy of destruction turned these harmonious refuges into scenes of suffering in a few decades.

He insisted that not only these communities but the whole nation faced the colossal problem of rapid, ruthless forest desecration. Deforestation might seem an obscure topic for group of scientists in a country seeking a way out of a complicated civil war, but this concern for forests reveals the patterns of belief that quickened the pace of revolutionary conservation and paved the way for national park creation.

Ruiz Velasco called this squander the "war against the tree" and placed blame squarely on the railroads and foreign capitalists.[4] Their waste and the conciliatory politicians who made destruction profitable with miniscule taxes and minor inspections reduced abundant forests while disregarding broader effects. Such critiques of the prior regime were familiar to revolutionaries who also attributed major national problems to its corruption, ineptitude, and lack of compassion. On the issue of forest conservation, Ruiz Velasco tried to separate himself from the ill effects of prior management but to simultaneously retain and even expand the validity of the scientific claims to manage the forests that arose during the prior administration.

The timing of Ruiz Velasco's speech marked a peculiar moment of transition that captured heightened concerns for forests as scientific forestry's elite practitioners aligned with revolutionary reformers expanding governmental ownership. The science of forestry (more than zoology, botany, metallurgy, meteorology, or astronomy) resonated in turn-of-the-century Mexico because of the immediately observable effects of forest degradation on erosion, flooding, and dust storms as well as the increased availability of scientific discourse on forests.[5] Indeed, the most prominent conservationists identified themselves primarily as foresters. Through their societies, Porfirian scientists advocated the rational use of forests yet became incensed when unrestrained logging decimated mountainsides. Revolutionaries likewise disapproved of woodland destruction and saw forests as spaces for the incorporation of greater territory and the people on it into the federal purview.

The study of forests provided a bridge between two political eras as foresters shifted roles from Porfirian experts to revolutionary administrators of environmental policy. For these scientists, national parks implied forests within them and the newly autonomous Forestry Department, whose life cycle began and ended with the Cárdenas presidency, administered the parks. National parks were tethered to the fate of this department, and their genesis owed much to the privileged status that forestry acquired. Only five of the forty parks declared and administered under Cárdenas did not contain forests.[6]

Scientists like Ruiz Velasco typified the people who molded initial revolutionary environmental policy, but their association with the dictatorship reduced their political clout. Instead of championing these experts alone, President Cárdenas encouraged the responsiveness of rural people and drew on a legacy of resurrecting prior claims to common property in the form of state-conferred ejidos. Articulated in the 1917 Constitution, this critical difference in revolutionary orientation fostered enduring "agrarian fantasies" that elevated the status of campesinos, privileged the moral work of rural people, expanded ideas of citizenship, and altered popular perceptions of government responsibility in the countryside.[7] Though preexisting, these fantasies expanded during the Cárdenas period and persisted to varying degrees throughout the century.

This chapter considers the origins of conservation science in Porfirian society and then explores how the revolutionary era reworked these scientific traditions, in particular that of forestry. Then it considers the transnational sources for the development of ideas about conservation and parks before examining the links between land reform and park creation. The idea of conservation itself marks the starting point for tracing the intellectual route from elite Porfirian societies to federally employed scientists managing national parks.

Revolutionary Conservation and Environmentalism

Ideas about nature conservation that emerged in revolutionary Mexico have certain characteristics that set them apart from prior efforts to protect nature. Most notably, revolutionary conservation implied a state responsibility to maintain the integrity of nature for the public. Examples of conservation stretch back to pre-Columbian civilizations and through the Spanish colonial period as do instances of individuals who advocated private conservation.[8] The revolutionary period laid new ground for conservation because of the way the state became involved managing nature for its citizenry. President Cárdenas best expressed his conservation objectives as a relationship in which "government action is important so that the Mexican people will receive the greatest benefits from the forest and fauna by providing enthusiasm and loyal cooperation in this work safeguarding and protecting Nature. True works of national conservation involve the regulation of use and exploitation that will create not only obedience but cooperation on behalf of local authorities, diverse social classes, and businesses to treat such indispensable elements well and foster trust in the government."[9] Regulating, safeguarding, and protecting nature were responsibilities commonly articulated by advocates of conservation, from the president to rural families. Yet conservation did not have a single meaning, and conservation efforts contained contradictory impulses that warned of the consequences of economic growth and at the same time advocated modern techniques for both the administration of forests and their scientific study.

Elite scientific organizations, especially the Antonio Alzate Scientific Society and the Mexican Forestry Society, contributed to a growing consensus over the importance of forests to national well-being. Indeed, members confidently asserted the need to regulate and manage forests, positing that "the precepts of the Forestry Law [of 1926], like those of science, do not prohibit exploitation but regulate use for the indefinite conservation of forests necessary for public wellbeing."[10] Organizations promoting conservation absorbed and reformulated foreign ideas through scholarly articles, conferences, and foreign study in tandem with transnational scientific conversations ranging as far as Japan and as near as Guatemala. This professionalization helped to increase governmental control and management over specific and clearly defined resources.

Revolutionary conservation privileged forestry, and it focused on the country's geographic center. Despite the diversity of biological areas, from deserts to rain forests, the landscape most intimately tied with national identity and the region described by Ruiz Velasco as tragically deteriorated was the Valley of Mexico. Known in pre-Hispanic times as Anáhuac, it included a series of islands and lakes in a peak-ringed basin on a central plateau nestled into the elbow of two mountain chains. Efforts to drain the lakes, to build on the unsteady soil, and to construct methods of transport all took their toll on the valley, but these efforts only reinforced the political authority of this central territory.[11] In 1929, the Ministry of Agriculture published a preliminary map of the country's climate regions that revealed this geographical hierarchy.[12] Ten climatic regions were labeled, with the southern and eastern lowlands described as having "monsoons like China" and the northern, "deserts like the Sahara." The central part of the country received its own prestigious identity: "high-altitude subtropical—typical of the Valley of Mexico." This was the only region described in reference to Mexico, not another world region, because this was the territory federal bureaucrats thought of as *truly* Mexican. Always the financial and political capital, Mexico City also proffered a cultural identity intimately tied to the landscape.

Revolutionary conservation had a cluster of traits. It drew upon growing trends of professionalization in transnational forestry science, wove these threads into an increasing federal state, focused attention on the central forests, and fashioned an ethic that drew upon traditions of common property. Arguments for conservation gave rise to a larger spirit of environmentalism. How these trends came together under Cárdenas had much to do with the preceding period.

Elite Origins

Federal forestry programs originated in the Porfiriato. Forestry was one of the many disciplines promoted by the *científicos*, or scientifically oriented advisors, including economists, engineers, and mathematicians, who made up the oligarchy advising President Díaz.[13] Trained mostly abroad, they contributed to a welcoming atmosphere for foreign capital as their expertise manifested into sophisticated modern factories, intensified agricultural plantations, and reinvigorated mining operations. Central to the views of the científicos was the idea that society functioned like a living being, subject to strict natural laws of evolution and change but also capable of development.[14] To improve this "national being," federal laws disentailed indigenous property and sentenced thousands of rural inhabitants to grueling work in haciendas.[15]

The rationalization of production also applied to the use of forest products. The increase in railroads, in public lighting, and in building construction all relied heavily on the consumption of forest resources mainly found in the central corridor.[16] Laborers laid thousands of kilometers of railroad track using the pine trunks for ties because of their proximity to the routes.[17] Modern advancements called for greater, not lesser, use of natural resources. The combination of elite social desires, liberal economic invigoration, and improved communication channels fostered a vigorous run of deforestation. Electricity increased the overall demand on the forests for lampposts and power-line poles as well as refined sealants made from tree sap. The heightened demand for processed combustibles in the capital city exposed a rift between users of raw firewood and users of chemically derived substances.[18] Such a divide highlighted the changing attributes of modern lifestyles alongside the persistence of ancient customs. Some of the most vocal foresters lamented the lack of attention by political leaders to such issues in the Constitution of 1857 or subsequent reforms. One argued of the laws, "Not one part protected these [forest] resources, and new rural property laws prohibited community lands (*bienes comunales*) and made their break up obligatory with no distinction between agricultural and forest lands or prairies or pastures. This egregious error brought ruin to communal forest properties and gravely endangered these pueblos principally in the mountains."[19] At the same time, the increased reliance on liberalized trade caused fluctuations in the price of agricultural staples that pushed peasants toward earning income from selling forest products.

As in other industrializing societies, the frenzied exploitation of primary materials took precedence over the maintenance of healthy surroundings. Porfirian officials made great strides attracting investments in Mexico's natural resources. By hiring private surveyors to complete extensive surveys of public lands, they facilitated the transfer of enormous quantities of government land into private hands but simultaneously created a stable central government capable of administering reliable titles and definitive property lines.[20] Public land transfers occurred most frequently in frontier zones that received far less attention by conservationists who were more interested in the private, collective, and public forests around the capital.

Porfirian científicos became concerned with conservation as they watched the habitability of their city decline. After attending the International Congress on Hygiene and Urbanism in Paris in 1900, one scientist lamented the pitiful lack of green space in the capital city compared to other urban areas. Mexico City appeared worse for the health of its inhabitants than London, New York, and Paris, but also worse than places like St. Louis, New Orleans, and Los Angeles. "Our capital figures last," lamented the scientist, "with only one hectare of free space for every 2,500 inhabitants, or just 4 cubic meters per person."[21] This embarrassing comparison sparked the redesign of several urban gardens, tree-lined avenues, and public parks.[22] Officials' urban concerns were explicitly linked to deterioration in the surrounding areas, and they began to write forest policies.

With increasing intensity, scientists studied the environment they perceived as fragile. Two societies' publications reveal the fervor with which members sought to know the natural world from the soils to the skies. *La Naturaleza* (Nature), the journal of the Mexican Natural History Society, printed reports, treatises, experiments, and notes on a variety of topics ranging from zoology and botany to meteorology. The articles announced new species, described animal behavior, studied the economic viability of plants, tested the chemical composition of minerals, and made general observations about the nation's geography. They also dabbled in the human sciences, printing articles on criminology, anthropology, and history. The editors, consisting of a rotating group of lettered men of science, preferred studies that centered on Mexico, especially reports on scientific excursions. These included expeditions to natural sites that later became national parks. For example, Manuel Villada described the vast stalactites he encountered on his trip to the Caverns of Cacahuamilpa (which became Guerrero State's first national park in 1936).[23] Investigations took scientists to the crater of Nevado de Toluca, up the slopes of Popocatépetl, and across the towering glaciers of Pico de Orizaba, all of which became park sites in the 1930s. They published some initial articles regarding forestry, but in the early issues, these mostly dealt with Bosque de Chapultepec within the Federal District.[24] They also reprinted articles from other countries on topics deemed relevant to Mexican issues, and they circulated the journal to eighty-three repositories worldwide. Members devoted sufficient time and energy to collecting a library and establishing a museum of natural history in 1910.[25] Over the course of the Porfiriato, this society shifted its focus from an elite social group that met privately to discuss studies of nature to an organization that envisioned itself as a public promoter of nature.

The Antonio Alzate Scientific Society followed a similar trajectory and shared many members with the Mexican Natural History Society.[26] When the Natural History Society dissolved early in the revolution, the Antonio Alzate Scientific Society expanded and went through a readership shift. Their journal, *Memorias y revista de la Sociedad Científica de Antonio Alzate* (Journal and Magazine of the Antonio Alzate Scientific Society) published articles in French and English in 1909, but in the heightened climate of nationalism by 1920, they translated similar foreign articles into Spanish. The interest in excursions remained, for instance, Elpidio Lopez and Fritz Weitzberg took a trip up the volcano Popocatépetl during Christmas in 1920, but the publications of forestry related articles intensified. The group published presentations from their society meetings, such as the one Ruiz Velasco delivered on deforestation in 1923.

The journals of professional societies reflected deeply held opinions about deforestation's origins. Primarily, foresters saw their work as differing from that of agriculturists. Whereas an agrarian engineer sought the propagation of plants artificially, silviculturists argued they tended to imitate the cultivation techniques of nature. Rather than planning for a short-term (one- or two-season) harvest, foresters claimed to look ahead decades, even centuries, for the realization of their work. Farmers annually cleared and restarted their fields, but foresters aimed to maintain the integrity of forests year after year. They advocated two related but opposed ends: the constant use of the forest and its perpetual conservation. Their work, as they saw it, connected to larger natural cycles, including climatic, soil, and hydrologic regimes as well as wildlife and human habitats. Additionally, the effects of forests in "elevating the human spirit" and protecting aesthetic landscapes weighed in the foresters' minds; they believed such noble endeavors were incomparable to the humble work of agriculturists.[27]

This tension between use and conservation existed in the ideas of the strongest forest advocates. The best illustration of this is the "Apostle of the Tree," Miguel Ángel de Quevedo. Born in 1862 in Guadalajara and educated in France, Quevedo learned scientific applications from medical researcher Louis Pasteur and Paul Laroche, an engineer of the Suez Canal. Returning home in 1888, Quevedo proved eager to apply his training. He worked for private industries and President Díaz while cultivating interest in forest issues among his peers. Yet, as his résumé demonstrates, his activities proved characteristic of the contradictions of the Porfiriato. He engineered for the enormous drainage project, the Gran Desagüe, that sought to control the waters of the central valley, but he also designed tobacco factories and served on a reforestation and dune construction project in Veracruz. In his later years, he planned tree nurseries and national parks. His writing reveals a lingering abhorrence of the popular classes who, he believed, failed to see the value of their forests, but he also harbored a great disdain for the tree-devouring greed of some industrialists.

Quevedo shaped and preserved more green space in and around Mexico City than any individual and led conservation and forestry campaigns for the better part of four decades.[28] Quevedo's commitment to forests shifted from private to public and heightened after the country plunged into political turmoil and violence. The revolution interrupted both forest uses and promises for conservation that stalled, but did not halt, his campaign. Quevedo helped organize the Junta Central de Bosques (Central Forest Group) in 1908. The first organization dedicated specifically to studying the nation's forests, it remained active through the presidency of Francisco Madero (1911–1913) but was driven underground when Victoriano Huerta took power in 1913. It reconvened as the Mexican Forestry Society, in 1922.[29] These wealthy, educated scientists continued to set the agenda for national forestry priorities well into the revolutionary period.

Revolutionary Reforms

Porfirian forestry took some time to mesh with revolutionary aspirations, although major revolutionary platforms made explicit claims on natural resources. The demands for "Mexico for Mexicans" and "land for those who work it" aimed to rectify the situation in the countryside and redefine

who deserved resources.[30] For instance, Emiliano Zapata articulated the
demands of the rural dispossessed, particularly those exploited by sugar-
cane planters in Morelos.[31] In his reform platform, the Plan de Ayala, Zapata maintained that communities deserved control over lands and usage
rights, proclaiming, that "because lands, timber, and water are monopolized in a few hands" a third of all monopolies should be expropriated to
provide ejidos, village territory, or municipal fields.[32] This is not to say the
Zapatistas were proto-environmentalists or nature lovers but rather their
social claims recognized the broader environmental dimensions of justice.

Because of their resonance with the rural populace, Zapata's demands
had to be taken seriously by other leaders. Amid fighting and civil war in
1914, Venustiano Carranza sought to bring order to the revolution and
solidify his own rule. Carranza carried out a series of significant reforms,
including the agrarian reform decree of January 6, 1915 (*Ley de desamor-
tización*), which mandated the return of communal lands and established
the National Agrarian Commission with branches in each state. Two further pieces of legislation, Article 27 of the Constitution of 1917 and the
Six-Year Plan for 1934–1940, explicitly regulated land, water, forest, and
mineral resources by enveloping environmental policies into larger plans
for the improvement of human resources.[33] Article 27 drew its strength
by placing the state between citizens and their resources. Proponents
believed the abuse of property rights caused the agrarian problem, not
merely the lack of irrigation, credit, or education.[34] Article 27 articulated
solutions to inequality in the countryside, including the expropriation of
private property for the public good, the restoration of communal land,
forests, and waters, the breaking up of haciendas, and the recovery of
public land privatized after 1876.[35] According to this new Constitution,
the federal government held the authority to adjudicate the ownership of
natural wealth and manage public property that used and conserved these
resources. President Carranza declared the first national park, Desierto de
los Leones, in a former Carmelite monastery near the capital city, on the
heels of the Constitution of 1917.[36]

In 1926, a landmark year for forests, the Forestry Society published a
formal declaration of the eighteen principles that undergirded their members' beliefs. These principles centered on the benefits that forests would
supply when conserved, cared for, and replenished. Members believed
that forests mediated floods, conserved soil, and maintained livable cli-
mates. They advocated restraining the expansion of agricultural territory
and argued that forest vegetation should never be destroyed to cultivate
crops. They promised rational harvesting of forest products because their

Walking along the road to Desierto de los Leones, 1925.

economics allowed for logging in a fashion that allowed the trees to re-
generate for the future. Finally, these foresters believed that the wealth of
forests demanded that all social groups receive instruction in the principal
elements of scientific forestry.[37]

Based on this platform, the Forestry Society, with Quevedo often serving as president, engaged in direct political activity. Quevedo's insistence
on conservation through forest protection allowed him to shape important legislation. While in self-imposed exile in Europe, Quevedo missed
the formative constitutional convention of 1917 but he added his part to
this increasing federal structure with the Forestry Law of 1926.[38] Quevedo
and the other members of the Forestry Society began discussing a national forest law in the early 1920s as part of their agenda to modernizing
resource use. This law, approved April 5, 1926, by President Plutarco
Elías Calles (1924–1928), sought to regularize conservation, restoration,
planning, and use while developing technical personnel to ensure the
same.[39] Forests could still be used, if users followed the new regulations
that included extractive limits, permits, and transit fees. The law claimed
to protect the public utility by regulating forests on municipal, communal, and private lands for the first time. It called for citizens to help with

enforcement by denouncing those who felled timber without federal permission. It laid the groundwork for forest reserves, immediately putting them into effect on national lands and established protocols for future reforestation, including regional nurseries and the creation of a forestry department. The law created the extensive framework that made possible regulating the use of forests nationwide. In many ways it provided a corollary to the land reform provisions in Article 27 for the comprehensiveness of its administration of the resource. By imposing regulations and monitoring mechanisms, the federal government staked its claim over all forests, even though it did not expropriate them outright. The implications of this forest policy cannot be overstated and should be compared to the nationalization of water and oil.

Members of the Forestry Society believed the only way to make forestry a legitimate issue was to get it out from under the thumb of the Ministry of Agriculture. Discouraged by what he perceived as the emphasis on agriculture above silviculture, Edmundo Bournet, president of the Forestry Society at the time, argued that forestry was the "older sister" of farming, both its "forerunner and protector."[40] Many foresters saw their mission as helping agriculture, in the long term, by assuring a stable climatic regime and protecting hillsides from erosion. In contrast, employees in the Ministry of Agriculture saw their main duty as freeing up and distributing land for farming as a revolutionary promise and an overall economic goal. In many places, the only available land remained covered with trees, which meant freeing space to cultivate food required clearing forests. Such rationalization frightened the growing group of revolutionary foresters. As Quevedo saw it, there would never be enough force behind a bureaucratic forestry division as long as it remained subordinate to the contradictory mandates of the Ministry of Agriculture.[41] Yet this reform would have to wait for a willing executive who recruited Quevedo into a prominent role.

Despite the radical nature of the new Constitution and changes made with certain areas, including forestry, the political atmosphere of the 1920s did not allow its full implementation.[42] Laws alone did not alter property rights countrywide; meaningful land reform required political will and a social context conducive to implementation. The effects of the worldwide economic downturn in 1929 shaped this context by weakening the power of large landowners and decreasing the profitability of export agriculture.[43] By 1930, only 5 percent of farmland was held by those who should have benefited from land reform, and much of this land contained forests.[44] The next major platform for federal resource administration came nearly fifteen years after the Constitution, as revolutionary fighting waned and political power concentrated around revolutionary strongman and former president Calles. Calles created the PNR as a solution to the problem of succession and as a foundation for bureaucratizing the revolution. The formal political party mediated the ambitions of the remaining generals and forcefully set out the direction for the national economy.

Formal articulation of the PNR's platform took shape in a time when state planning was in vogue around the world and the Six-Year Plan of 1934–1940 promised major changes.[45] Approved at the national convention on December 4, 1933, this act of deliberate planning for the future of the nation represented an important step in the expansion of revolutionary ideas into the daily lives of citizens. It elaborated on eleven specific areas, including federal watchfulness over forest use and the prevention of their destruction.[46] After decades of small steps, foresters and conservationists had the legal groundwork to proceed with halting deforestation and protecting landscapes.

By 1934, the appropriate political atmosphere for forest protection appeared. The Cárdenas presidency brought relief from the troubled politics of the 1920s and promised change. Cárdenas arrived as president with rich administrative experience and a soft spot for trees.[47] With room to maneuver, Cárdenas's personality converged with popular aspirations to extend reforms far, although their effects were never predictable or consistent.[48] He served as the governor of Michoacán (1928–1932), and there he had noted rates of deforestation similar to those around the capital. Cárdenas pointed to the influence of his teacher Hilario de Jesus Fajardo in shaping his ideas about forests. In weekend trips to nearby ranchos led by Fajardo, Cárdenas recalled that "on all of the excursions, the lectures from our teacher helped us to know the work of nature; he put special emphasis on talking to us about the trees, their importance, and the care with which we must guard them. It is the tree, he told us, that is the best friend of children, it blankets them with its shade, gives health and fruit and in general enriches all nations."[49] As he rose in politics, Cárdenas lamented the deterioration of Michoacán's forests, and he atoned for this with several national parks in the state. Some of his more personal actions also reveal his affinity for forests. For example, he first courted his future wife in an orchard named Los Pinos and later refused to inhabit the traditional presidential residence of Chapultepec Castle, instead adopting a nearby home, which he renamed Los Pinos.[50]

Once elected, Cárdenas faced mounting pressure from foresters for an autonomous forestry department. José V. Cardoso, a forester serving previous administrations, wrote a proposal for reorganizing the forestry division out of the Ministry of Agriculture in order to give foresters the resources and flexibility to respond to the preservation of forests. Cardoso claimed, "Conserving and restoring forests rebuilds the *patria*," connecting support for forestry with fulfilling the goals of the revolution.[51] Forestry Society members argued for greater attention to forestry issues in the new Cárdenas government. Quevedo, the president of the society when Cárdenas assumed power, applauded the new president who expressed enthusiasm for the forestry cause and promised to make it one of the dominant issues in his administrative program. Quevedo reiterated the position that "forestry conservation is the fundamental basis for economic equilibrium and social well-being in all refined nations." He then congratulated Cárdenas and offered the society's unconditional cooperation.[52]

For many, Cárdenas stood out as a messianic politician willing to adopt priorities of elite foresters and widen national attention toward forest issues. He understood bureaucratic conflict and as one of his first presidential acts, he created the autonomous Forestry Department, freeing it from the mandates of the Ministry of Agriculture.[53] "It is a fundamental vision of this Executive," the president argued, "to study and promote the related laws for the exploitation of the forest riches of our country so they align with social aims and unify collective wellbeing without harming the national interests." He promised greater federal control over forests would not mean eliminating wood products, but rather the Forestry Department would study methods for the "appropriate use" of natural resources, including fisheries and wildlife. Cárdenas claimed that states beyond Michoacán suffered from deforestation and promised to foster research into gas and other combustibles to replace the use of forest derived fuels.[54]

Cardenistas drank from the same trough as Porfirian scientists, but they also sipped elsewhere. The antecedents of radical forestry had liberal, elite, and intellectual roots in Porfirian social circles, but this did not mean foresters lacked potential for radicalization, although their conflicts with agriculture continued."[55] Scientific forestry in the 1930s no longer bore only promises of modernity; it now symbolized the possibility of rational equality. In a series of conferences about agrarian issues, the foresters Salvador Guerrero and Camilo del Moral argued that "the actual conservation of national forests and the suppression of private forest property will be the most radical solution to the forest problem."[56] Although their academic investigations and societies continued, the policies foresters advocated shifted in form to meet the revolutionary context and keep pace with the new president's priorities.

Creating the independent cabinet-level Forestry Department signified that Cárdenas aimed to protect the forests. The new department retained much of its organizational structure from its place in the Ministry of Agriculture, but it expanded its reach and scope particularly in areas of conservation. To the members of the Forestry Society and professional foresters, this move showed that their pleas paid off. To select a department director, Cárdenas overlooked Quevedo's Porfirian association and selected him because of his scientific training, conservative reputation, and practical experience.[57] Because formal forestry education had barely begun before the revolutionary upheaval curtailed its development, few candidates had the skills, experience, and commitment to direct this new department. No other forester even came close, despite the fact that Quevedo was seventy-three years old when he took the job. Quevedo supported revolutionary promises unenthusiastically, but his experience with forestry and conservation, as well as a certain amount of self-righteous egotism, convinced him to take the job managing the nation's forests and developing parks.[58]

Once granted autonomy, Forestry Department officials reorganized to better reflect a commitment to conservation and restoration. Removing forestry from its subordinate position allowed a culture of protection to flourish, including but not limited to national parks. The new department had six divisions covering the comprehensive scope of forestry management: an Office of Legal Affairs, an Administrative Office, an Office of Conservation, Propagation, and Restoration, an Office of Exploitation and Inspection, an Office of Research and Disclosure, and an Office of Statistics and Economics. Each had between two and ten sections; for example, the Section of Silviculture and Forest Nurseries was within the Office of Conservation, Propagation, and Restoration. Multiple sections expanded and moved location over the course of the Cárdenas *sexenio*. The Section on National Parks began attached to the Woodlands Section within the Office of Exploitation and Inspection and was later moved to the Office of Conservation.[59] The Forestry Department also maintained a number of delegations and subdelegations in state capitals and other important cities around the country. Both local and nonlocal employees staffed nineteen delegations in 1933, and by 1940 the number expanded to thirty-three. The delegations were later divided into regional zones with separate vigilance sectors.[60] The more senior positions in each office, section, and delegation went to professionals committed to the standard principles of forestry.

The institutional structure of the Forestry Department also proved fluid and flexible. It changed over time to reflect the variety of opinions that existed within the growing community of foresters that came to staff it. Because of its newness, the Forestry Department proved able to respond to criticism, from inside and out, about its effectiveness. One of the more vibrant philosophical divisions among the employees involved the issue of militarization and discipline. Edmundo Bournet, a technical inspector for the department and active member in the Forestry Society, advised a more rigorous and hierarchal structure within the department and the addition of an active police force, similar to a National Guard or rural police.[61] Bournet promised that such a Forest Service of disciplined soldiers would earn respect of communities for its ability to follow through on forest protection. The respect for and presence of the force would then reduce corruption found among ambitious local political bosses, industrial profiteers, and disgruntled foresters willing to collude with them. On the other hand, Carlos Treviño Saldana, an engineer who worked on protected zones, doubted the lack of discipline among foresters. He believed that oppressive administrative structures constrained well-intentioned employees from successfully complying with their duties. According to Treviño, policies proved too centralized and required too many signatures, which forced lower level guards and workers to feel irresponsible for their own actions.[62] He claimed that most foresters were "men of the country" who appreciated being outdoors, but the bureaucracy forced them to sit at a desk all day making conjectures without true knowledge about the extent of use in particular areas. Furthermore, the habit of rotating and transferring employees required them to "politic" for the most rewarding posts. For Treviño, foresters needed autonomy and responsibility, not militarization. Bournet and Treviño represent the frankness with which employees offered opinions about how to improve their department.

Bournet and Treviño's suggestions differed in substance, yet they both reveal a commitment to a sense of justice. Despite their somewhat elitist positions and formal training, their commitment to making forestry respectable reflected a larger desire to rebuild the rigor of their country. Bournet, Treviño, Quevedo, and many of the other officials believed that how a nation treated its forests was representative of how it treated its citizens. They made this point as a plea to President Cárdenas and the larger public for greater funding, publicity, resources, and support. In some cases, communities also absorbed this rationale. In response to the proposal in late 1939 to remove the Forestry Department from cabinet-level stature, a group of campesinos from the state of Chiapas attested to the value of conserving the forests. Their letter proclaimed, "If today we abandon our woods, tomorrow our children will have to humiliate themselves to foreigners making thousands of sacrifices to buy wood at the price of gold just to repair their huts or make household furnishings."[63] The Department of

Forestry, in their estimation, supported efforts of national sovereignty and prosperity. This link allowed forests and the parks that connected them to engage in a larger global conversation about conservation.

Transnational Scientific Dialogues

Foresters never worked in isolation. They absorbed suggestions, responded to critiques, and discussed alternatives as they managed parks. As the foundation of much of their authority, their scientific expertise drew from practical and theoretical applications. Educational institutions created crucibles of scientific thought, while international experiences enhanced the agendas of reformers committed to the conservation of forests and creation of national parks. Participating in a global community of researchers made Mexican foresters reinterpret, challenge, and confirm their own opinions. Exchanges with foreign experts strengthened domestic ideas about their natural patrimony and provided inspiration for forging a peculiarly Mexican form of environmentalism at a comparatively early stage.

Those who believed in the importance of forestry sought to expand their base of support especially by training youth. Several forestry schools existed in Mexico between 1908 and 1940. The first one, founded by

The nursery at Viveros de Coyoacán, ca. 1920.

Quevedo and located in a wealthy neighborhood of Mexico City known as Santa Fe, employed French foresters as professors because of the lack of national experts. It opened August 20, 1909, in a modest building with few amenities, but with a select group of teachers and the dedication of Quevedo behind it.[64] The school moved to Coyoacán in 1912 and remained open with thirty-two students until 1914 when political turmoil closed the school and Quevedo went into exile. By 1932, Quevedo convinced the national university to sponsor forestry training, and they did so until 1935 when the new Forestry Department sponsored the Instituto Superior de Enseñanza Forestal (Superior Institute for Forestry Instruction) in Coyoacán. This time, Mexicans, with few foreign teachers, staffed the forestry school. The three-semester curriculum emphasized discipline, honor, and a "forest spirit" as essential skills equal to technical knowledge. Teachers believed that foresters had to fight propaganda and enter political battles if they were to achieve respect for and conservation of the trees to which they dedicated their work.[65] In 1937, the school was transferred to Perote, Veracruz, where it remained until 1939 when the school was incorporated into the National School of Agriculture and forestry became one of many majors available for agronomists.[66] Despite the emphasis on formal professional training, forestry education extended far beyond forestry schools. Within national parks, various didactic activities took place ranging from signs and pamphlets to camps and festivals (see chap. 2).

Policies developing in the United States influenced Cardenistas, as did those from the long emulated country of France.[67] Quevedo had himself been trained in France, and the proximity to the United States inspired periodic exchanges.[68] Quevedo and two associates attended the North American Conservation Conference in Washington DC in 1909, and park planners even credited the League of Nations accord as a partial inspiration for park creation.[69] Negotiations for several border parks brought officials from both nations into contact repeatedly in the 1930s.[70] Department employees Quevedo, Daniel Galicia, and Hans Zimmerer took tours of American parks, including Carlsbad Caverns in New Mexico, the Grand Canyon in Arizona, and Sequoia National Park in California. These trips gave them the opportunity not only to see the way U.S. national parks were run, but also to discuss ideas and philosophies of park management. There were several attempts to use a theme similar to the U.S. Park Service's "See America First" campaign as Mexican officials called on their fellow citizens to "Know Our Mexico."[71] Quevedo also created a popular museum, the Museum of Flora and Fauna, in Chapultepec Park in Mexico City, to display information about his department's activities. In

1936, Ángel Roldán, an engineer from the Forestry Department, attended the Congress on Silviculture and Carbon Fuels, in Brussels. In addition to the conference he toured French, German, Swiss, Austrian, Czechoslovakian, and Polish parks and reserves, making observations on each and bringing back ideas on how to improve the new parks in Mexico.[72] Shortly thereafter, Quevedo took a tour to Guatemala to foster friendship with the southern neighbor, and he proposed an international peace park along the border, including the Suchiate River in Chiapas.[73]

Perhaps less expectedly, Mexican engineers, bureaucrats, and scientists looked outside the United States and Europe for techniques. Employees of the fishing division of the Forestry Department took an extensive tour of Japan and invited Japanese experts to Mexico to improve fish cultivation.[74] Japanese experts did not limit their contributions to fish; one Japanese professor sent 100 cherry trees to be planted in Lagunas de Zempoala National Park. The trees were to help with erosion around the lake, but also to exemplify the exchange of knowledge, friendship, and nature between the two countries.[75] In addition to reaching out to Japan, a special series in the forestry journal *México Forestal* (Forested Mexico) featured a twelve-part article on the trees of South Africa and the cultivation of Mexican pines in that country.[76] While Mexican foresters prided themselves on their methods, often derived from European and American techniques, they also adeptly sought other sources and they believed in their own contributions to the world of forestry.

The flow of ideas about forestry and national parks went both directions. The Forestry Department officials and the government publication agents took special measures to publicize national achievements in the realm of natural resources. The director of the National Parks Office, Daniel Galicia, wrote an article explaining the new national parks and their merits that he had translated into English and sent to Uruguay, Poland, Italy, and England, among other places. When the article appeared in a Czechoslovakian newspaper, the foreign publication made news in Mexico.[77] Besides written descriptions, trees themselves were sent as ambassadors of friendship. Mexico sent an *ahuehuete* (Montezuma Cypress, *Taxodium mucronatum*) seedling to Peru, and the California Avocado Association made a trip to Atlixco, Puebla, presenting a bronze plaque in recognition of "the shared wealth generated by the avocado tree."[78] Individuals also came as ambassadors of goodwill toward trees and natural resources. The acclaimed Chilean poet Gabriela Mistral was given honorary membership in the Mexican Forestry Society, and she wrote a special entry in their magazine entitled "Hymn to the Trees."

Building national parks formed a remarkably international endeavor. Contact with and tours to other countries involved crafting the messages and collecting information for incorporation into new projects. By interacting with officials in other countries, foresters promoted their achievements and became ambassadors of a revolutionary environmentalism. Far from copying the ideas that sprang out of forestry schools in France or national park development in the United States, Mexican foresters and officials created programs, meanings, and constituents of their own. Undoubtedly they were influenced by international developments, but more consistently they were shaped by local circumstances and domestic suggestions tied to revolutionary social reforms, the most widespread of which involved land redistribution.

Land Reform and Park Creation

When developing parks, planners had to take into account the compositions of land tenure regimes. Of all the promises for social change emanating from the revolution, land reform most dramatically transformed the landscape and altered property holdings in expected and unexpected ways. The remarkable speed and scope of change resulted in the redistribution of eighteen million hectares of land to 800,000 recipients. By the end of Cárdenas's term nearly half of the nation's cultivated lands and a fifth of the nation's forests were transferred to communities.[79] Land redistribution added concrete actions to complement ideological claims to revolutionary justice.[80] Moreover, the reclassification of lands from private hands (largely haciendas) into community hands (mainly ejidos) brought rural dwellers into contact with a federal state in a repetitive and binding manner that commingled modern forestry science with the demands of rural peoples who had previously managed the forests. Reclassifying land reform parcels and forests as parklands or ejidos secured the participation of residents while furthering their subjectivity to state control.

It is useful to view the increasing governance of the forests and the transformations in use through the lens of what Arun Agrawal calls "environmentality."[81] Environmentality, a combination of environment and the Foucaultian ideas of governmentality, brings attention to the various relations of power mediated through access to the natural world. For instance, regulations reshaped harvesting practices, but also and more insidiously, they reformed meanings of the forest. The production of knowledge about natural spaces occurred in tandem with the incorporation of rural communities into tighter state control and resulted in transformed environmental identities. In Mexico, the ecological rootedness of communities gave them both legitimacy and autonomy for a time, and the insertion of federal power into this dynamic came tied to social and environmental understandings of forest functions. The simultaneous redefinition of the environment and its subjects reshaped the countryside as popular demands for land came to echo in the aims of revolutionary planners.

Land redistribution reached its apogee under Cárdenas when its process and function involved federal policies with intimate local repercussions. But this period neither invented nor monopolized rural land claims. Historian John Tutino argues that the "ecological autonomy" of a rural community proved essential to the outcomes of revolutions.[82] In this sense, revolutionary participation hinged on the ability of a community to produce basic subsistence and to turn the rudimentary tools of rural life, like machetes and hatchets, into weapons of war. From indigenous people to common landholders, Catholics to union members, multiple and overlapping markers denoted the social positions of rural dwellers vis-à-vis other rural dwellers.[83] Yet collective identities tied to work, ownership, and history were rehabilitated when communities confronted federal agents mediating new policies over natural resources. Recovering some of these campesino identities and evaluating their relative differences shows that park creation involved more than pitting scientific outsiders against unified rural dwellers. More complex traditions were at play.

Land reform and national park creation both stemmed from transformations to legal designations tied to communal property.[84] Setting aside land in parks and giving land to peasants to work may appear paradoxical, but both resource claims stemmed from the same source: a state-supported (if only for a time) tradition of collective property and a desire to forge a common cultural patrimony. But this did not make parks and ejidos equivalent designations. In fact, ejido distribution could (and did) proceed without any acknowledgment of the parallel efforts to create parks. But the opposite is not true—parks came to exist because of the formulation of common property as a source of national pride. Without a deep commitment to land reform, park creation might have appeared a land grab. Instead, parks unfolded in tandem with ejidos because ejidos reinforced the federal mediation of land stewardship for rural people. In the public recognition of ejidos, scientists discovered a mechanism for saving forests and spreading their message of conservation more rapidly. In other words, ejidos contributed to changing technologies of government and opened up new mentalities that created space for the parks. By interpreting the global concept of a park through the lens of the revolution that elevated the idea of communal resources as a means of benefiting the poor, a completely different style of park creation unfolded and alternative meanings developed. This requires a consideration of how the complimentary, and at times conflicting, land use designations of ejido and national park drew upon a network of laws to reinforce communal property and federal authority, encourage stability and settlement, and promote economic development alongside cultural preservation.

Reforms to land tenure aimed to rectify the increasing accumulation of resources to benefit a few people at the expense of a vast majority and triggered unprecedented interference by a burgeoning state. As one historian notes, "They had fought for *tierra y libertad*—land and liberty. They got *tierra y el estado*—land and the state."[85] Receiving an ejido required multiple formal steps in a thicket of agrarian legislation regarding eligibility, properties affected, appeals, and administrative structures.[86] Generally, the applicants first needed to decide to apply for a grant (*dotación*) or a restitution (*restitución*). If they could prove with historical documentation and under the scrutiny of a land survey that they had recently (since the 1856 Lerdo Law) lost their land, they were (in theory) vindicated by having the hectares returned. If villagers had not previously owned the land, whether or not they had actually worked and resided on it, and they wanted to carve out a portion of it according to the provisions in the Constitution's new agrarian code, they went through the granting process. Some found success wresting land from foreign owners during the most violent years, but for most communities gaining access to land was a lengthy, tedious, and uncertain course, one full of possible violence and destructive repercussions.[87]

As part of the process, campesinos faced limits on where they could request an ejido, as they could expand only within a seven-kilometer radius of the original ejido. With their potential landholdings fixed by the state bureaucrats, landless people found themselves impeded from any sort of pioneering migration for the best lands.[88] Grants were carved from property held in excess of specified limits on the size of private property holdings, usually more than 300 hectares per owner. If villagers could prove that an owner had more than the allotted territory, they could file for the grant in a request directed to the governor of their state, and if he approved, it passed to the president. After the governor and president published their decisions, aspiring ejidatarios took possession of the land in a provisional grant. It required anywhere from a few months to several years for a grant to move from provisional to definitive status through intense scrutiny. The request went to the national agrarian officials, where an agrarian official conducted a census of heads of households and current holdings. The survey and census then served a crucial purpose in the allocation of property. The number of heads of household determined the amount of property in the ejido, generally calculated at four to six hectares of land per household, depending on the type of land and quality of irrigation. Some communities painstakingly tried to enhance their numbers to supplement the overall size. The census and survey, written exclusively by agrarian officials, held the community's future resource prospects.[89] After federal officials confirmed the grant with another publication of the notice, ejidatarios could apply for enlargements (*ampliaciones*) on their granted lands.

Land allocation created conflict because few ways existed to divide the land. Giving to one party often meant taking from another. Bureaucratic rules, for example, that enlargements could be requested only within seven kilometers of the original grant, ensured inevitable conflict with surrounding landholders. Once the government declared an ejido, the legal agrarian structures paved the way for enlargement and in fact encouraged ejidatarios to seek out extensions. By allocating land in steps, allowing for enlargements, and making size restrictions universal, the federal government created a system that encouraged permanence.

These procedures marked the proscribed manner of acquiring land, although the actual process of dispensing national territory often proved more complicated. After resistance by hacienda owners, the most common conflicts over designating ejidos came from communities petitioning for the same land. Less frequent were ejido requests overlapping with other federal designations including forests and parks. Bureaucrats differed on the issue of whether or not forests could be redistributed as ejidos. Agrarian Department employees in charge of land reform saw any unclaimed land as potentially available for redistribution, with the most plausible plots being land near existent communities. Forestry Department officials, Quevedo especially, objected to the possibility of redistributing forests to campesinos who wished, or were instructed, to clear forests for agriculture. "Those who have communal forests guard and respect them with moderate operations," Quevedo claimed, "while those who have received forests of good quality but lack tradition and attachment exploit with un-halting frenzy."[90] He further elaborated that "the Constitution's authors did not intend to redistribute forests but to return them to those dispossessed of them." In a few cases, such as La Malinche National Park (see chap. 4), sections of forests designated national parks were also redistributed to ejidatarios. Such overlap reveals the inexactness of custodianship and the ambiguity of bureaucratic control. The resulting negotiation of use wound through several rounds of claims, counterclaims, denunciations, and debates, yet in some cases both the park and the ejido persist, demonstrating that the two forms of property were reconcilable.

Cardenistas did not envision a nation exclusively of collectivities and cooperatives; they also saw the need for private property and for federal holdings. Parks were one example of federal holdings that could be highly symbolic, tangible political assets. Designating parks was a relatively low-budget, high-yield gesture that went beyond conservation and aimed to ameliorate broader tensions around the delicate issue of land ownership. While private societies and individual foresters had long spoken of parks, only when commitments to land reform took center stage were parks able to be reframed to fit the promises of a new society. By emphasizing communal rights and federal stewardship, Cárdenas became able to use the complimentary designations of national park and ejido to much success. He cannot be credited with complete innovation on this front as the ideas for both emanated from the past. Instead, Cárdenas's effectiveness lay in his ability to use preexisting concepts to make radical changes.

In contrast to local demand for ejidos, outsiders requested national parks.[91] Groups of scientists within the Forestry Department identified sites, conducted studies, made recommendations, and then wrote declarations for the president to sign. Once the study and decree had been written, they drew a sketch of the area, identifying major landmarks. No size, content, or ownership specifications existed for the parks, but patterns emerged, including preference for pine, oak, and fir forests, historic landscapes, and small sizes. The decrees specified whether property needed to change hands and how the park would be administered, either solely through the Forestry Department or in conjunction with other federal or municipal authorities (see app. A). The president signed the decree and published it in the *Diario Oficial*, making it law. Decrees provided a streamlined process for creating parks, one that proceeded more quickly than ejidos. Decrees averted debate and discussion in the legislature and sidestepped permission from the affected population. Through this authoritarian process, park decrees designated sites that belonged to the nation, not to individuals or even communities, and in doing so contributed to an expanded idea of common property, including revolutionary conservation.

Ejidos embedded a local collective property in a federal structure. Decisions about how the land would be worked remained with the elected members of the ejido, and while they did not have the title, their land was not public property. Parks also embedded local property within federal structure, but it was national property. Federal planners chose a location, sometimes private or municipal property, then declared their authority to manage it and returned it to the public in a limited sense. As forestry engineer and department employee Edmundo Bournet described, "Forested land is the true communal and national collective reserve."[92] Foresters wove their aims of conservation into broader land reform projects by appealing to the idea of common property. Many of the parks rewarded local communities with material benefits for preserving the forests or landscapes worthy of park status. This encouraged outsiders to visit the park, bringing additional sources of income to residents. In complementing local management practices and promising the economic stimulus of tourism, parks encouraged settlement and stability.[93]

Despite their near religious reverence for forests, Forestry Department employees did not maintain an unequivocal commitment to preservation of some imagined wilderness. While certain individuals, such as Quevedo, argued for abstaining from forest use, Cárdenas strove to mitigate the potentially exclusionary impacts of rendering forests off-limits. This negotiation between protection, restoration, and use appears in the trajectory of national park administration. For the first two years of the Forestry Department, decrees creating parks universally usurped the lands into federal domain while owners were promised compensation for their property. This model, similar to that of national parks in other countries, proved unworkable because of Mexico's complicated position in the middle of a comprehensive land reform program. Cárdenas found that allocating lands with one bureaucratic arm (the Agrarian Department) and taking it away with another (the Forestry Department) provoked confusion among the citizenry and the bureaucracy. There were also financial constraints: the Forestry Department simply did not have enough funds to comply with the compensation.

By 1938, the decrees were changed to allow ownership to remain in its original hands, as long as the proprietor abided by park regulations. This situation expedited the creation of parks, but its lack of rigor weakened the parks in the longer term. Cárdenas also stepped in to respond to citizen concerns over forest policy, arguing for changes to the Forestry Law because "activities involved with forest vigilance have impeded development and harmed the campesino classes."[94] Laws restricting use in areas deprived some populations of their livelihoods, and taxes on forest goods proved a particularly contentious issue for poor residents. In return, the Forestry Law was changed to allow campesinos to sell up to fifteen pesos worth of firewood, untaxed.[95] Just as all users were not equal, Cárdenas differentiated among various land designations when he responded to the Forestry Department's request to make all forested lands unavailable for ejidal restitution. Seeking a compromise, the president declared parks off-limits but left forest reserves open on a case-by-case basis.[96] This willingness to concede extraction but maintain notions of scale limited the entry of residents to the larger market, resulting in a radical compromise.

Ejidos and parks rewarded permanent and long-standing communities and encouraged others to become stable.[97] Although not equal in scale, ejidos affected millions of hectares of land and parks only hundreds of thousands, their formal creation processes and the intentions driving their construction intertwined. Both ejidos and parks contributed to the idea of a unified national heritage and fit into a revolutionary impulse to reconsider the roots of Mexican culture. Ejidos were unambiguous expressions of ethnicity tied to traditional tenure patterns and contingent on legitimization by the federal bureaucracy. Ejidos represented a particular social class of campesinos, whereas parks aimed to include all citizens. Revolutionaries chose to protect lakes, not swamps, and they selected sites near the capital, not on the periphery. This meant that parks reflected stories of descent and heritage by monumentalizing particular spaces and reformers created multiple tiers of a national patrimony that embraced the tension between traditional culture and modern habits. Historian Enrique Florescano credits the revolution with the creation of a notion of national patrimony accepted by much of the population.[98] Parks formed part of the revolutionary patrimony because they bridged natural resources and cultural preferences.

In their policies, Cardenistas looked to combine elite and popular culture to move beyond antagonistic ethnic divisions. Their actions were not merely rhetorical—they involved vast material changes. Often, these policies carried a human face like a teacher, a forester, an agronomist, or an anthropologist or had material markers such as a school, a field, or a park. Scientists and social scientists employed by the state carried the nationalistic message of cultural inclusion and in doing so transformed their subjects and themselves. Various new constituent groups, from women to peasants to workers, made vocal claims on their government, and in doing so these groups helped redefine what citizenship meant and shape the consolidation of a reciprocal state.[99] In the process of constructing citizenship, activists drew from liberal notions of participation, long-established expectations of patronage, and revolutionary processes of collective mobilization in order to gain access to the array of benefits now extended.

In this way, cultural politics grafted ideas about citizenship onto plans for agrarian reform, industrial development, rural education, and, at issue here, natural resource management.

Reforms accepting more expansive interpretations of citizenship aimed to unify these constituencies. As part of this spectrum, ejidos and parks played a role in fusing collective identities into a national character. Both property arrangements were future-oriented in their rhetoric but backward looking in their authority. The crafting of ejidos and parks simultaneously reveals how the government changed: rather than a rush toward an unspecified and foreign modernity that left behind a rural, Indian, and natural past, social policies in this era aimed to preserve distinct national attributes to showcase the special position Mexico had among the nations of the world. As the project of including rural people in the nation proceeded, the corollary project of elevating their lived landscapes kept pace.

Conclusion

At the chronological midpoint between the reign of Porfirian science and the social reforms of the Cárdenas period, the forester Ruiz Velasco called on his audience to bear in mind the transformation of their remarkable forests. He addressed a cadre of experts unmoored by their shifting social prestige and eager to fasten their knowledge to a new agenda. He and his audience saw the opportunity to shape the future in the new era of revolutionary thinking that sought a break with an exploitative past that had benefited few. Foresters hitched their aims to the activities of reformers who declared intellectual and cultural autonomy from a decrepit and alienating regime in favor of a platform of social equality. Cardenistas offered an idealistic plan for reworking society from the ground up, yet before long Cardenistas realized that to follow through on their promises, they needed expertise from an educated elite in certain technical areas. This tension proved especially visible within the development of forest policy, where the goals that fit the revolutionary paradigm required salvaging the least undesirable Porfiran scientists.

Mexico came to have more parks than any other nation in the world due to the flexible heritage of conservation ideas that grew in the nation's core and changed with the political context. Prerevolutionary foresters engaged with foreign theories but rarely dialogued with ordinary citizens. After the revolution, scientists could no longer only talk to each other; they had to take their understanding to the people. By the mid-1930s, park creation epitomized the complicated intellectual path trodden to administer the nation's resources. Parks marked cultural spaces, yet because of their natural qualities, they provided an intriguingly neutral template for incorporative environmental policies intertwining the revolutionary reforms with nature. Land reform affirmed communal property, providing the opening for interpreting parks as public rather than elite spaces. Reorienting prior scientific expertise to buttress these reforms became a foundational process that supported park creation. A new focus on nationally directed education, one that relied in part on scientific ideas, gave foresters justification to push toward a common cultural patrimony of nature. Besides believing in their own rigor, foresters sought opportunities to extend their explanations for the function and fortitude of forests through educational activities tied to national parks. In Lagunas de Zempoala National Park, these activities merged recreation and education in a place that soon became the epitome of national nature.

CHAPTER TWO

Education

Restoring Nature and Rebuilding Society in Lagunas de Zempoala National Park

The fog lingered on the lakes in the morning. It rose slowly past the evergreens shrouding the seven substantial lakes and dozen fleeting lagoons, then ambled past the open meadows beyond them. Full with waters from the nearby volcanic ridges, the lakes absorbed thick sediments and pushed the forests back to create a landscape that dramatized the tension between the water and the woods. Such a beautiful site beckoned park proponents and became an important template for national park creation. Situated in the southwestern range of the Valley of Mexico, sixty-six kilometers from the capital and just fifteen off the highway, the lakes of Lagunas de Zempoala National Park (hereafter Zempoala) may have been breathtaking, but they were never devoid of people. Tourists and picnickers frequented on weekends, while youth groups and campers enjoyed the park for longer trips. They hiked, fished, and swam in this area targeted for reforestation, wildlife restoration, and minor development. The park's landscape appeared in films, brochures, and newspapers and even entered into educational curricula. Also present in this humanized natural park were the producers' cooperatives, refreshment stands, and patrolling arrangements negotiated with local residents, who viewed the park with suspicion at first.

That this park protected lakes—not ranchlands or agricultural fields—made it a particularly compelling locale in which to instruct both rural inhabitants and urban workers about appropriate, modern uses for the rural landscape. These uses involved leisure, not extractive labor. Park promoters conveyed the idea that a trip to Zempoala was not a return to

A lake in Lagunas de Zempoala National Park, ca. 1937.

the farm but an enactment of modern citizenship. In this way, visitors to parks earned a sense of respectability in the revolutionary regime as they lounged on the lakeshore, sent their children to summer camps, or participated in tree planting festivals. Parks were mechanisms of social change judiciously and strategically popularized by the federal government.

Three social groups—federal officials, rural residents, and urban tourists—participated in the mutually constitutive creation of Zempoala in overlapping and sometimes contradictory ways. Federal officials promoted and publicized national parks as a way of inscribing their authority to manage the nation's natural resources. Federal officials, in this case mostly foresters, drew upon the history of Porfirian science and the newfound bureaucratic authority of the Forestry Department to establish park policies claiming and redefining land use. Rural residents found parks declared on lands that were part of their daily lives, and many took advantage of additional opportunities from these new creations. Rather than empty receptacles, rural inhabitants proved opinionated participants in the parks' creation. Alongside their rural compatriots, urbanites became the subjects of federal officials' educational campaigns to reform opinions about nature and redeem the rural landscape. Urban tourists sought out parks to display their increasing affluence and mobility. Weekend excursions and planned visits provided recreation that expressed solidarity with revolutionary causes without resurrecting Porfirian elitism. This nascent national tourism built up economic arguments for park development and made urban tourists subjects of federal publicity and willing supporters of reforestation projects.

Efforts to reshape the ways citizens used natural spaces also reveal paternalistic tendencies and conservationist prerogatives of the Cardenista state. Restricting and limiting everyday activities of rural inhabitants went hand in hand with promoting "modernized" reinterpretations of similar park activities that sought to socialize country folk and naturalize urban dwellers. For instance, Boy Scouts learned to cook over rustic fires even though domestic cooking fires were restricted; residents were banned from bathing in the lakes, whereas tourists were encouraged to take boats out in them. Yet, to focus too tightly on these restrictions limits the broader view that included redefining the rural landscape as the nexus of moral renewal. Policies that restricted rural inhabitants concomitantly constrained urban tourists and attempted to shape them both. Through the process of using the parks and articulating their desires, both groups in turn reshaped the state. No direct negotiation around a table or formal opinion gathering took place; instead, by actively engaging in the use of park space, scrutinizing policies, and objecting to unsatisfactory changes, diverse constituents shaped the evolving purposes for the parks. This chapter uses Zempoala to consider local encounters with national park design, tourism development, recreational programs and festivals, and restoration activities. Let us first consider the origins of the park itself.

The Milieu of Huitzilac

Miguel Ángel de Quevedo, head of the Forestry Department, and Edmundo Bournet, president of the Mexican Forestry Society, proposed the creation of Zempoala in March of 1936.[1] A few weeks later, José Peralta, Marcelo Rodríguez, and Teofilo Vazquez wrote President Cárdenas on behalf of dozens of residents of Huitzilac, the closest village to the proposed national park.[2] Upon hearing of the proposal, these residents objected because it prohibited their planting of corn on the fertile grasslands around the lakes. Peralta, Rodríguez, and Vazquez argued that this prohibition would force them into wresting subsistence from the woods, causing a "great injustice for our families." To them, the lakes' scenic qualities meant less than the confluence of resources available nearby. They had grounds to be hopeful about their request. In 1929, Agrarian Department officials had granted Huitzilac an ejido out of restituted lands, and Huitzilac maintained a forestry cooperative, also established in 1929, that periodically exploited dead wood by making charcoal.[3] There is no direct evidence that the president himself read the telegram, but it was forwarded along to the Department of Forestry, where Miguel Dehesa, the forestry delegate in charge of their region, took up their complaint.

Dehesa felt passionately that "sites of natural beauty," particularly those that captured the pastoral harmony between the lakes and forests, merited "vigorous protection."[4] He also maintained confidence that the park would bring opportunities beyond lumbering and agriculture to Huitzilac residents. His conviction proved cogent. After its formal creation, the park boasted thousands of visitors and built a reputation for park recreation among diverse groups.[5] Zempoala became a weekend destination for urbanites, many of whom brought money to spend. The Treasury Department held a retreat for their employees in the park, and the first youth summer camp in Mexico likewise took place there.[6] Dehesa refused to budge on the prohibition of farming, but he instead validated another activity entrepreneurial residents had already taken up: they replaced their cornfields with stands selling refreshments to tourists. Dehesa negotiated an exclusive vending contract with the community of Huitzilac and denied nonlocal requests, mostly from residents of the Federal District, for restaurants and developments.[7] This lucrative permission to sell prepared foods and beverages grew to include additional positions as enforcers of park policies. Dehesa hired Huitzilac campesinos to monitor restrictions on vending, such as keeping all stands a minimum of fifty meters from the lakes' edge, to enforce the swimming prohibitions, and to pick up garbage from the area, among other duties.[8]

Later evidence shows that the same community that initially objected became enthusiastic about its park. The arrangements for vending and vigilance provided a margin of profit to the community, and two years later when President Cárdenas sat down with villagers to ask what their government could do for them, the community no longer objected to the park.[9] Instead, they requested fruit trees be planted to give them readily available produce to vend. They also asked that the vehicular lot for the park be extended to accommodate the crowds, which proved especially heavy on Sundays. Quevedo immediately dispensed the fruit trees, expanded the permission for refreshment stands, and proceeded with the vehicular lot extension.[10] Although they never wielded equal power, the conversations between the Forestry Department and the community of Huitzilac reveal the coexistence of federal and local uses of the park and the ability of park advocates to provide acceptable incentives to alter local usage patterns in ways that coincided with the long-term interests of conservation within the park.

This shift must be viewed in the context of changing governmental institutions. Three brief examples demonstrate how policies became buffers around competing objectives. In January of 1939, Zempoala's park director Eduardo Madero installed a large sign in plain sight of the largest and most inviting of Zempoala's lakes. The sign explained that bathing or swimming in the lakes would no longer be permitted without written permission from the Forestry Department.[11] The creation of this restriction grew out of a tragedy: Consepción Hernández, a teenage boy from Coyoacán, drowned in the lake. Three weeks earlier, Hernández had made his way to the deepest part of the lake, more than eight meters, and then suffered stomach cramps from the food he'd just consumed. His position in the lake made him unreachable, and he succumbed to exhaustion and drowned. The trip director who brought Consepción to the park argued that if the deep section of the lake could not be cordoned off, swimming should be restricted. Up until that point, the lakes had been used by local residents during the week to bathe and by tourists on the weekends, especially young boys. Foresters enacted the restriction, allowing local residents to get written permission to use the lakes during the less crowded weekdays. Rather than merely circumscribing local use, this restriction came about from the failings of urban visitors.

Regulated lakes illustrate the controlled scenic locale, but it was the forests in Zempoala that received the most restrictions. The park designation prohibited sawing wood inside, but the forests on all sides of the park increasingly were managed by peasant-run forestry cooperatives. Huitzilac had a cooperative, and so did neighboring Ocuilán. Because neither maintained jurisdiction over the park, both cooperatives held a latent suspicion of the other regarding access to the woods within the park. In response to this suspicion, members from both cooperatives offered their services, readily accepted by the Forestry Department, to patrol the park and ensure others were not exploiting it.[12] Both Ocuilán and Huitzilac residents offered to periodically send members to inspect the extent of the park's territory and report regularly. Park director Eduardo Madero paid them sporadically for these efforts, and he used the patrols as a source of information and recorded their findings. As they checked up on each other, the cooperative members also strengthened the legitimacy of the federal designation by acting as enforcers.

Although every park had a slightly different relationship with its surrounding communities, around Zempoala the residents had a working relationship in which they perceived benefits from the park. In some instances, park officials used surprising techniques to encourage activities that complemented those that the officials prioritized. For example, in May of 1937 the head of the Office of Parks and Reserves, J. Manuel Corona, received complaints from some park visitors that the woods were filled with fallen branches and needed to be "cleaned."[13] While the Forestry Department lacked a budget for the removal of the understory debris, communities such as Huitzilac used the wood for their domestic needs. Corona asked the forestry delegation to remind the Huitzilac residents that until they cleared out the fallen wood in the park, no permit for the extraction of more profitable wood elsewhere would be granted to them. In a sense, the villagers became low-cost laborers "cleaning" the park for city visitors who preferred not to see a forest full of fallen branches. Yet, the villagers kept the gathered wood for their own purposes.[14]

Restrictions on public bathing, functional patrolling, and understory cleaning provide glimpses into the multidimensional custodianship dynamics developing in national parks. Foresters created, promoted, and designed the parks, and people recreating in them or living around them also contributed to their meaning. Ongoing debates about what activities were appropriate in the park contributed to the democratic process of state development, even when the results seemed authoritarian. To be more than just symbolic, conservation programs involved restrictions on levels of use, and determining those restrictions in this case involved the participation of multiple constituencies.

The preferences afforded to Zempoala's local residents exemplified government aims to protect both defenseless nature and vulnerable citizens while furthering a forestry education campaign. The recreational focus of the park typified early arguments for tourism as part of a transition to a modern economy. From the start, the park aimed to provide alternative incomes to residents that reduced the extractive use of the forests. These alternatives, largely tied to a tourist economy, favored local enterprises but served outside visitors. Foresters promoting tourism used their professional specialization to advocate for the park as a means of incorporating these citizens into the national patrimony and furthering ecological aims to protect the Valley of Mexico. Today, such efforts might be categorized as *ecotourism*, but to these scientists and campesinos, managing the park by limiting its economic activities simply seemed fair.

Park Tourism

In late 1938, Claudio Díaz, a movie producer based in Mexico City, asked the Forestry Department for permission to film scenes in Zempoala. Díaz maintained that the park would make a perfect panorama for his dramatic film *My Pueblo's Campaign*. Daniel Galicia promptly gave permission as long as the movie crew did not "modify the park in any permanent manner" and "left all trees in place."[15] The cinematic use of the landscape solidified foresters' claims that the site had scenic value. Just as movie scenes redefined space through a camera lens, tourism redefined nature through the interpretive power of reclamation—the exalted status of a national park drew more and more urban visitors into scripted areas to display their affluence and reenact rituals of modern citizenship.

A dedicated group of boosters in private and public institutions worked diligently to redefine the nation's reputation as a tourist destination in the 1930s. This set the stage for what would become a global destination for recreation that drew largely upon prehistoric sites and museums.[16] Although some connections existed, park planners stood on the margins of these developments because conservationists dealt more with agricultural and forestry interests. Yet the park planners' efforts hold resonance with a newer form of tourism that aspired toward more environmental aims: ecotourism. Although there is no direct intellectual link to the early national parks, the Mexican architect Hector Ceballos-Lascurain coined the term *ecotourism* in 1983.[17] Defined as "responsible travel to natural areas that conserves the environment and improves the well-being of local people," it arose as a critique of conventional tourism's impact on the environment and as an attempt to bridge the aims of enjoying nature and supporting local communities that protect that nature.[18] In most explanations, the emergence of this idea corresponds with the accessibility of airplane travel, the growing environmental movement in the United States, and the rise in international conservation organizations, all in the 1970s.

Cardenista aims to combine tourism and local development predated the boom in traditional tourism and the later critique of it. Overlooking historical, homegrown ideals in countries that later became destinations for ecotourism reinforces the idea that environmentalism in any form is an import from the United States or Europe. Such an oversight impoverishes understandings about which societies can build institutions that value nature and social justice. The views and actions of early Mexican park promoters demonstrate that participants in the social revolution attuned their plans to the economically sound links between nature and culture. They saw tourism as a scientifically responsible and socially just mechanism for conserving nature and respecting rural livelihoods. They overlooked—or could not anticipate—the cumulative effects of vehicular travel and road building, but they aimed to minimize the negative effects of logging by providing alternative sources of income.[19] These steps toward ensuring local people's incorporation in parks helped create a template for permanence, if not pristine protection.

Visitors who traveled to Zempoala provide important texture to the development of tourism in tandem with the parks. In May 1937, less than one year after the creation of the park at Zempoala, the director of the National Parks Office, Daniel Galicia, requested funds from the secretary of public works, who administered roads for the country. He followed through on the expansion of the parking lot at Zempoala Park because the size was insufficient for the number of tourists who visited.[20] Park employees reported that their staff spent all day every Sunday regulating the parking lot for all of the "metropolitan people" who were trying to park their cars. Galicia personally verified the demand on Sunday May 8, 1938, when over 250 cars came to the lot, even though adequate space barely existed for 100.[21] Uneven and haphazard parking exacerbated by rains caused tires to spin in the mud and ruts to form in the roads. The lack of vehicle parking highlights the eager public inspired to visit the parks in accord with the Forestry Department officials' preliminary hopes.

Who were all of these tourists, and what were they doing in the park? Park officials kept visitor logs that help to profile the average tourists, including their origins, occupations, and comments on the site. Records were not kept (or do not survive) for every year, yet it is possible to derive trends from nine months of logs kept during 1938, one of the peak years of park creation. During these months, Zempoala saw 11,846 total visitors, or 1316 average monthly visitors.[22] Most people arrived in groups of six or seven, although some entries identified up to thirty-six companions. Although the park officials claimed that one of the reasons to have a park was to give citizens a place for solitude, only a handful of visitors came alone, and they had little chance for quiet on popular holidays or Sundays. Seventeen people registered more than once, included one woman, Gilberta Valle-cillo, who claimed, "I've come five times and each time I admire more the beauty that is our Mexico."[23] Although some visitors drove from as far away as Dallas, Texas, or Monterrey, Nuevo Leon, most made only a day trip from the capital. The vast majority of visitors (88 percent) came from

A group enjoying an excursion to the lake at the future Lagunas de Zempoala National Park in 1935.

Mexico City, with only 10 percent from elsewhere in Mexico and 2 percent from the United States. In addition, visitors came from Russia, France, and Cuba to the park. Tourists were typically urban families of professionals and workers who came in cars for single day trips on the weekend.

One of the more interesting components of the visitor logs comes from the list of visitors' occupations. That park employees solicited this information attests to their sensitivity to whom the park would serve, and it served a diverse crowd. Visitors self-identified their occupations listing 110 separate jobs, and when grouped into like professions, these overwhelmingly urban occupations demonstrate the range of park visitors, from business professionals to agriculturists and domestic workers. The occupations identify only about 10 percent of the actual visitors because one person signed the log for the six or so people who accompanied him (rarely her).[24] Nevertheless, these nearly 1600 identifications confirm that the park appealed to a constituency far beyond the foresters who designed it.

The range of occupations attests to a far-reaching appeal for national parks, in particular to those involved in the expanding service sector and skilled working-class occupations. Business professionals, including lawyers, merchants, and bankers, made up the largest group of visitors, but they were closely followed by industrial workers, including factory workers, construction employees, and mechanics. The majority of jobs had some degree of upward mobility, indicative perhaps of the aspirations of weekend visitors. People involved with education, such as students and teachers, frequented the parks, but so did engineers, nurses, jewelers, and public employees. Eighty visitors did not identify their occupations, listing only that they were tourists, climbers, or travelers. These discernable patterns reflect large numbers of visitors from a range of social positions.[25]

The variety and concentration of occupations demonstrates that park visitors did enter a space where they could mingle with people outside their daily social circle. Indeed, a trip to a park likely offered a degree of respectability for people in skilled working-class occupations. Mechanics could eat picnic lunches next to lawyers, or painters could walk around the lakes with chemists. Based on the people who patronized the park, foresters succeeded in crafting a national space in the sense that it appealed to vast numbers of citizens. A park visit confirmed the accessibility of leisure to popular classes once excluded from respectable recreation. Not surprisingly, rural peoples remained more interested in how the park could provide a livelihood, not an escape.

How visitors felt about the park also comes through in the logbooks. The most frequent comment on the park was "beautiful," followed by *political*

"marvelous," "magnificent," and "pretty." A few visitors made more lengthy comments. Roberto Clemente, a tailor from Mexico City, expressed nationalistic pride when he wrote in the comment book that the park was "one of so many beauties that unite my fatherland." Dr. J. A. Roate remarked that the park's healthy climate provided a perfect cure for persistent sicknesses. The businessman Juan de la Pérez claimed that the park was impressive but bemoaned the terrible road that impeded a relaxing trip. These men saw in the park reflections of the importance of their own social positions and professions. The doctor saw health in the climate, the tailor was concerned with appearance, and the businessman noted opportunities with road construction.[26]

To make tourism viable, forestry officials had to meet the needs and desires of citizens outside their circle of scientists (a scant 8 percent of the visitors). Many park visitors did not hesitate to make their wishes known, either in visitor logs or in letters to the Forestry Department or the president. Some suggestions fit well with policies underway, like the comments of foreign tourist Maurice Cumskeep, who lamented the state of forests around the capital city and encouraged the planting of more trees.[27] Other interested parties demanded increased reforestation. Pedro Pérez, the municipal president of Tangancícuaro, Michoacán, near the National Park Lago de Camécuaro, complained that the park was not getting enough attention from the federal government despite the many tourists that visited. He feared that the state of disarray of the older trees, full of fallen branches, as well as the empty holes dug for new saplings that were never planted, gave visitors the impression that the park had been neglected and discouraged them from visiting the lake for which the park was named. In his opinion, even though the park was located on the highway from Mexico City to Guadalajara, passersby had no reason to stop because of the unfortunate shape of the park.[28] Visitors and residents alike saw the conditions in the parks as critical to the development of tourism.

Tourism then justified construction projects and programs encouraging park use. For example, planners adorned the highway from Mexico City to Tijuana with national parks. They intended parks to encourage highway use and for the highway also to encourage use of the parks. The Pemex (Petroleos Mexicanos) travel club published brochures with trip routes describing excursions. These travel club guides were distributed throughout the nation and given to the U.S. consulates to encourage highway travel—and, of course, the accompanying use of gasoline. The highways and parks were featured in the brochures—along with lodging, restaurants, and shops.[29]

Smaller tourist amenities—mainly benches, tables, parking lots, garbage cans, cooking grills, trails, signs, and lookout sites—were developed in the parks. In addition to the parking lot expansion in Zempoala, Forestry Department officials repeatedly suggested building projects to show that the parks contributed to the growth of the national economy.[30] Kiosks, fences, and signs served functional purposes, while ambitions of floating docks and cabins repeatedly surfaced.[31] Such developments aimed to make visitors more comfortable while they enjoyed nature.

Many visitors mentioned the strength of life they found in the parks and the tranquility and peace that put them in good spirits.[32] Visiting parks, rather than living around them, allowed urbanites to develop a different orientation toward the rural landscape. Tourism provided not merely an economic activity but a cleansing of the social soul and a rejuvenation of the national being. Forestry officials hoped that a visual and tactile experience would cultivate support for the parks. In their vision, parks would encourage tourism from urban constituents and stimulate the economy in the surrounding areas by the purchase of food and amenities. Tourism also provided some justification to halt logging activities or take forests out of production. By vending an experience, tourism extended the federal government's promise to create a new revolutionary citizen.[33] Education, recreation, and tourism sat nested within plans for social change reinforcing one another.

Redemption through Recreation

When José Sánchez and Gabriel Reyes, residents of the Federal District, asked for permission to spend three days camping at Zempoala, Director Galicia responded enthusiastically by requesting that "these men be provided with every consideration because camping proved an important bridge" between rural residents and urban visitors in the park.[34] Camping, or spending several days pretending to live in the park, symbolized important things. It romanticized rural life and elevated the rustic over the modern. It demonstrated that enough wealth had accrued to redefine leisure pursuits in revolutionary, rather than Porfirian, terms. And it blended the moral certitude of campesino life with the popular social impulses of capital residents. Sánchez and Reyes were independent campers, enjoying the park of their own accord, but most of the camping activities that used the parks involved organized youth groups. Foresters largely supported camping and aimed to expand its appeal. For example, the Boy Scouts largely involved urban middle- and upper-class youth, but camps run through the

Secretary of Public Education (hereafter SEP) focused on rural working-class children. Recreation provides the best example of foresters' hopes for the use of park spaces to erase distinctions and merge "representatives of all the social sectors and working groups, military, schools, and scientific, cultural, and sporting institutions" into a cohesive populace.[35] Recreation also provides an entry point into public discourse over the environment. Two examples of organized recreation — camps and festivals — demonstrate the ways federal officials used national parks to redeem rural landscapes and to unify social groups.

By Cárdenas's presidency, rural communities were no longer riddled with the chaos of war and political instability or haunted by the prospect of economic devastation. This is not to say that the countryside transformed into a bastion of peace and progress, but a number of reforms enabled rural people to participate in state-driven mobilizations and, by doing so, secure various benefits. The organization of campesino federations, the creation of ejidos, and even the construction of rural schools, began to soften, co-opt, and direct local concerns away from direct conflict and to-ward the consolidation of a single party state that oversaw development projects. Foresters worked to promote forested lands as a locus for national redemption that bridged conflicts among communities and between rural and urban constituencies. In doing so, foresters promoted civic recreation, including visits to national parks.

From the first decade of the twentieth century, Mexico boasted a group of Boy Scouts (Tribus de exploradores), modeled after the Boy Scouts of Great Britain and the United States.[36] By 1939, there were nearly 12,000 boys enrolled in the youth organization. The capital city had at least four active troops known as the Tequihua, Tomochic, Tlacopan, and Texcucana and the SEP encouraged the troops. The members, mostly elite young men guided by older male leaders aspired to learn about nature, science, and discipline through a series of excursions and training exercises. They had troop flags and offered merit badges for mastering skills. The troops took excursions to several national parks, including the truncated corridor of parks of Zempoala, Cumbres de Ajusco, and Miguel Hidalgo.[37]

Ironically, the Scouts confirmed the importance of youthful patriotism by teaching city youth the skills associated with country people. For example, cooking dinner over a campfire was a survival skill, one well known by rural residents in and near the national parks, but one less common for city dwellers. Rather than a daily necessity, constructing a fire was a skill to be employed as a demonstration of technical knowledge. Fires conveyed conflicting symbols as campers constructed them as part of their educational rituals but also promised to control fires set by campesinos to clear forests for pasture or fields. In their newsletter, *Cumbre* (The Summit), Boy Scouts from the Tequihuas troop proudly displayed themselves in front of campfires and wrote about the importance of youth in the historical moment in which their nation found itself. Amidst translations of Greek poetry and inspirational quotes from Hegel and Socrates, the newsletter espoused political views about nature, youth, and society. "Rather than sit idly by," the newsletter claimed, "today's circumstances demand that youth intervene directly and forcefully in national life, infusing it with arts, natural and social sciences, and technical philosophy."[38] The members even recognized the labors of the Forestry Department. The Tequihuas troop congratulated Quevedo and his team of specialized engineers for their work "developing constructive, healthful, and beneficent policies for the national interests."[39]

Such compliments might have had a deeper agenda. The Tequihuas troop applied to the Forestry Department for permission to construct a cabin within Cumbres de Ajusco National Park, adjacent to Zempoala, to use for their weekly meetings. The cabin was to be constructed of wood, mostly from already fallen and dead trees but also from a few they would need to cut down. The Scouts argued that cutting a few trees provided a better alternative to using concrete, which would disrupt the beauty and intentions of the park's natural state. The Scouts proposed to care for the cabin by spending one night there at least every eight days, but they would not exclude others from its use. The proposal extended the use of the cabin, "out of a moral duty, to fellow outdoorsmen."[40] Members expressed their desire to support, not challenge, the conservation works of the Forestry Department and their hopes to collaborate with the department, especially by putting out forest fires. Having the cabin would help the troop to reside "in the heart of the national park, attentive and ready to extinguish any unconscionable individual's criminal act of fire-setting."[41] These young men dramatized their promise to risk their lives to protect the nation's forests.

After first denying the solicitation because of the prohibition on closed structures in national parks, in September of 1938, forestry engineer Salvador Guerrero approved the proposal with the rationale that encouraging time in nature matched perfectly with the objectives of the Forestry Department. He asked for modifications to the cabin's design to eliminate enclosure on all four sides, but he argued that the structure would provide shelter for tourists and serve as a site of scientific investigation.[42] Guerrero explained that similar proposals would be looked upon favorably in the future. The willingness of officials to concede to their constituents and, in some cases, place broader objectives above technical rules demonstrates the flexibility of park regulations. Although closed structures were known to cause problems with vigilance, the cabin's role in developing youthful interest and appreciation for forests outweighed the prior prohibition.

The Boy Scouts were not the only campers in national parks; Zempoala hosted several varieties of camps. Professor Alfredo Basurto conducted the First Community Camping School in Zempoala during May of 1938. Just as the Boy Scouts sought to mold young men, other professionals saw the enhancement of the future for children by giving them structured contact with nature. Unlike the Boy Scouts, this coeducational camp included boys and girls of various ages. Basurto developed this idea of a summer camp for popular education from suggestions made by the Special Delegation for Popular Education in Querétaro. He began working through various federal departments and acquiring the necessary tents, supplies, and funds for the camp. He established a directive staff, which included himself as director, a doctor and a nurse, a professor of physical education, two music and choir teachers, an agronomist, two forest guards, and a carpenter. Three military instructors and various vocational students also assisted.[43] Five regional rural schools from the states of Hidalgo, Mexico, Puebla, Morelos, and Guerrero were invited to send delegations of twenty-two students each for a total group of 110 students. Once assembled, the opening ceremony on the principal patio of the SEP's main building began with the raising of the national flag and the presentation of the children's respective state flags, symbolically merging regional identity into national. Similarly, students were transported from their regions into the capital to unite before they ventured together out into nature.

Basurto's report captured the energy and enthusiasm, but also the chaos of the camp. The trip out of the capital took four hours due to various stops to pick up equipment, get gasoline, and make purchases, and then another two hours passed unloading the vehicles. Upon arrival, young campers with scarcely sufficient clothing became cold and hungry. Some children ate their beans and bread voraciously on the picnic tables while others sat at the base of the mountains. After a restless night in the stark cold (slightly above freezing) of morning, the physical education teacher led the boys and girls in marches, exercises, and gymnastic games. When these exercises ended, the children explored the lakes, where some swam and others walked along the edge. In the evening, the forest guard accompanied them on an exploratory hike with instructions on the art of camping. Before bed, the camp held its first fireside lesson, which included music, theater, and jokes, followed by a story about Aztec mythology.

Camp overseers saw their work in concordance with the revolutionary government. "Around the campfires," Basurto explained, "were the most fitting occasions to talk about the objectives and aims of the Camp, the eminent revolutionary work of President Cárdenas, the betrayal of the Patria by the Cedillista faction, the role of youth in the development of the revolution and in its immediate future, the ideals and claims of young people in the present moment, the problems of sex, and the professional problems of future teachers." With a dramatic flourish, Basurto further made his point: "In the heat of the campfires, the minds of the kids were better disposed to hear and to think deeply about the great questions that face their generation." The natural setting became a metaphor for revolutionary struggles: the storms and the squalls that came through the mountains were obstacles the campers faced, just as illiteracy and disorganization challenged revolutionary progress.

During camp, students practiced technical skills that held particular application to the new industry of tourism and park recreation. The camp carpenter constructed two latrines and commissioned several boys to learn his construction techniques. The campers also received instruction on the creation of orchards and reforestation projects around the country. After a week of camping, half of the campers visited Huitzilac for a basketball tournament and the other half served as guides for park visitors, giving explanations about the camp's objectives. Forestry Department officials Galicia, Quevedo, and others came to the park and invited campers to view the forestry cooperative in Huitzilac. Foresters claimed that the cooperative had afforded the community skills and money to refurbish the municipal building and to add a public clock tower.[44]

Concluding the camp, Basurto reported that no sicknesses and no accidents had occurred during the camp, which solidified his belief that parks were peaceful oases in a country still grasping for stability. He noted the superior behavior, enthusiasm, and camaraderie of the campers. In Basurto's mind, the camp proved that young men and women could live and be educated in a tranquil and natural environment because "classes and lessons given within the forests where you can concentrate perfectly have excellent results." He determined that the national park provided a healthy place to camp, a beautiful site near water, magnificent excursions, and safety from assaults and robberies.[45] Camping in national parks tied youth to nature and nature to the nation while providing a showcase for federal policies aimed at conferring a sense of belonging.

For those who could not attend overnight camps, daytime festivals proved a compelling alternative to engage with the parks. The Forestry

Department assisted with the promotion of activities associated with Arbor Day (Día del árbol) and the Forest Festivals (Fiestas del bosque). More than frivolous events, festivals express deeply held cultural affinities and reveal priorities.[46] Most holidays highlighted the federal government's recognition of specific constituencies, but some festival days, such as Arbor Day, involved more neutral symbolism. The widespread participation in and promotion of Arbor Day demonstrated that trees had an emblematic importance. Arbor Day had been celebrated sporadically since the inaugural festival in 1912, but beginning in 1925, the Forestry Society sponsored annual Arbor Day celebrations in various locations throughout the country during February and March.[47] By 1935, the main force behind the celebration transferred from the private society to the Forestry Department and celebrations were held in every state capital and at numerous federal schools. Federal administrators did not hesitate to enhance the festivals with popular activities such as live music and dancing, and events included children planting trees and listening to speeches in honor of trees.[48]

Over the course of the Cárdenas period, trees came to have a cultural significance that linked nature to the nation. In addition to formal national holidays to celebrate trees, the planting of specific trees frequently marked special occasions. For example, in 1938 the Forestry Society planted a tree in Mexico City's oldest park, Bosque de Chapultepec, in recognition of the work undertaken by Quevedo. The tree, an ahuehuete, was planted with soil sent from all the states to symbolize national gratitude for the work Quevedo had undertaken in behalf of the forests. Four kilos of soil were sent in from Cárdenas's hometown of Jiquilpan, Michoacan, to complete the ceremony. The tree was even named "the Apostle" to honor Quevedo's legacy and service to the nation.[49] The location of the tree ensured its viewing by thousands of visitors and demonstrated how officials considered the effects of tourists on the spaces they shaped.

Nourishing Restoration

Foresters saw that uniting the production of new trees with new citizens provided the best way to reach their social goals. Some parks, like Zempoala, maintained healthy forests, but others required major reforestation works. Foresters planned reforestation by creating a nationwide tree nursery system within the Forestry Department. Known as "stations of forest repopulation" by the scientists, they were popularly known as *viveros*, or nurseries.[50] After a failed attempt to import saplings from France and California,

Quevedo founded the first national tree nursery in Coyoacán in southern Mexico City between 1907 and 1913 on a portion of his family property. He called it simply Viveros and boasted that it "contributed powerfully to public education as a practical school for arboriculture visited by a great number of schoolchildren and the general public."[51]

In Forestry Department activities, Viveros served as a national focal point for tree, sapling, and seedling distribution to nurseries across the nation at low or no cost. In addition to woodland species such as pine and fir (*oyamel, Abies religiosa*), seedlings included ornamental and fruit trees along with Australian species of eucalyptus and casuarinas, seen as particularly useful for their rapid growth in reforestation projects. Although students of the national forestry school voted the ahuehuete the official national tree, many reforestation works used foreign species that engineers believed provided more rapid growth and greater success.[52] The planners called for the creation of nurseries in municipalities, schools, and ejidos to be the recipients of the federal growths.[53] Individual nurseries then would disseminate and plant in the appropriate spaces near government buildings, in plazas, and surrounding schools. For the country to be reforested, trees had to be available, but in addition to its practical application, this process of nursery development reflected the Cárdenas government's centralization as far-flung nurseries were linked to administrative centers.

Foresters focused diligently on the quantity of trees provided for reforestation as evidence of their revolutionary works. They boasted that between mid-February to mid-March 1937, the Forestry Department provided over 150,000 trees to citizens. In addition to two national and thirty-eight regional nurseries, foresters managed 709 school nurseries in cooperation with the SEP. For the project of reforesting the Valley of Mexico, they established thirteen nurseries in the area, producing over a million saplings. The final count for repopulation stood at 4,720,032 seedlings and 1,212,900 kilograms of seeds.[54] They counted trees as diligently as they counted park visitors.

National nurseries with local counterparts distributed trees nationwide, but individual citizens also propagated trees on their own private property with the encouragement of foresters. Incentives for private nurseries appealed particularly to hacienda owners who were threatened with losing their property to agrarian reform unless they used their lands in productive ways. For example, Julia Piñedo de Rojas owned the hacienda La Encarnación, that formed part of the protected zone declared within the Valley of Mexico. The hacienda's inclusion in this protected zone placed it within a logging ban that effectively prevented Piñedo de Rojas from exploiting any of the forest resources on her property. Instead, she was encouraged to create a nursery and provide trees for propagation for the government and for surrounding properties. She established this nursery, agreed to provide the wages for two laborers to work the area, and remitted 25 percent of the plants to the Forestry Department. The nursery's production covered more than 2,000 hectares, of which 300 were ceded by the property owner to the department. In exchange, her property remained untouchable and she was allowed to sell the saplings from of the rest of the nursery. With this precarious relationship, the widow retained the security of her property and the allegiance of the federal entity. By 1942 the ejido Villa Nicolás Romero also supported the nursery, donating ten hectares of their ejidal land because they believed that the nursery increased the water available for irrigation making their lands more productive.[55]

Trees were not the only species propagated by revolutionary reformers in the Valley of Mexico. Zempoala became an experimental station for the restoration of fish in the lakes and wildlife in the forests. These projects were much less developed and less successful than reforestation programs, yet foresters undertook them with enthusiasm. Park administrators at Zempoala stocked the lakes with trout and the forests with deer and quail to augment the connection of humans to wildlife within the park. In May of 1937, the director of fishing stations requested two workers to dig and develop the ditch alongside the lake to feed young trout introduced and cultivated there.[56] By 1939, foresters employed residents to correct the streams between the lakes to make them more hospitable for trout because only about 60 percent survived in the ditch. The new plan involved introducing incubation pools for trout eggs they hoped would begin to self-reproduce, to no avail.[57] Zempoala was not alone in wildlife restoration efforts. Roberto Barrena led the white-tailed deer, antelope, and bighorn sheep reintroduction project in northern Sonora. Barrena championed a similar project in Zempoala, which would start with building a fence to keep the wildlife inside the park.[58] While some animals, mainly deer, were introduced, the expense for this project outweighed the benefits as locals hunted them and the deer fled fencing. The relationship between park ideals and the reality of managing nature rarely matched up. Parks were for people; animals entered as an afterthought.

Educating and Enacting Authority

Zempoala, and other parks like it, provide texture to the national efforts at building a public patrimony. Parks could be used to educate citizens about the value of both the environmental conservation program and the legitimacy of the government. The centrality of education to the construction of a revolutionary state has not been lost on historians. As Mary Kay Vaughan argues, in rural schools, "central state policy makers, provincial teachers, and men, women, and children of the countryside came together in the 1930s to forge a national culture."[59] Such a process reached far beyond intellectual circles or federal policies to tether elite ideas to the daily lives of ordinary men and women. Educating citizens on nature conservation combined modern sensibilities and traditional values and involved far more than proper schooling. Foresters used formal and informal instruction to reform peasant behavior, universalize standards of citizenship, and create a common patrimony with reverence for specific ecological features.

Much attention has been given by historians and sociologists to how federal governments, their representatives, and their plans universalized, homogenized, and erased local variety and eradicated difference. James Scott has argued that the ways in which authoritarian states "see" has had catastrophic effects on alternative worldviews and customary manners of organizing resource use by standardizing everything from surnames to pine trees in order to better collect fees, impose controls, solidify power, and direct social programs.[60] Such an approach to state functions is a useful — but incomplete — entry point for understanding the actions of the Forestry Department. To better administer nature and people, Cardenistas marked the landscape with their own scientific priorities and attempted to shape citizens' understandings of the natural world, but both changed rapidly given the social context. For example, ambitions for federal schools were developed in consonance with plans for tree nurseries in ways that blended paternalistic managerial principles. Seedlings from federal nurseries were distributed for sowing nationwide because planting trees had two purposes: to reforest the woodlands and to perform a symbolic and instructive act teaching the importance of forests.

Despite the conservation programs' paternalism, Cardenista plans stopped short of running roughshod over competing agendas. Rather than quash local engagement, revolutionary programs required flexibility. On the one hand, it is important to refrain from universalizing the power of the Cardenista state to reform and subsequently erase local, independent, or dissonant thought. Policies regulating new uses of the natural world, particularly recreation and leisure, provided buffers for more sensitive areas of regulation, such as agricultural land or workers' unions. State-derived policies and their application were neither as fixed nor as rational as Scott's model would suggest. On the other hand, the superiority of Porfiran science and a strong dose of arrogance shaped bureaucrats' ideas and created a cadre of men who believed so deeply in what they were doing they determined to shape the world to their will. Park regulations sculpted authority over landscapes and inhabitants, yet their avariciousness was tempered by a revolutionary ethos and urgency afforded to restoration.

The Forestry Department influenced rural schools mainly through the distribution of pamphlets, magazines, instructional cards, and other publications. Various departments under the Cárdenas administration enacted public campaigns, and each department reported regularly to the president with the activities they promised enhanced life for the everyday person.[61] Although the Forestry Department was not far from the norm of other departments, the ideas diffused through their literature give insight into the kind of information—and moral fortitude—they wished to foster. Such educational material aimed to "awaken in children love and respect for trees" and promote "respect, protection, and sympathy for the role of nature in improving the lives of humans."[62] According to the Forestry Department, conserving forests equated to conserving and improving the lives of citizens because a revolutionary citizen was only as healthy as his or her surrounding environment.

The Forestry Society and the Forestry Department made obvious and repeated connections between growing trees and cultivating citizens. Besides providing saplings for ejidos, foresters designed the national nursery system to support cultural diffusion. Children and campesinos were interchangeable symbols of this diffusion and provided a constant analogy to justify the importance of both to the future. In this manner, foresters infantilized campesinos by linking the two groups to a supposed need for guidance. Quevedo took the analogy between gardens and kindergarten, or *jardines de niños*, literally. He advocated structuring city parks in a manner consistent with preschools, complete with supervision and boundaries.[63] From "nourishing the sources where water comes forth" to "opening founts of wealth and production," references to the fertilization of the revolution abounded.[64] While schools metaphorically sowed the seeds among citizens, foresters literally sowed the seeds and saplings of a prosperous future by growing forests.[65]

Through nursery programs, the federal government sought to grow a new citizenry surrounded by healthy forests. Equating children with trees, some curricula went as far as to suggest that classes should be held outside in the open air because many children were desperately malnourished, and they needed the benefits of "pure air and sun" just like their arboreal brethren.[66] While the Forestry Department dominated reforestation efforts, other entities were also involved. SEP distribution also standardized trees. Each tree contained a tin certificate attached to the trunk that identified its number, species, and specific steward. Both the tree and the citizen were identified, linking the behavior and condition of both nature and society. Furthermore, as part of the tree campaign, teachers taught pupils to love trees and instructed patience and perseverance learned by caring for trees. A contest judged the trees from the campaign on a range of aspects, including symmetry, height, health, and other features determined by a forestry expert. Three monetary prizes were given for the best tree, along with a 200-volume compilation of arboriculture literature, and a trophy. In giving prizes for "tree champions," this contest sought to manipulate and encourage participation and reward participants who aligned their thinking with the national policies.[67] Proponents also regulated the normalcy or shape of trees to meet the desires of national policy makers. A tree and its shaper were celebrated as makers of revolutionary promises because such celebration had the potential to create a particular type of nature and inspire others to strive for such uniformity.

Nevertheless, the creation of national parks was a federal project that involved gathering places and peoples into the national patrimony. Federal officials labeled the landscape and marked the forests with tangible indicators of governmental authority, such as roads and signs, and because marks are meaningless unless their symbolism and power is understood, campaigns used demonstrative activities and didactic forms, from Boy Scouts to tree planting. The Forestry Department sought to establish the permanence of both forest resources and national administration through parks like Zempoala.

Conclusion

An early park with typical features, Zempoala National Park contributed to a common cultural patrimony of nature. Its creation combined rational science and federal policy to manage natural resources for rural residents and urban visitors. For foresters, the park marked a site where people could enjoy peace and contemplate nature in a national landscape.[68] The accessible lakes promoted the value of trees and importance of popular recreation as they drew crowds in the thousands. The park struck a popular chord, and citizens visited Zempoala, earning the park program publicity and praise.

Forestry Department officials sought to shape rural and urban citizens, neither of which passively absorbed their commands and in turn both influenced the Forestry Department with their actions and demands. Park scientists promoted a rational version of management, but mechanics, office workers, and taxi drivers brought their own values each time they visited the park. Educators designed curricula to infuse young people with physical health, but children participated in the outdoor experiences that suited them. Perhaps most importantly, the park provided a series of compromises to rural residents that held prior claims to the land. The success of the park in bringing visitors and the exclusive rights to provision these visitors caused residents to make the switch to service jobs—vending food and drink, participating in vigilance, or clearing areas for scenery—rather than subsistence activities. Local residents accepted the imposition of a park for a key initial period, which allowed other citizens to visit and institutionalize its establishment. Changes to restrictions and the flexibility of management meant the park served less and less to rigidly protect nature.

The creation of parks reached far into the federal restructuring of the government's and individual's relationships to natural resources. Foresters convinced many people of nature's importance and locked away chunks of land for the presumed good of the country, at times offering alternative occupations for rural residents tied to what promised to be a fruitful tourist economy. In Zempoala, this agenda met with enthusiasm, accord, and sometimes ambivalence, but in other locales park creation faced deeper obstacles because of the sophisticated range of forestry enterprises that took place within and around proposed parks. The high-profile volcanoes Popocatépetl and Iztaccíhuatl boasted deeper ties to national history and more profitable industries on their flanks. This park shared similarities with Zempoala in that it marked a popular site of recreation and a focus for scientific forestry, but it differed in the economic importance of the landscape proposed for protection and the multilayered cultural interpretations of the volcanoes themselves.

CHAPTER THREE

Productivity

Forest Industries and National Landscapes in Mexico's Popocatépetl-Iztaccíhuatl National Park

[handwritten margin note: Cárdenas 1st Nat'l Park]

Imagined into shapes of treasure chests, half-moons, and even supine women, more than 3,000 volcanoes punctuate the political and economic axis of Mexico's central valley. This scattered chain of fiery mountains invites creative interpretations as it rises from dissipating lakebeds to create ecological areas ranging from wetlands to high-altitude grasslands.[1] But no volcanoes figure more prominently in the history of Mexico than the adjacent peaks of Popocatépetl and Iztaccíhuatl, popularly envisioned as a smoking warrior standing at attention over a sleeping woman.[2] Glacier capped and permanently snow covered, these two famed volcanoes, affectionately known as Popo and Izta, merge cultivated fields, working forests, alpine extremes, and invented profiles in a fixed landscape representing the careful symbiosis of nature and culture.[3] Though they earned their reputations long before, on November 8, 1935, President Cárdenas declared the deeply revered and intensively used landscape around Popo and Izta his first national park. This move indicated that at its heart, Cardenistas resource management approach sought federally guided economic use and forward-looking conservation by advocating compromises.[4]

The park's presidential decree articulated this vision by giving several justifications for the park and forming a template for future parks.[5] The decree first noted the location of the volcanoes, identifying the "portentous and significant setting of them in the principal center of the Republic." The "existence of populous cities in their valleys" and the importance of protecting "the soils that contain degraded, maintained, or restored forests" justified the social and scientific aims of conservation. The decree

Popocatépetl (right) and Iztaccíhuatl, with forests, fields, and Amecameca in the foreground, ca. 1930.

further explained that protecting these mountains with afforestation and maintenance would preserve climatic stability. Listing eight additional cities that would benefit from the park, the decree claimed, "for all of them [the cities], forest conservation on these mountains is necessary to assure to the rich valleys and watercourses essential to agriculture and industry." Keeping soil in place and ensuring ample water resources contributed to economic goals. After addressing the relevance of parks, the decree laid out the ways the park would create new enterprises, including promoting the park as a "living museum to nature," to bring tourism to the area.

Most significantly, the decree stated the imperative for federal stewardship. "Conservation cannot be obtained in an effective manner," the decree explained, "if those that prevail are the communal or ejidal property holders or private interests that tend toward excessive exploitation of these same forests." Left alone, the forested volcanoes would suffer undue exploitation and only the federal government could save this historic swath of national territory for the groups who were unable to protect it themselves: campesinos and private industries. In creating this park, the federal government became the intermediary between these groups, and in effect treated them similarly. Evicting either group proved politically infeasible and undesirable because each wielded considerable clout. Instead, the park became a mechanism to bring various constituencies into the federal fold, mitigate conflict among them, and increase supervision of their activities.

The creation of Izta and Popo National Park created a bridge between multiethnic national imaginings and economic activities in several ways. First, a variety of economic activities, including firewood collection, resin processing, and paper production, formed a spectrum of economic engagement in and around the park. Next, how federal authorities regulated conservation in the face of such use proved a considerable challenge with its own innovations. But the authorities alone did not revere the mountains, as various artistic representations and retellings of excursions to the volcanoes linked the landscape to the nation and captured the promise of conservation. Finally, the combination of extractive industries alongside a venerated landscape defined the park's purpose as a program integrating rural groups into the growing national patrimony, while simultaneously seeking to reform and modernize them. Even in this most central and famous park, compromises happened because the revolution meant local people could not be excluded and had to be integrated into park management. This made Popo and Izta a showplace for revolutionary ideology—not just for nature—as park creators strove to demonstrate their openness to and acceptance of a type of environmentalism mediated by revolutionary goals.

Economic Activities

From the rooftop of Cárdenas's presidential residence in Mexico City, the volcanoes' profiles loomed large. Less visible were the lucrative enterprises transpiring on their slopes, ranging from sulfur extraction in Popo's crater to melting snow for irrigating the valley's corn and wheat fields.[6] By far, the most profitable, most plentiful, and most attention-getting of the industries in the area involved the coniferous forests. Lumber could be sawed from tree trunks; firewood proffered from branches; charcoal processed by roasting wood debris; resin produced from sap; shingles sliced from bark; and paper pulp distilled from the cellulose matter of the trees. This spectrum of economic activity in the park ranged from postindustrial (tourism), to industrial (paper manufacturing), semi-industrial (resin processing for turpentine), basic (charcoal), extractive (sulfur and firewood), and agricultural (cornfields). These activities reflected the larger national economy, as did their unequal distribution and various levels of market integration. Different scales of consumption, technology, and skill involved dynamic relationships between agriculture, forestry, and industrial production and blurred identities of rural and urban citizens.

The park became a slow brake on this landscape of production. Similar to Zempoala, scientists here expressed deep concern that the forests immediately around Mexico City had been ravaged for firewood and charcoal. Yet they hesitated to resort to universal prohibitions of use; in neither the resin or firewood industries did the federal government seek to squash the practice despite the apparent conflicts with conservation.[7] On the one hand this may signify a feeble commitment to conservation, but on the other hand it reveals that rather than invoke authority, foresters desired to keep open other options for fear of alienating their logical allies. Federal foresters viewed forest industries as legitimate, vital for the time, and necessary to meet consumer demand.[8] They did see rustic resin and firewood collectors as needing modernization and warned of risks to the forest from unscientific harvesting methods. Their solution did not involve evicting residents or erasing the industries, but instead inserting federal techniques, guidance, and supervision into the process and monitoring the scale.

Each component of this complex medley of production within and around the park had at least one main group of producers, although the range of people involved in each activity varied widely.[9] The industries of firewood collection, resin processing, and paper production most clearly reveal the differences among these producers. Firewood collection involved campesinos, including women and children gatherers. Resin work involved more intermediate groups of rural people, some campesinos but also townspeople with necessary skills, and over time resin collection involved federal bureaucrats as well. Paper production as a manufacturing enterprise involved industrial workers and included elite industrialists who requested access to forests, transport concessions, and tax relief on imported machinery.[10] Many workers in the factory, some local and others not, resided in on-site company housing and actively agitated for higher salaries, shorter work shifts, and better housing conditions. These three products—firewood, resin, and paper—and their producers highlight the complex economic activities transpiring in this newly nationalized space.

Firewood and charcoal provided major sources of cooking fuel in the central area of the country. Many rural people made money from selling firewood bundles to local markets that eventually made their way to streets in Mexico City or Puebla for daily consumption. Many collectors harvested fallen wood and branches in the forest as a supplemental economic activity in addition to working a small plot of land and caring for livestock. Forest residents lacked the transportation to gather enough firewood and sell it in the locations it would fetch the highest price, so they opportunistically sold firewood to intermediaries in addition to using it for their own domestic needs. According to the Forestry Department, fallen, dead wood was eligible for collection while "green" or live branches broken off trees were prohibited and often fetched lower prices because they burned less well. In practice, collectors used axes and hatchets to break low and dying branches and viewed this as their right.[11] Many foresters advocated this collaborative arrangement so campesinos could continue their economic activities while cleaning forests of the irritating debris that increased the chances of forest fires.[12] Some foresters, like Mexico City's Lorenzo Aizpuru, came to view campesinos' access to fallen wood as part of the exchange between a government and its people.[13] Aizpuru claimed that permitting campesinos to gather firewood in the park encouraged them "to provide their services of vigilance" and turned them into the "eyes and ears of the Forestry Department," which lacked the funds for full-time surveillance against larger scale extraction and suspicious individuals thought to be setting forest fires. Aizpuru even suggested that this economic relationship—trading firewood for vigilance—could be expanded if a system were developed to also allow campesinos access to small, regulated amounts of chopped wood.

Property disputes constantly plagued the firewood collection process. Competing claims on property among communities and private owners led to numerous accusations of unauthorized wood gathering. For instance, the village of Tlalmanalco's mayor claimed that residents of the neighboring community of Santa Isabel Chalma got up in the middle of the night to cut branches from their property.[14] Tensions also existed between resident populations and the paper factory, San Rafael. Residents of Amecameca, claimed that the paper company harvested wood on their communal property without any compensation for the villagers, who claimed the rights to that firewood.[15]

Issues of firewood collection consistently strained the abilities of forestry officials, who tried to control and standardize its extraction. Foresters often tried to extend rational measurement techniques to practices that were much less precise. Two foresters, H. Arthur Meyer (a Swiss expert) and Carlos Treviño Saldaña (an employee with the Department of Forestry), attempted to account for the many ways of measuring firewood in the Valley of Mexico. They explained that bundles came in sizes of twelve, fourteen, eighteen, twenty, twenty-four, and twenty-seven inches. Firewood was also sold by cart or truckload instead of bundle, though it might be sold by the mound, especially with skinny twigs of irregular shape. In exasperation, Meyer and Treviño concluded that a standard measure proved impossible because it depended on the cart or truck's size and the method of stacking, among other variables.[16] Gatherers and vendors knew the value of the wood and could negotiate a price based on the dryness, texture, straightness, and age, but a scientific calculation of this process eluded the forestry officials. Foresters, such as Meyer and Treviño, who searched for an orderly system of bundling, overlooked the expertise of wood gatherers and the skills of the sellers to make these determinations. Although a uniform system might have simplified and rationalized this industry, making the state's purview easier, it also would erase the complexity of nature and the ingenuity of local methods. Meyer and Treviño illustrated foresters' desire to apply quantifiable standards to a process of firewood collection that had evolved in less formal transactions of trust and honor rather than seemingly objective measurement.

There was good reason for emphasizing measurement: size and transportation costs had real bearing on financial returns. A forest products distributing company purchased firewood sized twenty-four inches for four-and-one-half pesos for a bundle of 400 sticks, or sixteen pesos per bundle, including the freight charge. They sold the firewood for thirty-eight pesos a bundle, making a considerable markup. Smaller bundles, those of eighteen inches, were purchased for two pesos, with the retail price of sixteen pesos.[17] The significant difference between the bundle prices highlights the impulse for standardization. Furthermore, the freight charge reveals the considerable difference between the price campesinos received for their work and the profits for intermediaries with access to transportation. The sale of firewood could prove quite lucrative yet it hardly profited those who gathered it out of the woods.

In addition to limbs and branches, residents utilized the trees' liquid resources. Skilled harvesters refined sap gathered from pine trees for use in numerous products, including turpentine, creosote, and, most commonly, a type of sap-filled torch (*tea*) burned for public lighting. Resins also provided railroad-tie sealants and industrial chemicals.[18] To get the resin, harvesters made deep incisions across part of the trunk of a mature tree, usually at a height of one meter, and then hooked a bucket underneath the cut. Depending on the particular method the harvester used, the cut would be vertical or diagonal, going with or against the cellular grain of the trunk's fibers. Unlike rubber trees, pine sap does not flow quickly into a bucket, so the harvester would check the tree every few days to scrape the sap gathering in the cut, opening it again for more flow. Gatherers needed secretion from approximately 100 trees for a twenty-kilo bucket of resin.[19] At some point, depending on the health and size of the tree, the trunk hardened around the cut and stopped the sap. The harvester would then make another incision at a different location on the tree. Whichever slicing method he used, a harvester generally managed several dozen trees at the same time to collect enough resin to make a living. In areas with many collectors, entire stands of trees might be marked with sap slashes. This enterprise slowly bled out the sticky fluid from the tree and required patience and diligence on behalf of the harvester. Over several years, this process weakened the tree, which eventually died and was cut down for wood.[20]

Due to the widespread demand for resin products, foresters suggested new and purportedly advanced methods to make collection more efficient. Engineers working for the Forestry Department, like Carlos Castro Flores, recommended leaving a space of about a dozen centimeters between the vertical incisions to keep the tree alive longer and the resin flowing more regularly. Castro also advised, based on his readings of French resin experts, that the harvester follow the grain of the wood carefully, making incisions along the exact direction of tree growth to ensure the most efficient harvest from the tree's veins. According to these experts, sloppiness and overlapping weakened the tree, killing it before all resin was extracted and effectively wasting the tree. Castro belittled harvesters with such techniques, claiming their "greediness, ignorance, and improvidence" joined with their "absurd and inadequate system of resin harvesting" to kill thousands of trees each year.[21] He believed that adopting standard methods was the only way for the industry to survive.

Unlike firewood, resins required sophisticated and lengthy processing to make marketable products. For professional foresters, like Francisco Almendaro, resin gathering presented a dilemma. Almendaro, the administrator assigned to the district of Río Frio, an extension of the Popo and Izta Park, knew the pros and cons of resin work.[22] Like many foresters, he objected to bleeding the trees because sap extraction weakened individual trees and made forests more susceptible to fire, but he also knew how valuable—and lucrative—resin products were to the recovering national economy. Almendaro and his colleagues recognized the uses of the resin and even oversaw the necessary proceedings to have the Forestry Department take over the resin distilling plant in Río Frio. Almendaro used his expertise, and that of other department employees, to apply for federal bank credit of 50,000 pesos and a presidential decree giving permission to the Forestry Department to use the resources needed to turn the small processing area into a larger industrial plant. The plant proved successful for a time by filling a foreign contract for colophony as well as meeting the regional demand for resin products.[23] The Forestry Department also created a forestry cooperative in Río Frío to provide lumber and resin for the factory.[24] The federal government undertook the contradictory role of supervising and regulating residents' use while fostering a forest industry as an investment for the Forestry Department.

The prices for the various products manufactured by this resin facility indicate why the federal government got directly involved. Almendaro explained that the factory purchased unprocessed base resin for seventy pesos a ton, including the costs of freight. Colophony and turpentine oil, made from the refined resin, sold at wholesale for between twelve and twenty centavos a kilo for colophony and twenty-five to thirty-six centavos a kilo for turpentine. This represented a processed price up to three times the cost of the raw materials.[25] The initial harvester rarely profited from the high value of the sap he gathered when it was sold in larger markets; instead he often traded his harvest for "eggs, beans, and corn while those with access to transport made larger profits."[26] But forest products were profitable for many.

The paper industry added more complexity to how the federal government regulated natural resources for multiple ends. Paper production, distinct from long-standing industries like mining, had only begun to offer significant potential for growth.[27] The demand for paper increased dramatically with the expansion of literacy and a growing demand for magazines, comic books, and newspapers. Although paper production required substantial technology, its capital requirements were low compared to auto industries, petroleum refining, or heavy manufacturing. To this end, the capacity to meet the nation's paper needs seemed possible. The location of thousands of acres of forests at a convenient distance from the capital further invited development.

Paper had been produced in Mexico since the sixteenth century, but it had been a rare commodity until heavy (mostly foreign) investment came in the late nineteenth century. Like many other industries during this period, paper companies underwent a process of consolidation and monopolization. As technology advanced and demand crept forward, old mills and concessions fell into the control of two major companies: Loreto-Peña Pobre and San Rafael. In the late 1880s, Alberto Lenz, a German immigrant, purchased Loreto-Peña Pobre, which produced high-quality writing and magazine paper on the southern outskirts of Mexico City.[28] The second company, San Rafael y Anexas, formed from the remnants of an ironworks plant when Andrés Ahedo and José Sánchez Ramos transformed the company into a wood-pulp-based paper factory in 1890. Located on the skirts of Izta, the site had access to enough water to power the factory, making it the first completely electrified paper plant. The De la Macorra family acquired the major interests by 1900 and oversaw San Rafael's development until 1948. These owners purchased several smaller paper companies in 1904 and 1905, and successfully fought attempts by the legislature to lower the tariff on foreign paper imports. Under the ownership of the De la Macorras, the company increased production from one mill to twelve, reaching a peak of 250 tons of diverse papers daily. San Rafael produced such a volume of available newsprint that publishers complained the De la Macorras were monopolists.[29] San Rafael administrators denounced the need for competition, claiming that their location and complexity afforded the company authority over producing the cellulose base. They also claimed that the drop in imports, due to the worldwide economic downturn and then global war preparations, stimulated the need to produce domestically.[30]

Like all other large industries, paper production faced serious disruption during the violent stages of the revolution and the economic crises of the late 1920s and early 1930s. Nevertheless, Loreto-Peña Pobre and San

Popocatépetl smoking, with forests below and a view of the San Rafael paper factory and fields, ca. 1910.

Rafael remained the highest producing and most capitalized paper industries through the decades that followed. Both moved away from recycled cloth fibers and toward the sole use of pine and fir trees in their production. Although these advances proceeded in fits and starts, by the time of the Cárdenas presidency, they had sufficient machines and processing equipment.[31] During this period, domestic industries, including paper, received renewed attention.

For the federal government, companies proved easier to regulate than millions of individual users, but they also demanded significant benefits. A national paper industry required trees and capital equipment to process them into paper, and both demanded substantial investments. San Rafael also required human resources and quickly expanded its employee base. By 1936, the company employed over 1,000 workers, including mechanics, electrical operators, paper cutters, and processors. The development of wood paste and sulfite cellulose expanded the range of products the factories could make, which led to a desire to expand the factories' forest consumption. The Forestry Department granted special concessions to the companies, including permissions to extract in and near the parks.[32] The flanks of Popo and Izta were full of oyamel trees that manufacturers preferred for their lengthy, firm fibers. Yet federal foresters complained about the deforestation caused by the company and sought greater involvement in overseeing the company's use of the resource by declaring protected zones in the most ravaged areas.[33] Rather than a contradiction, or an undoing of the park decree, support for San Rafael fit into the spectrum of state involvement in the economy that aimed to manage multiple constituencies and the natural world.

But paper production was a controversial industry. In 1937, the Forestry Department officials noticed that oyamel trees had become scarce and were on the brink of disappearance in the park. San Rafael officials accused firewood gatherers of squandering potential resources, although foresters acknowledged the affinity that paper producers had for oyamel.[34] These were not the only tensions between the factory and workers or local residents. In addition to trees, the factory needed water for hydroelectric power and a place to dump residues from pulp processing. As early as 1911, nearby residents had complained about the hazardous wastes from the factory and San Rafael's monopolization of water resources.[35] In 1944, a labor dispute was settled between the Confederation of Mexican Workers (CTM) and San Rafael, resulting in a large monetary settlement for the workers. The settlement was made possible in part because the company doubled production to over 1,000 tons of paper a year between 1918 and

1944 and the workers demanded a share of the increase. Several strikes, in 1923, 1935, 1936, and 1947, brought additional benefits, including salary increases, company housing, and a day of rest each week.[36]

However monopolistic paper corporations seemed, Cárdenas decided not to confront the industrialists head-on to dismantle them. But neither was he willing to let them proceed unfettered; instead he proposed a compromise in keeping with his practice of statecraft and federalizing profit-making enterprises. Cárdenas designed an entity to insert the federal government into the core workings of the industry while leaving the businesses in private hands. In 1935, he created the Production and Importation of Paper Board (Productora e Importadora de Papel, or PIPSA), which regulated the publishing industries and set prices for the paper. In this manner, an industrial monopoly changed to a state-supervised corporation that benefited the federal government and the monopolists, with minor changes for both.[37] PIPSA allowed the expansion of the paper companies and also kept foreign paper out of Mexico by imposing stiff tariffs. The success of the paper companies in meeting local demand and providing sophisticated products proved that with federal oversight and certain concessions, the goal of fostering domestic industry could be met. Although they differed in scale and profitability, the Cárdenas administration meddled in both campesino and private forest industries to eek out a space for conservation.

Constructing Conservation

Although productive activities dotted the landscape, opposing but not incompatible forces promoted alternative conceptions of use. Revolutionary ideas about conservation provided a bridge between unbridled use and rational reductions. Creating adequate conservation policies entailed negotiating a series of flexible arrangements that built cumulatively on the social context. In this way, conservation united the interests of different social groups already using the lands and incorporated each into a national vision for the future. To construct conservation, the park first gained legal status as a defined and delineated entity.

In its first iteration, federal foresters constructed parks as emblems of conservation through revolutionary policy. Laws, decrees, and regulations organized the park framework to keep the general features of the land intact. These rules put a hold on the conversion of forests to fields, slowed the rate of tree felling, and halted plans for harnessing the glaciers into irrigation systems. The first action involved ordering and reordering land tenure patterns around the volcanoes as part of a nationwide land reform effort. In this first park, foresters hoped to claim supervision of communal and private lands, reimburse the owners, and place the territory in public custodianship. The park's decree claimed that forest conservation could not be effective if private interests exceeded public needs. Initially, founders prohibited private lands within the park and worked to limit communal and ejidal lands by providing restitution for transferring them to park property. In various places, this undermined foresters' aims to have residents conserve because it angered the residents and created animosity between administrators and residents. By 1937, foresters moved away from the expropriation model because nationalizing communal land proved a political pitfall and a logistical nightmare. Instead, later parks allowed tenancy to remain but demanded that residents comply with forestry regulations. The reluctance and inability to evict residents led to a more integrated model of conservation and use, although this flexibility caused complications.

This is not to say that compromises came easy. Creating a park by declaration added a tangible legal character to a vision of conservation. Boundary descriptions allowed park promoters to argue for the need to safeguard the territorial integrity of park spaces, and in some cases from existing custodians. Quevedo recognized that not all ejidatarios proved equivalent forest managers. He first asked Cárdenas to allocate ejidos on forest lands only to campesinos already residing there because those campesinos had experience managing the forests. Quevedo felt that giving new grants to campesinos with no forestry experience destroyed forests.[38] Quevedo later argued successfully for the prohibition of ejido grants within parks, although he recognized that he could not disentail those that already existed.[39]

But federal officials were not the only people who defended park integrity. Residents came forward, arguing that administrators sometimes became part of the problem. A forestry cooperative member, Agustín Rayón, denounced a forestry delegate for giving away lands within the national park. Rayón wrote to President Cárdenas, "We are making accusations against the actions of Forestry Delegate Mr. Francisco Fernández Almendaro of Toluca, Mexico in the sense that he has allowed an ejido extension [*ampliación*] inside the National Park lands and the region that has been reforested by the Forestry Department."[40] Rayón went on to request that Fernández be removed from his job and the reforested area be left to recover. For Rayón, defending the park ensured his cooperative's stability and became a way to prevent further occupation of the lands. Although federal foresters defined parks, local residents sometimes defended them.

After declaration, the next stage of conservation and subsequent point of contention involved restrictions on the use of forests within and around the park. Many complaints claimed individual or collective losses because of the conservation-based restrictions. For example, on May 12, 1936, Florencio Muñoz wrote on behalf of "numerous others" from Amecameca to President Cárdenas to "protest that the Forestry Department has not resolved the prior request where they asked that Popocatépetl and Iztac-cíhuatl not be declared national parks."[41] Muñoz explained that the park restricted their livelihoods by limiting firewood gathering. Rather than outright dismissal by administrators, the repetitive nature of such complaints led to more lenient restrictions to forge a middle ground between total restrictions and unchecked use.

President Cárdenas responded to this and other initial protests about national parks by allowing certain campesinos—those quantifiably desti-tute—permission to harvest products on a small scale. To formalize this exception, in 1937 Cárdenas issued a presidential decree that modified the Forestry Code of 1926 in three ways. First, recognizing that some con-servation programs stunted the development of campesino livelihoods, Cárdenas authorized permit-free and tax-free exploitation of forests by campesinos geared for a local market. Second, the free exploitation ap-plied only to those without economic alternatives (for instance, members of cooperatives were not included). And third, the decree strictly prohib-ited and punished the resale and monopolization of campesinos' prod-ucts by intermediaries.[42] These reforms made the conservation restrictions more flexible by creating an exception for the most destitute residents, yet they remained heedful of conservation by limiting the scale of use.

Local forestry representatives had concerns that the decree would be interpreted too broadly and lead to haphazard extraction, so they issued a clarification explaining the specifics. Small-scale exploitation meant a value of less than fifteen pesos a week, and it meant that the products had to be sold directly to consumers. Furthermore, in the interest of conserva-tion, people found destitute could remove only debris from the forest floor; they could not log live trees in critical areas. The clarification encouraged owners to allow people to clean their woods of debris to reduce the risk of fire and produce charcoal and firewood.[43] Such policies proved astute as they gave reason for residents to stop protesting the federal government and start supervising their forest.

In places, this agreement led to a defense of national parks in order to defend community rights. Asunción Juárez and other members of the nearby community, Santiago Cuauhtenco, supported the new exception.[44]

They saw it as a way around suspected corruption and a way to defend conservation in the park and also their own livelihoods—neither of which proved mutually exclusive. Showing this support, Juárez denounced Loreto Rodríguez, a resident of the same community, who produced charcoal on a large scale in Chuauhtenco's woods and offered to split half of the profit with Juárez for not being denounced. Rodríguez claimed the woods where he made the charcoal belonged to him, explaining that he'd purchased the land in a prior transaction. Understanding his rights and the new exception, Juárez aggressively responded to Rodríguez that not only was such a transaction unrecognized, it was impossible, "because the part of the forest in reference belongs in actuality to the Supreme Federal Government, forming part of the National Park of the Volcanoes." Juárez went on to explain that as soon as Rodríguez made these claims, community members presented themselves to the forestry delegate because "in no manner does the pueblo of Cuauhtenco recognize as valid any operation conducted among private individuals on land exclusively and legitimately of the pueblo, which is now Federal property, which is the forest." This denunciation speaks to an acceptance—or at least a tolerance—of the park and a view that saw the federal property as an extension of community authority or at minimum a means to denounce violators of village norms.

While many objections at first reveal hostility to the park and overt resistance to conservation, some of the more surprising complaints involved defenses of conservation against outsiders or uses that compromised other activities. Carlos Pichardo, secretary general of the State of Mexico, explained to the municipal president of Amecameca that he had received complaints from residents. Pichardo remarked that residents articulated their claims in juxtaposition with outsiders. They explained that they had observed Miguel Moisén, Carlos Muñoz Silva, and Lorenzo Guzmán, who were neither destitute nor residents of their community, manufacturing charcoal in their woods.[45] Thanks in part to Cárdenas's exception to the Forestry Code, these residents continued to see the forests as belonging in their own patrimony and were willing to police the area to ensure their own small-scale use fit within the larger mission of conservation.

But not everyone was satisfied with such flexible conservation. Some of the harshest critics of the parks claimed that the government was not doing enough. A series of newspaper editorials by an anonymous writer, The Correspondent (*El Corresponsal*) remarked that clandestine logging continued despite the park's creation. The author's claims are worth quoting at length:

Despite the fact that the woods encircling the region of the volcanoes have been declared a national park by the President of the Republic, these woods have been subjected to merciless exploitation. Forestry authorities have conceded permission for the exploitation of firewood in various cases, but it is doubtful that those receiving permissions have obtained authorization to finalize this extent of destruction. Every person that tours the highway of the volcanoes can easily see below the region of Popocatépetl trucks full of firewood, all day and all night. The indigenous [*indígenas*] of the region also transit through the streets of this town and other villages with their beasts of burden carrying beams or lumber brought from the zone declared a national park. It is certain that much of the lumber that leaves these forests in danger of disappearing, is transported to the Federal District by night without the awareness of those in charge of forest vigilance or with their complicity.[46]

The Correspondent points out several important critiques of the park's effectiveness. He is careful to wage his accusations at both those people who have access to trucks as transport and those who can use only animals, thus universalizing the responsibility for conservation. He then blames the forestry officials for their ineffective enforcement of forestry restrictions that not only sent the wrong message, in this reporter's eyes, it allowed an important asset to slip away from the public. In another editorial, he claims that for the time being, the forest extraction took place clandestinely at night, but given the scandalous consistency it would not be long before the exploitation moved into the light of day.[47]

There are numerous ways these editorials could be interpreted. Notably, the author does not pretend that the national park instantly created a pristine oasis with steadfast protection. He calls for more and stronger conservation, and his critique of both campesinos and entrepreneurs reveals a more widespread claim to conservation rather than overt class-based exclusion. The author's dissatisfaction with flexible conservation policies, such as the concessions to firewood gathering, speaks to sentiments approving more rigid park boundaries. The critique of the foresters' lack of vigilance also contributes to a vision of conservation with stricter enforcement. The editorial's tone expresses a desire to expand conservation and prevent future loss, making apparent that although some conservation occurred, it was not nearly enough to meet this author's demand. What is clear is that the issue of conservation made it into mainstream media, into popular discussions, and into the awareness of thousands of readers. Conservation became a common topic, with a rightful place in deciding the fate of the

land, because the creation of these parks emerged in a contested and conciliatory manner rather than a hegemonic fashion.

Yet the question of actual conservation lingers. If a goal of conservation included reducing extractive use, how much did the national park
conserve? The park today maintains one of the largest contiguous forests
in central Mexico, but whether or not this is a result of the early national
park is an extremely difficult question of historical ecology. The available
evidence does not provide simple answers. Determining accurate, clear
measures of the forests from historical sources is fraught with difficulty
since proponents and opponents blatantly, and sometimes more subtly,
make their agendas known by amplifying the catastrophic destruction to
promote their vision of conservation. Similarly, those profiting from timber harvest had reason to downplay the deteriorating forest conditions.
However, because these peaks have beckoned to climbers, artists, and scientists, historical descriptions allude in vague terms to the condition and
size of the forests, providing glimpses into the changing dynamics of the
forests and their resiliency.

To give one brief example, travelers' cumulative observances suggest
that the amount of snow coverage on the volcanoes had decreased since
the late nineteenth century (although what this meant for forests is less
clear). In 1886, American naturalist A. Packard noted that the snow continued to reach about 4673 meters on Popo, which was near where Humboldt noted it. He described the prior profundity of certain trees, including
an axe-felled tree one and a half meters in diameter, but most subsequent
travelers failed to measure the forests in any standard way.[48] The amount of
snow and the snow line continued to earn descriptions. In 1896, the American scientist O. Howarth remarked that the two peaks were seen with a cap
of snow extending down 2000 or 3000 feet (about 610 to 915 meters) from
the summits. He also remarked that upon ascending Izta, he saw no snow
at 11,000 feet but instead "abundant and varied" vegetation, including a
"delicate maidenhair fern." He remarked that on Popo the snow would
disappear in the latter months of the dry season, to heights of 17,000 feet
(5181 meters).[49] Below the snow, Howarth observed that the twin volcanoes
stood in contrast to the limited amount of pine forest on the ranges encircling Mexico City further north and west from Izta, stating by comparison,
"These ranges are almost entirely devoid of the pine-growth which clothe
the mountains on the south, and vegetation is far more scanty."

In February of 1919, for the first time in 200 years, Popo began to emit
fire, fumes, and ash, which continued sporadically throughout the next
decade.[50] The effect of these explosions on the forest or the snow cover is

not clear, although many writers noted the changes. The self-taught volca-
nologist and artist Gerardo Murillo, or Dr. Atl, chronicled and interpreted
these explosions in his paintings and even speculated on the eruption's
origins with an overeager sulfur extraction company.[51] A group of scientists
from the Antonio Alzate Scientific Society went to investigate the erup-
tions in October of 1920 and noted the paucity of snow at 15,000 feet (4572
meters), unusual for the end of the rainy season. Aerial photos from the
1940s depict impressive forests but without specific dates identifying the
season, they are hard to correlate with these earlier descriptions.[52] More
recently, in 1962, ecologist John Beaman drew upon prior descriptions of
the timberline to postulate that the highest vegetation on the volcanoes
remained constant for at least the prior century.[53] What these observations
and others contribute to understandings of climatic change in the valley,
species migration within the forests, human extractive use, or the effects of
conservation remain questions open for investigation, but the issue of how
conservation entered into the construction of revolutionary social reforms
requires attention here.

Experiencing and Depicting the Volcanoes

Forest change can be measured using scientific methods like pollen
counts and dendrochronology, but the idea of conservation remains tied
to the fluctuations of cultural values, which change over time in less precisely measurable ways. These can be seen in tax laws, economic policies,
and tenure arrangements, but they can also be seen in the fabric of how
people make meaning of their lives with art, music, and leisure. Regard
for these volcanoes developed in tandem with their productive capacity as
they earned repeated reverence in various cultural forms before and after
the Cárdenas period. Alexander von Humboldt noticed the peculiarity
of the snow-capped mountains rising out of tropical vegetation and the
possibilities for profitable enterprise found around them.[54] During the Porfirian era, foreigners delighted in expeditions to the summit of Popo and
slid down the slopes on straw mats.[55] Visitors consistently lauded the landscape's beauty, like the scientist Howarth who claimed, "It would be hard,
I think, to discover in the world a scene more sublime than is presented
for an hour before and after sunset, from the terrace of the Holy Mount
of Amecameca, facing the two great mountains." He extended the enjoyment of such majesty far, explaining, "Neither scientific nor technical
knowledge is needed and . . . for that one sight alone life has been worth

living."[56] Others built the cultural weight of the mountains by diffusing legends, stories, pictures, and dramas about the volatile and increasingly humanized peaks.

Throughout the twentieth century, intellectuals remarked upon the prominence of these volcanoes. The Argentine revolutionary Ernesto "Che" Guevara found himself drawn to the volcanoes. When he lived in Mexico City in 1954, he climbed to the crater of Popo and was able to "peer into the entrails of Pacha Mama [Mother Earth]."[57] In 1968, on tour to Mexico, the Duke Ellington Orchestra played a song to honor the volcanoes but avoided their difficult pronunciations by calling the song "The Sleeping Lady and the Giant Who Guards Her."[58] Carlos Fuentes, novelist and social commentator, remarked in 1988 that the volcanoes gauged the modernization of the capital city, explaining, "An afternoon in Mexico City, so different from an afternoon in Paris, but so different also, in 1959, from the afternoons in Mexico City today. You could see the volcanoes, Popocatépetl the smoking mountain and Iztaccíhuatl the sleeping lady, as you drove down Insurgentes Avenue."[59] And more recently, journalist and writer Elena Poniatowska explained that they created a gateway to the nation's past: "The two volcanoes . . . have been well traveled by ancient Mexicans and also by visitors; even Hernán Cortés crossed them to enter great Tenochtitlan and in doing so converted them into the mysterious door that opened and shut the country's history."[60] Cultural references to the volcanoes are ubiquitous, and such persistence contributes to their significance as Cárdenas's first national park.

But did people in revolutionary Mexico also revere the volcanoes? Many did through artistic expression and excursions to them. Conservation earns salience from cultural values created by experiences—both personally held and popularly retold. Numerous visitors sought to capture the majesty of the mountains with description and to absorb the environment with their bodies. Travelogues and guidebooks consistently mentioned the volcanoes, and young male travelers saw the peaks as challenges to be conquered.[61] Ascensions of the peaks were rare, making accounts of them bolster the physical prowess of the climbers. Although most excursions aimed at the higher peak of Popo, climbers reached the summit of Izta on the filled crater, which, "snow-covered, is one of the 'breasts' of the mountain."[62] Mountaineers routinely remarked on the views of Popo provided from the top of the sleeping woman because such an exploit demonstrated the strength and vigor of the masculine travelers.[63] But the trips often became expressions of nationalism more than gendered conquest. For instance, young men in the Exploration Club summited Popo

Climbers on Popocatépetl, with Iztaccíhuatl in the background, ca. 1910.

on Independence Day in 1936 and reported their achievement to the national daily newspaper *Excelsior.*[64]

Other men depicted their trips as journeys of triumph. Octavio Benavides, an engineer with the Forestry Department, went with several adventurers to the summit of Izta in November of 1938. His description, published in the magazine *Protección a la Naturaleza* (Protecting Nature), sought to contribute to the process of "improving the physical and moral condition of the national character" by encouraging engagement with nature.[65] Unlike the foreigners venturing up the volcano in earlier years, this account profiled domestic climbers, who depicted their adventure with paternalistic passion and fervor. They interspersed detailed commentary on the prodigious vegetation and landscapes while describing the difficulty of the trip that "taxed their lungs and exhausted their muscles." They likened the fresh smells and pure air to an injection of life into their weary bodies and drew an analogy between their own lifeblood and that of their country. They also noted that just as the mountain air gave them new life, the water that flowed from the mountains coursed into hydroelectric turbines and provided the San Rafael paper company with power. In this volcano story, their personal health related directly to the economic health of their country, and both improved through the natural wealth of this park.

On the second day, after resting in the Vicente Guerrero Lodge built by the National Exploration Club, the visitors rose early and climbed to the summit of Izta, enjoying the marvelous view. The hikers took time to lament that not every Mexican had been to the peak, as they claimed it transformed "patriotic love from a light sentiment into a filial affection." To these men, the words *sublime* and *magnificent* were too human to match the divinity of what they saw from the top of the volcano. The parallels between environment and individual, landscape and society, and moral adjustment and physical improvement underlined the account intertwining social processes of reform with the magnificence of the territory.

The park's array of economic activities might give cause to overlook the fact that the landscape, including Popo and Izta, officially marked a monument to the nation. In fact, considering only the forested components of this park would neglect a critical reason that this particular space became Cárdenas's first park: namely, that Popo and Izta provided an instantly recognizable landscape that reflected the majesty of a resurgent Mexico. According to the presidential declaration, "Of all the mountains in the national territory, those of Iztaccíhuatl and Popocatépetl are without a doubt the most significant for their location in the principal center and most populated part of the republic."[66] Revered spaces, according to this logic, resided in and around the nation's citizens and not in isolated and remote areas. Such locations also proved sites for strengthening the nation. As one official described, "Without a doubt, it is a laudable idea from our government to declare the most beautiful natural areas in our republic, National Parks. The purpose of this endeavor is to provide individuals of all social classes with places where they can improve their health . . . and read from the immense book Nature has to offer."[67] Making the volcanoes a national park did not create their symbolic importance; rather, the federal park officials seized on the cultural weight of the volcanoes to reinforce their growing government.

Artistic uses of the volcanoes afford insight into cultural expressions of conservation, and Popo and Izta loom large in the mythologies that represent national history. Their shapes, a flawless smoldering cone and a jagged female profile, evoke the main characters in a popular folktale that explains the presence of the two volcanoes. Many versions render the tale similar to the Shakespearean tragedy of Romeo and Juliet in which the Aztec warrior Popo fell passionately in love with Izta, the elegant princess daughter of a rival leader. Popo valiantly defended the city Tenochtitlan with the hope that his triumph would allow him to return to his love. Izta watched the battle and saw her beloved fall. Believing he had died and unable to live without him, she took her own life. Shortly thereafter, Popo recovered to find Izta dead. Heartbroken, he picked her up and carried her to the valley's highest point and laid her body across the horizon. He stood guard to protect her eternally by morphing into volcano form.[68]

The precise origins of this legend remain unclear; although the stories claim an indigenous context, the legends seem to have appeared only after the Spanish conquest.[69] This helps explain the European attributes that are further solidified by paintings that enshrine this romanticized aesthetic of the human places within nature. The early landscape paintings of José Velasco in the late nineteenth century documented an idealized pastoral countryside including the volcanoes: uninhabited, but replete with national symbols like the eagle with a serpent perched on a prickly pear cactus. In 1910, Dr. Atl designed one of the most complex works of art ever produced on the volcanoes, the Tiffany crystal curtain at the Palace of Fine Arts in Mexico City. This fragmented mosaic brings millions of crystal pieces together in a representation of the valley below the snowy summits of Popo and Izta on a stage routinely used to showcase interpretations of national dances.

By the mid-twentieth century, landscape depictions began to have inhabitants, and importantly, these inhabitants embodied *mestizaje*, a cultural blend of European and indigenous features that fit into the promises of equality and unity promoted by Cárdenas. This artistic change also marked a larger political shift that occurred in the late 1930s, the slow and incomplete process of popular incorporation into a redefined national narrative. Jesús Helguera produced the painting *La leyenda de los volcanes* (Legend of the Volcanoes) on the heels of Cárdenas's tenure in 1940. This work solidified the peaks' position as a shared cultural symbol representing the national landscape. The popularity of the painting brought the two volcanoes and their human likenesses (rather than their forested slopes) to mass-marketed calendars, tapestries, T-shirts and other items of popular consumption. The painting depicted human figures of Popo and Izta with the mountains behind them, mimicking the human profiles. In this painting, both Popo and Izta have light skin, narrow facial features, long silky hair, and tall muscular bodies. Popo appears in an Aztec headdress of feathers with a warrior chest plate, nobly crouched near his fallen love. Izta's beauty and innocence, marked by her thin white dress, emanate from the painting's center. Their sensuous bodies surrounded by the natural scene humanize the landscape, and Helguera silently captures the combination of European and Indian features within this indisputably Mexican backdrop. By including people as part of the natural scene,

Helguera allowed a broad array of viewers to insert themselves into the romantic legend by empathizing with the love story and imagining their own royal indigenous heritage or glorified European physique. With valiant and proud personas, the two volcanoes provided the setting and the historical background that marked the legend as a national story.[70]

Although they symbolized unity, the appropriated volcanoes also revealed constant fissures. Not only does the legend inscribe much repeated gender roles—a passive woman and heroic man—it served to civilize powerful and mysterious nature by endowing the volcanoes with human characteristics. Seen as participants in a romanticized affair of young love, the fiery and destructive volcanoes became tempestuous repositories of unrequited dreams.[71] The legend spoke of promise and desire, but revealed disappointment. The painting looked beautiful, it resonated with familiarity, and it struck a popular chord of tragedy. Helguera's painting marked the disappointments—the heartbreak—of the Cardenista revolution for various constituencies. For women, Cárdenas promised and ratified the female vote, but it failed to translate into enfranchisement in federal elections until 1958. Like Izta, women were painted passive by the revolution.[72] For campesinos, land reform reconfigured resource distribution but inscribed a bureaucratic state in place of a domineering landowner. For indigenous peoples, the admiration of a distant indigenous past (as presented by Helguera) obscured the harsh realities of a persistent racial divide. Cárdenas administrated a radical, but also traditional and paternalistic, state. This transfer of subjugation proved tragic for many involved, and it led to competing ways of remembering and recognizing national landscapes.

Through art, the volcanoes had been woven tightly into imaginings of the nation to the point that it becomes difficult to tell which referents spoke louder. Rita Macedo, a recent visitor to the Tonantzintla Observatory in Puebla, glimpsed the actual volcanoes and exclaimed, "Look, it's just like the curtain in Bellas Artes!"[73] The volcanoes depict a particular setting, the Valley of Mexico, but by the late twentieth century, the ubiquity of Helguera's paintings themselves became a backdrop verifying the Mexicanness of the viewer. Owning and displaying the volcano legend on a calendar, a postcard, or even a dashboard meant expressing pride in the nation, particularly as Mexican immigrants moved to the United States. Catrióna Rueda Esquibel examines the use of Helguera's volcanoes in calendar art and the calendar's reappearance in Chicano movie scenes.[74] She argues that instead of a painting of volcanoes denoting the physical location, a Helguera painting in a movie set, much like an image

Reproductions of Helgura figure types for sale in a Mexico City marketplace in 2010.

of the Virgin of Guadalupe, denotes the authenticity of the space as Mexican. Through artistic reproduction, the national became personal. The prolific appearance of replicas of Helguera's work in various media over the six decades since its original painting attests to Popo and Izta as symbols of national identity and sources of collective romanticizing about the past. Their resonance went deeper than the forests and soils and into the soul of the national imaginary.

Conclusion

Crafting parks contributed to the legitimacy, both structurally and ideologically, of the federal bureaucracy. The forest economy grew under Cárdenas, in tandem with park creation, but this growth did not signal homogeneity. Small-scale and large-scale industries competed with each other for access to the resources they needed, and revolutionary bureaucrats successfully positioned themselves as the providers of these resources.

Through park and other federal designations, forestry engineers gained a point of entry into the lives of thousands of campesinos and dozens of aspiring industrialists. Material projects also reached into the lives of rural people who were unaccustomed to federal attention. Forestry laws put in place the authority to regulate forests on private property and to supervise the use and extraction of resources within parks. Permits, measurements, techniques, fees, and other tentacles of government control supported the administration of parks and reinforced the strength of federal managers, despite their weaknesses.[75]

Parks also provided a framework for articulating national pride. Park creation, industry development, and landscape depiction reveal the centrality of the environment to government policy and to cultural expression on the heels of the revolution. Reformers of various sorts reclaimed the prominent features of their nation's landscape for the patrimony, through paintings, parks, and paper industries. Popo and Izta, and the many representations of them, captured the extreme, the unique, and the dramatic, for posterity. The volcanoes formed a symbol of the nation and at the same time an encapsulation of the natural resources that created and made possible the nation's material demands. The volcanoes had many owners and even more users over the years. Multiple plots of land covered the flanks of the mountains and supported farming, grazing, and forestry. Campesinos used the forests for daily energy needs, while industrialists developed paper industries. Climbers and tourists periodically scaled the peaks, and artists depicted them in various ways. These volcanoes provided symbols of national wealth and revolutionary promise that identified a commitment to natural resources benefiting the majority.

If Popo and Izta epitomize a confederation of industrial uses alongside measured restrictions for conserving forests, other parks had less harmony. Struggles over property rights proved the most contentious arena for national park promoters. In La Malinche National Park, revolutionary rhetoric justifying community land ownership proved a mechanism that residents could use to reject and defame plans for parks. The absence of satisfactory alternatives and the ferocity of local disputes made La Malinche a landscape of conflict unable to re-create the ways Lagunas de Zempoala and Popo and Izta promoted dialogue and incorporation.

CHAPTER FOUR

Property

Ecological Plagues and Legal Frameworks in La Malinche National Park

The mistletoe was a plague, claimed the Forestry Department employee, Antonio Sosa, and plagues should be exterminated. He recommended that a brigade of foresters attack the epidemic to clear out the epiphytes that slowly drained the woods of their vibrancy. By stopping the growth of the parasite, the affected trees would be released of the unwanted burden and the health of the forest would rebound. As Sosa explained, "It [the forest] must be better treated, protected, and cleaned to be freed of the sickness that has invaded it."[1] He argued that a rapid and comprehensive annihilation of the mistletoe would rehabilitate the healthy forests that the La Malinche volcano had long supported. For Sosa, threats to these woods merited immediate attention and action. But why was this forester so intent on eradicating a common woodland parasite?

Although the use of ecological arguments to advance the park earned foresters less local support, they chose this justification because of the lack of political room to advocate the expulsion of campesinos themselves. Sosa's position on mistletoe—vaguely militaristic, deeply confident, and aimed at restoration—reflected his approach to not only forests but also the communities around the national park. Sosa linked the spread of mistletoe with the extractive activities of campesinos, explaining, "The abuses are committed by *indígenas* in the region that do not respect any laws, causing the forest all imaginable damages." Such recklessness allowed the lands to "develop the sicknesses and plagues that ruin the forests."[2] In his formulation, the mistletoe plague and the residents' activities were interrelated threats to a neglected forest that required federal intervention. It

94

may seem inconsistent that a park proponent would remark so vehemently on its poor condition, but foresters saw parks as mechanisms for the restoration of degraded forests as much as for the protection of pristine areas. By emphasizing the consequences of neglect in dramatic terms, Sosa aimed to build stronger arguments for foresters' authority and to prevent future degradation.

Empowered by initial successes in parks like Lagunas de Zempoala and Popo and Izta, foresters deepened the extent of their park program but quickly faced challenges from complex patterns of land redistribution. By the creation of La Malinche National Park (hereafter Malinche) October 6, 1938, foresters advocated federal claims to conserve land in terms tempered by the political context. Although not always successful, the call for mistletoe eradication and its corollary, the protection of woodlands, became a way for foresters to position nature conservation as favorable to the rights of rural people. If only they could get citizens to follow the rules, these foresters believed, they could orchestrate a path to environmental and social equilibrium. Calls to action that blamed forest destruction on mistletoe gave foresters a way of critiquing "rampant agrarianism," or the political claims to resources made by "radical" rural people without attacking them head-on.[3] As Nancy Jacobs has demonstrated with the policies of donkey control in South Africa, sometimes the management of nature says more about the relationships among peoples than it does about disruptions in the nonhuman world.[4] In fact, foresters discussed mistletoe eradication in the same breath with concerns over ejidatarios' actions in the woods. Conflating the two allowed this seemingly neutral botanical outbreak to stand in for a larger critique of campesino practices that belied foresters' convictions that unrestricted use would surrender the park. In Malinche, this approach met with disdain and dedicated resistance, giving the foresters their toughest fight for a park of the period.

Malinche became the most controversial of all of Cárdenas's parks because its creation entered into long-standing local disputes over land redistribution. Residents objected to the large park in tandem with fierce property disputes, dissatisfaction with federal regulations, and the absence of adequate alternative economic enterprises. Rather than a rejection of the national park program writ large, objections to this particular park reveal important facets of local and extralocal negotiations over early environmental policy. When Forestry Department officials confronted this fragmented social landscape filled with defiant local groups, they tethered the park project to an ecological goal filled with moral righteousness based on the employment of legitimating science. Yet scientific legitimacy alone was never enough for foresters to create or maintain a park. As shown in chapter 1, scientific arguments for protection circulated decades before the creation of parks, but proposals for conservation during the Porfiriato achieved little public resonance and thus never translated into a common national patrimony. Instead of science alone, to gain traction foresters had to translate their agenda into the language of campesino justice and modify their intolerance to maintain approval within the Cárdenas government. Scholars have long concluded that marginalized groups that came to speak the language of bureaucracy gained access to greater rights and resources.[5] Revolutionary conservation proves exceptional because in contrast, scientists had to push their agenda to fit within the discourse shaped by and for campesinos.

This did not mean that foresters became egalitarian champions of the rural poor. Quite the contrary, many maintained lingering prejudices about the abilities of rural people to appropriately use or adequately conserve forests. But during this interlude fixated on social reforms, proving an agenda valid through the lens of science was not enough if that agenda excluded and marginalized the social groups Cardenistas came to defend. Instead, conservationists had to adopt a stance on nature protection that proved conciliatory to human demands as much as ecological ones.

How this played out in the woods is the subject of this chapter. First under consideration is the terrain, both natural and cultural, around the park that helps appropriately contextualize the conflicts that unfolded. Then the chapter turns to the dynamics of land reform, with particular attention to the representative demands of the communities Ixtenco and Zitlaltepec. Layered on top of these fractured debates over redistribution was the problem of forest destruction, a problem increasingly relevant to the park's creation but one without consensus on its origins or solutions. Some viewed the problem as having social causes, and others articulated ecological reasoning. As a result, this park's creation inserted federal foresters into local contestations for power and in doing so complicated the picture of custodianship with the multifaceted problem of forest destruction.

A Contested Landscape

The idea that Tlaxcala's forests faced an invasion raises several larger legacies of colonialism linked to this landscape and stretching back to the arrival of the Spanish. Historians for the past five centuries have grappled with explanations for how a few Spanish conquistadors could march through

Tlaxcala and into the heart of the Aztec empire in Tenochtitlan, where they encountered a sophisticated warrior culture yet were able to seize power.[6] Violence, disease, ambition, luck, and timing all played significant roles, as did the actions of individuals. Malintzin, a native woman the Spanish called Doña Marina, served as a guide and translator to Hernán Cortés in this conquest. An indispensable collaborator who ensured negotiations with native groups, her role, physically and symbolically, changed the course of history, and for this she remains a controversial character.[7] As Octavio Paz explained, "Doña Marina becomes a figure representing the Indian women who were fascinated, violated or seduced by the Spaniards."[8] Over time, Doña Marina became better known as La Malinche, a name that came to signify betrayal or, as Paz explained, "to denounce those who have been corrupted by foreign influences."[9] La Malinche is the embodiment of weakness and force, a victim and a power broker, the conquered and the conquering, a complicated and multifaceted symbol. Despite her significance and the historical traditions that remember her, only one monument to La Malinche exists in all of Mexico.[10] This monument is the national park declared around a volcano by the same name situated on the boundary between the states of Tlaxcala and Puebla. The traces of why this mountain bears her name are blurred in the historical record, and her story is tangential to resource politics in the 1930s, but her complex importance embodies the patchwork of meanings that frame the landscape named for her.

The national park endowed with the cultural significance of La Malinche also held a natural landscape worth noting. As the park decree claimed, "The mountain named La Malinche is a majestic silhouette with a beautiful profile crowned with snow in the wintertime. This makes it a monument of exceptional beauty."[11] These claims only begin to describe the landscape where the 4462-meter jagged peak dominates the skyline south of Tlaxcala City and north of Puebla. The volcano occupies 750 square kilometers, nearly one-eighth of the total area of Tlaxcala, and its forests form one of two woodland areas in the state.[12] The nation's smallest state, Tlaxcala, sits on the eastern edge of the central plateau near the Sierra Madre Oriental range and is wedged politically between powerful Puebla, México, and Hidalgo. By the late nineteenth century, railroads crossed the state, linking the Federal District to Puebla and Veracruz. Despite these trunk lines, the state remained rural, and in 1910 only five localities had populations over 4000 people.[13]

The span of the volcanoes' flanks formed an extended natural and social topography—an area from which individuals and communities utilized natural resources. Unlike other parks with volcanoes, Malinche's decree relied mainly on descriptions of the landscape and discrete locations rather than a boundary line unilaterally designating protection at a certain altitude.[14] In fact, the boundary-marking engineer, Humberto Vidal Romero, explained the boundary's intent: "The limit of the national park stays localized at the edge of the forest and agriculturally cultivated lands, leaving outside the small strips and forests without importance."[15] The park decree meandered around communities in the region, stretching between socially recognized settlements and landmarks and encompassing an area nearly twice the size of Popo and Izta.

The first fourteen national parks expropriated the property, or called for its expropriation but never secured it. By early 1937, the idea of reclaiming such lands for the nation through a transfer of title proved unfeasible, economically and politically. Park planners, however, did not let this discourage their program. Instead, they altered the format of the decrees and began to call for communities to retain ownership of their lands within the park boundary, and this was the case at Malinche. Such property maintenance retained the caveat that owners were still subjected to forestry regulations. Overall, the landscape encompassed a variety of peoples, activities, and resources yet coherently provided the template for a national park largely because of the ample forest lands.

Malinche's base had been historically forested. The forest included mainly conifers and some deciduous trees, with a majority of pine and fir species. Hernán Cortés's chronicler, Bernal Díaz, described it as so thickly forested that when they traveled through in the sixteenth century, the Spaniards were unable to use their horses in large sections.[16] During the Porfirian period, the number of haciendas in the area greatly increased and the subsequent removal of trees and exhaustion of soils proceeded unchecked for several decades.[17] According to foresters, less than 300 square kilometers (about 40 percent) remained forested by 1932. Irregular logging and haphazardly extracting trees compromised the condition of the forest, particularly in the lower zones. Few pines over a meter in diameter remained, mistletoe set in, and rare was a trunk without bark removed for shingles or cuts for resin extraction.[18] This volcano's forests became known for their degradation, not their pristine condition.

By 1930, Tlaxcala was the most densely populated state in the republic. New ejidos added to the pressure already taxing the forests as many communities made their livelihoods from a combination of agricultural and woodland products. In a pattern similar to the economic activities in the forests of Popo and Izta, agrarian communities grew mostly corn in their fields, although many also grew wheat, despite the unsatisfactory conditions, because it fetched a higher price. Hacienda lands concentrated their production in cereal crops, although a few maguey fields existed for the fabrication of alcohol.[19] Some residents pastured livestock, while others extracted resin from the woods, gathered stacks of firewood for cooking fires, or constructed underground ovens to make charcoal. These extractive, primary industries increasingly relied on the dwindling forests, and at the time of the park's creation many parts of the forest were thinned beyond recognition, making erosion and flooding predictable seasonal problems.

Although the forested area historically protected the watershed of the surrounding valleys, few substantial water sources remained on the mountain, none of which were rivers. In its largest extension, Malinche's watershed included the cities of Huamantla to the east and Puebla to the south. Water proved such a recurrent concern that by 1939, when the waters that fed the city of Puebla became degraded beyond use, the governor agreed to support the conservation of the forests shielding their origins.[20] The area's springs were used for domestic consumption, which did not leave enough water for irrigation projects of any scale. When abundant, the forests provided an important means of capturing the seasonal rains that fell from May to October, but as they decreased, the damage to soils triggered torrential flooding. As the forests were cut, more sand and scree slopes appeared and agricultural bounty declined. The extensions of land appropriate for agriculture shrank because of the dearth of water, which sent more people into the forests to scrape for survival. This spiral of degradation amplified the strain on waters, woods, and agricultural lands and exposed the area's dire ecological vulnerability.

Resource degradation reveals more than nature's backdrop; the interactions among social groups guided the construction of this natural space as much as they participated in its alteration. Scientific concern with protecting a degraded environment provided a leitmotif for orchestrating a plan of conservation that would include diverse and disputing social groups. The coherence of such a plan faced challenges from local disputes related to the social revolution's commitment to redistributing land.

Land Reform

Land reform and resource possession formed a fluid mosaic along the slopes of the volcano. As this later map shows, the sizes and allotments of communities within the Malinche forest varied, as did their access

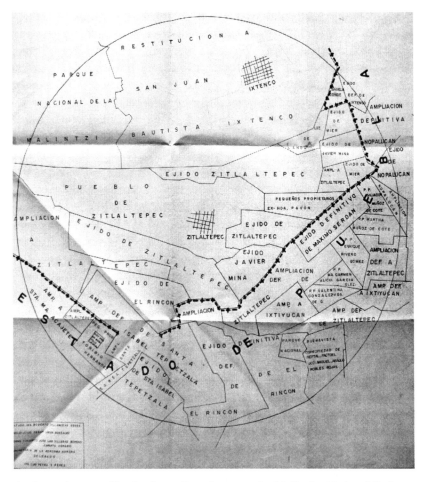

A schematic map of land-reform allocations near La Malinche National Park, ca. 1965. Note the national park labels on parcels at the top left and bottom right. The larger park extension is not pictured. The bold border line in the center is that between the states of Tlaxcala and Puebla.

to resources. National park parcels sat nested within territories claimed by competing groups. Two particular communities, San Juan Bautista Ixtenco and San Pablo Zitlaltepec, stand out for their heated rivalry.[21] Ixtenco residents prided themselves on four centuries of residency on the mountainside, while those from Zitlaltepec thought of themselves as true revolutionaries because they used the agrarian reforms of the new federal constitution to acquire hacienda land and constitute their new community as an ejido. Part of the reason for animosity between Ixtenco and Zitlaltepec stemmed from the different types of communal property each community claimed. Ixtenco was a self-governing community with lands held in common dating back centuries, and only a portion of their lands constituted an ejido. Zitlaltepec was created as an ejido by disaffected landless campesinos from former haciendas that had never been given communal rights. The manner in which ejidos were created shaped schisms among campesinos and distinctions in their orientations toward resource stewardship. Each community constituted a closed commons, one in which membership mattered and distribution was internally regulated. Contestation accrued within each place as agricultural parcels were divided among eligible heads of household. Experiences of retaining and acquiring property elucidate the complexity of resource redistribution, and the comparative stories illustrate the complex relationship between conservation and land reform.

One common way rural villagers expressed their rights to an area was by describing the length of their possession of resources.[22] Some communities traced their legal rights from the first Spanish documentation of their area. Francisco B. Mendez, a self-proclaimed village historian of San Juan Bautista Ixtenco, claimed the village became legally constituted on January 8, 1532, and was named after Juana Bautista, the mother of the viceroy, and Ixtenco, which signified the woodlands in the skirts of the volcano.[23] Ixtenco residents boasted of their careful custodianship of the woodlands that had been in their hands for all but a few decades in the late nineteenth century. Ixtenco's ejido came about through a restitution that rewarded their ability to articulate long-standing ownership. Residents made their case by describing their stewardship of the forests—for instance, Mendez explained the village had always united "in defense of our forest" because it proved "the foundation of the village's interests."[24] Longevity, custodianship, and justice undergirded Ixtenco's claim.

Ixtenco walked a comparatively easy path to legalize property rights. Rather than a grant, in 1916, they requested the restitution of lands that had previously composed their communal patrimony. The inspector of the proposed restitution described them as a "hard-working and industrious" community that had been subjected to the persecution of anti-agrarian neighbors, ruthless local politicians, and vicious hacienda employers.[25] In the inspector's view, Ixtenco had been the victim of scheming outsiders who first sought to corrupt them with alcohol, then swindled their lands with a mortgage. In February of 1919, the Agrarian Commission identified 2245 hectares already belonging to Ixtenco and 5686 hectares available for reclamation, including both agricultural and forest land. Six months later, the governor of Tlaxcala found the request reasonable, but the presidential resolution took three additional years to reach its conclusion. In that period, one of Ixtenco's neighboring communities, Zitilaltepec, protested the proposed allocation. Inspectors witnessed this protest when lands allocated to Ixtenco were not respected by their neighbors after the restitution (in particular, residents of Hacienda Mier and Zitlaltepec clandestinely cut trees). Federal agents viewed giving forests to Ixtenco as a way to protect the forest but became alarmed when neighbors did not respect the allocation.[26]

Ixtenco residents had a tradition of forest management that allowed them to receive forest lands in their restitution.[27] They successfully argued that their stewardship set them apart from other residents and that the care they had provided to the forests was the main reason trees remained. They took this logic of custodianship further by asserting their rights as both political subjects and appropriate stewards. They argued that in contrast to haciendas and ambitious individuals, they engaged in only small-scale exploitation on a level barely noticeable in the health of the forests yet that exploitation provided them with economic supplements to their meager incomes. These residents did not concede that they compromised forest health; rather, they claimed they had found a sustainable medium between small-scale use and conservation. In keeping with this strategy, Ixtenco ejidatarios refused to admit to any forest destruction and instead consistently blamed either Zitlaltepec for invading their forests or local haciendas for catastrophic exploitation. They explained these claims to the agrarian inspector, Ramón Corral, who reported, "The forests of the lands belonging to the ejido of Ixtenco have not been carefully respected by the Hacienda de Soltepec and San Juan Mier [and] these haciendas continue logging through their associates." Corral went on to demonstrate that it was not only the *hacendados* who took advantages of Ixtenco's property: "In the lands and the forest that were restituted to the same pueblo of Ixtenco and have not yet been turned over, residents of Huamantla and Zitlaltepec have also taken up exploitation by calling themselves owners and then selling the charcoal and firewood indiscriminately to the markets in the region."[28]

Repeatedly, Ixtenco ejidatarios claimed their historic legacy in the area and defended their long term commitment to stewardship by pointing out their role as conservationists in juxtaposition to other groups. Ixtenco residents also appealed to President Cárdenas to request that their small forest products be exempt from limitations.[29] "We know there is a group of individuals that in bad faith are already cutting firewood and producing charcoal on federal lands of Malintzi," they maintained, "[and] we oppose these methods that have no noble or healthy ends."[30] Yet, despite the admission of a problem, these ejidatarios felt that restricting small, sustainable forestry production by appropriate custodians was unjust and insulting. "As the legal residents recognized by the national government . . . we only ask for the guarantees of forest interests enough to live humanely . . . because these provide the sustenance for our families now suffering for the lack of bread, a situation intolerable under this revolutionary government." Portraying themselves as mature, skilled, and conscientious residents, Ixtenco ejidatarios articulated a position in contrast to other rural people, one that privileged their own stewardship and claimed they could be trusted to act carefully. Such moral certitude also vilified the orchestrations of their neighbors in Zitlaltepec.

Instead of claiming capable stewardship, the people of Zitlaltepec proffered their claims in juxtaposition to domineering haciendas. The existence of unjustly sized haciendas advanced the community's right to acquire more property because large haciendas represented a counterrevolutionary distribution of land. For instance, the hacienda San Diego Pinar held 3146 hectares, San Diego Pavón had 820, and San Juan Bautista Mier had 1617. Each of these widely exceeded legal ownership regulations, and as aspiring ejidatarios knew, owners were legally allowed to retain only 300 hectares.[31] Beginning in 1916, Zitlaltepec requested ejidal lands and the initial agrarian survey found them eligible for 600 hectares based on the number of households. After seven years of requests, in June 1923, the villagers finally received a provisional right to 400 hectares. Certain they deserved more, the community chose not to agree to this allocation.

Instantly, the owners of the Hacienda San Juan Bautista de Mier filed an injunction to stop the grant. The landowners, Sebastian Mier and Guadalupe Cuevas de Mier, contended that the ejidal request contained false information and was compiled incorrectly. A judge voided the objection, but the community members accused the hacienda of having undue influence in the process of requesting land, particularly at the state level (which caused the original seven-year delay in processing), and of having bribed several community members into obstructing the land reform process by refusing to give their names to the agrarian census.

The granting of ejidos often meant taking away someone else's property, which in turn provoked a legal response. The Mexican legal tradition afforded special attention to the defense of individual rights. The forum for this defense, the *juicio de amparo* or *amparo*, gave private citizens access

to legal recourse to prevent ordinary legislation as well as violations of constitutional rights.[32] Amparo literally meant "protection" or "shelter," and
it constituted a way of shielding one party from the pending legal actions
put into motion by another. The amparo acted like a hold, and it had to be
dealt with before the original action could continue. Amparos were often
filed against ejidal endowments by persons having their property rights
rescinded. The amparo stopped the land from changing hands, although
in practice many ejidatarios occupied lands once the provisional grant was
approved.[33]

An amparo filed by José Mesa y Guitérrez, the owner of a hacienda,
helps illustrate these transactions. Mesa protested the ejidal grant given to
Zitlaltepec over certain irregularities with its declaration, which he used
to argue for the grant's unacceptability.[34] He claimed that some families
within the initial ejidal census population objected to the ejido and that
the local agrarian commission failed to investigate incongruities with the
census's total count. In effect, he claimed there were families who declined participation in the ejido but were counted as claimants regardless.
Mesa further argued that the resources and transportation routes of the
area, such as the location of Zitlaltepec along the railroad and the abundant and regular precipitation they received, made the local situation less
dire than how ejidatarios portrayed it.

The attempted compromise—giving ejidos less and letting haciendas
keep more—pleased no one, yet it relates the dynamics of governance at
work in the process of land reform and reveals the strength of rural communities' ability to demand change. The residents employed their knowledge of the laws to argue for their full rights to the land, refusing to settle
for an appeasement when they felt they were owed more. Ultimately, these
campesinos succeed with this strategy: on November 29, 1923, Zitlaltepec
was endowed with 1154 hectares of land, nearly double the original allocation.[35] Zitlaltepec's agrarian rights officially began with the presidential
resolution in late 1923, but their struggle for land did not subside. The
campesinos of Zitlaltepec continued to plead to the Agrarian Department
with evidence of their population and the expanded acreage they required.
When their actions resulted in an attack by the haciendas in court, they
fought back with allegations of wrongdoing and corruption.

After the allocations, the Agrarian Department required the filing of a
survey of the parcels' distribution to members. Numerous ejidatarios in
Zitlaltepec protested that not only was the document not on file, no survey
ever took place. If it had, they claimed, it would reveal that some people
received parcels of 12,000 square meters while others barely got 5700.

They claimed that the adjudication of parcels had not been verified and moreover, it failed to comply with the law.[36] The ejidatarios protested that these illegitimately allocated parcels came about because a few members paid off the ejidal president. They referred to their rights within the Agrarian Code repeatedly in their accusations against him. In this way, ejidatarios used the law to make formal accusations against an elected leader and then to ask for federal intervention to correct this local conflict. Surprisingly, then, they called on the authority of the federal government to interfere in village-level corruption and weed out the illegal decisions with a professional inspection. Not only did the allocation of ejido lands often result in conflict with surrounding communities and previous owners, ejidos endured heated conflict from within.

Beyond the internal wrangling, ejido land designated by the federal authorities provoked complaints. In 1936, a group of 200 ejidatarios from Zitlaltepec wrote to the Agrarian Department pleading for an enlargement because they felt they unfairly received poor land.[37] Major issues that arose included the quality of land for agricultural production, the amount of land, and access to ancillary support like roads, railroads, water, and housing. They claimed the territory that the original engineer declared for them was subject to frequent landslides, which left it impossible to cultivate. Ejidatarios did not want to give up lands they had already planted and fertilized "with thousands of sacrifices that left our families without food to eat many times, just to make the land more productive."[38] They wanted a solution to the irregularity and inequality of the distribution. Demonstrating that they too could use studies to their own benefit, ejidatarios offered to pay for another technical study of the area. The ejidatarios' fervor increased to the point that another local resident wrote to President Cárdenas, explaining that he had no where else to turn and he feared the problems in the ejido were quickly escalating into violent struggles.[39]

Such vocal contestation gained the attention of bureaucrats and got results, for a time. On June 9, 1937, the grant was provisionally enlarged by 1325 hectares and again on June 29, 1938, by 953 hectares with land from the haciendas. Only eighty-six hectares of the enlargement were agricultural land (*temporal*), while the rest were high forest (*monte alto*). The Agrarian Department determined these enlargements based on the updated general census that found 593 people eligible for parcels within the ejido.[40] Yet this final enlargement never took effect because of other federal agendas for the area. Although the documentation reveals little, it is likely that these enlargements were made when the Agrarian Department decided to allocate forests with the idea they could be cleared and turned into agricultural land. Although it may have seemed like a reasonable solution to exuberant local claims to property, placating ejidatarios with forests hardly salvaged the region from conflict. Zitlalepec's new grant was soon contravened by other bureaucratic interests.

Land reform appeals took place nested inside an ever-changing regime of federal resource management. Just as savvy bureaucrats sought resolution to Zitlaltepec's demands, other employees scrutinized the implications of conferring forests to agriculturalists. They decided that such impulses would prove hostile to the greater cause of land reform. As a result, a presidential declaration on June 7, 1937, prohibited giving away forest lands as land reform parcels leading to the reversal of earlier decisions.[41] In addition, most of the forest allocated to Zitlaltepec was declared part of the park before the final approval of the enlargements. The Agrarian Department only partially authorized Zitlaltepec's enlargement and did not survey and mark the woods. The park decree restricted this allocation and made the woods completely unavailable for future grants and restitutions by ejidos. While Zitlaltepec succeeded in getting an ejido, the national park declaration impeded the community from realizing the enlargements they determined to acquire. The park did not take away their territory, nor did it push them out, yet it succeeded in stopping the enlargement of their ejido onto forests the president had declared off-limits. Instead of leaving the forests, the ejidatarios ignored the presidential restrictions and proceeded to log them in belief that they had to take advantage of the resources before they were forcefully taken away.

Zitlaltepec's ejidatarios viewed their use of resources within and around the park as protected social and political rights. As campesinos, the central subject of the revolution, and because they were economically destitute, they believed they retained the right to use any resources put at their disposal. Furthermore, Zitlaltepecos were agriculturalists, not foresters, and as such they saw federal restrictions as a hindrance to cultivation. Forest destruction, in their conception, was a necessary outcome that stemmed from their rights. Because the creation of Zitlaltepec proved a politically difficult undertaking, the residents harbored deep suspicion for federal authorities. They also despised neighboring haciendas, which they viewed as illegitimate usurpers. Zitlaltepec's ejidatarios sought to justify their actions, even those that resulted in forest destruction, with a political explanation: Zitlaltepec had no other choice than to destroy forests because the federal government afforded no other options and their neighbors retained all of the rich resources.

Land redistribution proved a process fraught with inconsistencies, inequalities, and conflicts. Reform requests brought varying ideas about the value of different landscapes (lands with forests versus lands with fields) in direct competition. Yet it also proved a remarkably resilient process and one that sought to involve communities in advocating for their own position. At times, this empowerment rewarded the most extreme communities by pacifying their actions with more land or greater extensions. Land reform must be seen as a contentious process on multiple levels, within communities, among communities, and between communities and the federal government. Each level contained institutions that mediated common lands through varying degrees of restriction, and the effects for the conservation of this land played out differently.

Ixtenco's and Zitlaltepec's experiences represent two stories of the larger land reform process. Ixtenco used an ecological argument—that they cared for the forests—as a means to expand their holdings. Zitlaltepec proved less concerned with the area's ecological management and instead used the authority of social justice to argue for expanding their holdings. Competing bureaucratic arms of the federal government had enormous weight in this process. Once the legal rights were laid down for ejidatarios, foresters were limited by these rights. Rather than an empty tablet unto which they could paint their agenda, park planners were restricted by decisions already conferred. Their entry point into a circumscribed property regime then became the amalgam of exigencies relating to the forests and making them fundamentally different from agricultural land. Given this context, framing the problem of forests as a transcendent and urgent issue underlay the creation of Malinche.

The Problem of Forest Destruction

Although water and agricultural land proved historically important, conflict in Malinche during the late 1930s revolved around a single penetrating problem—the destruction of the forests—and its rippling effects. Federal foresters described destruction in order to further their authority over the region as agrarian reform parcels expanded. Sosa, the federal forestry expert on Tlaxcala, reported his assessment of the state's forests in 1926, arguing, "I'm convinced of the need to end the destruction of arboreal vegetation on our soil. The ruin of our mountains, the desiccation of our rivers, the sterilization of lower valleys, the depopulation and misery of our mountain zones all inspires me to fight for the diffusion of forest

theories to wake up my compatriots and Mexicans in general to the interest of conservation."[42] This framework of "destruction," rather than the
more neutral "use," fostered notions of scarcity, waste, and tragedy. Framing the issue as a crisis drew upon unifying emotions about the importance
of the forest that precariously refrained from direct blame. Such a view
also constructed a transparent agenda: forest destruction necessitated forest protection. The urgency of ending the purported devastation caused
Sosa to speak in dramatic terms, and he went on to deepen the cause for
his authority by explaining that he had worked in the area for years. He
concluded with the caveat that the problem did not necessitate the "ab-
solute prohibition of any exploitation of trees."[43] The proper antidotes to
destruction, as framed by foresters, were reforestation and conservation,
not total restriction.

Rather than immutable critiques of campesinos, foresters learned to
hitch their claims to larger purposes. Sosa called for forest protection as
part of a comprehensive plan of rebuilding the countryside: "Right now
the federal government is full of transcendent objectives like fostering irrigation, construction, opening roads, the Agrarian Problem and others
and it is already time to think about assuring stability in the works that
are started." For Sosa, forest protection could be insurance for other enterprises: "Each dam that is built, each canal constructed should be done
after guaranteeing the conservation and improvement of the hydraulic regime where the currents originate. Each road that is opened should be
bordered with trees that, more than constituting ornamental shade, will
give strength to the roads. Each ejido that is granted should fraction a
separate zone dedicated to a true forest reserve, conserving the existing
vegetation and regenerating what has disappeared. This is what our *patria*
needs."[44] Sosa saw the problem of forest destruction as the potential down-
fall of all plans for national reconstruction—and resolving the problem, in
his mind, would also provide for a more stable future.

Nonetheless, foresters were not the only people who observed the problem of destruction. In fact, the foresters' hesitation to lay blame created
an opening into which campesinos could explain their own conceptual-
izations of the causes of forest destruction. A brief anecdote reveals the
complexities of interpreting forest destruction. Adalberto Cortés, a representative of pueblos on the western slope of Malinche, noted the history
of his community, Coajulmulco, by explaining, "The lands that occupy
this territory have always been covered by forests. Our great grandparents,
grandparents, and parents have always lived from the products of our parcels of forest and to this date we conserve with pride and satisfaction the

forests that have always been cared for with true zeal."[45] But Cortés admitted that by 1938, such conservation was not possible. He went on to explain that he and his fellow campesinos destroyed the forests in an unsustainable and shameful way because they had no choice—the federal Forestry Code *caused* them to destroy the forest. Before the laws, he argued, no permitting or transit fees existed and campesinos could harvest one load of firewood and make enough to sustain their families. After the enactment of the laws, "economic necessity required them to harvest two loads to pay for permits and taxes with no increase in the amount of sustenance they could provide for their families."[46] Instead of simply monitoring activities, the economics of the Forest Code provoked an increase in the cutting of trees. This tool of rational science aimed to conserve provoked the opposite results.

In this telling testimony, Cortés forcefully makes the case for understanding the problem of forest destruction. Namely, he points out that the forests were conserved when they remained in the hands of their long-standing stewards, the campesinos. Rather than dismiss the importance of forests or advocate solely for legal rights, Cortés was among the many campesinos who came to adopt frameworks and terminologies similar to those articulated by foresters. This pervasive environmentality tethered foresters and campesinos to each other in order to resolve the problem— namely, the need to conserve the forests. Their defense of local autonomy came in the language of stewardship and subsistence, an appeal that resonated in the revolutionary government. Yet campesinos used these same frameworks to critique the methods—particularly permits, fees, and even parks—employed by the foresters. Cortés explained that the forestry law increased the burden on the residents and the forest, amplifying the pressures on both. He emphasized the residents' obedience to whatever the government imposed and their willingness to learn new techniques of extracting forest products. He then made his final and most pressing request, "because we have always been committed to the obedience and observation of forest dispositions there exists no reason to take our property in the forests of Malintzi and we ask you this favor: that the forest authorities retire their proposition to declare a national park in the forests of Malintzi."[47] Cortés and his colleagues viewed the park as an attempt to take away their property in addition to regulations that had already compromised their livelihoods. If, as they believed, the Forestry Code had produced more destruction, a park would annihilate the forests and the remaining residents.

Campesinos' arguments were not proverbial voices in the wilderness. Their claims were taken up by others, in this case on the editorial page of a major Mexico City newspaper, *La Prensa*. Here, the author discussed the conflicts unfolding at Malinche in 1938, explaining that residents had indeed organized themselves to request justice. The editorial, signed with the byline One of Many, reported, "The claimants have presented themselves to the President of the Republic, asking that he intervene with his rank and influence so that the forestry authorities withdraw their project to declare a national park in the mountains of La Malintzin. If the foresters are able to proceed, the claimants will be in danger of losing their lands and being condemned to the most disastrous of miseries."[48] Just as foresters subtly accused campesinos of wanton destruction, foresters earned critiques for the undesirable social effects their actions would conceivably cause. Yet the contrasting opinions on method belied the same guiding problem of forest destruction.

As both campesinos and foresters grasped for deeper authority over the properties around Malinche, they began to inhabit a similar discourse. In fact, embedded in their contestations were shared values. Campesinos, especially from Ixtenco, enumerated their long-standing stewardship and desire to retain the forests "as part of their patrimony."[49] Foresters made reciprocal claims to protect the forest for the greater good. Both came to view the forests as part of a broader system, one component of a productive, resilient, and functional rural resource regime. Inadvertently, through conflicts over rights to the forest, both foresters and campesinos supported an oddly similar, broadly envisioned ecological landscape that maintained both communal rights for long-standing residents and public property for the protection of the national patrimony. The striking concord over the need for conservation revealed a point on which both groups found common ground. This ecological agreement began to create a discourse on which compromise could emerge. Yet, divergent understandings of the cause of forest destruction—particularly where the blame for the problem lay—rendered the agendas of campesinos and foresters oppositional. How these groups encountered each other and the ways in which foresters were tempered by active campesino demands reveals the salience of both ecological understandings and arguments for campesino justice.

In addition to revealing fissures among social groups, Cortés's accusations highlight important questions about resource use. Did federal regulations destroy the forest rather than protect it? Did long-standing communities already conserve the forests? The question of destruction begs an inquiry into both how destruction was understood and what exactly was destroyed. Determining just how forest use proceeded proves a difficult task for historians. Accusations of "destruction" that appear in written sources are loaded with social prejudices and political preferences. One person's right to use becomes another's catastrophic decimation. Little objective measure exists through which to parse the rapidity with which forests declined. Yet patterns of scale and repetition can be deduced. The cacophony of voices at Malinche did not dispute that the forest were declining, that woods were getting scarcer, waters less reliable, and parasites more rampant. If series photographs, satellite images, pollen samples, or other material sources existed for this particular forest, more concrete trajectories of change might be inferred. Because none have surfaced, witnesses must be scrutinized and the framework into which they placed the forests' condition problematized.

Private property owners felt pressures as they lost their land to the Agrarian Department's social reforms and were quick to accuse campesinos of misguided and ignorant use. Private property owners appealed to the same federal government that allocated ejidos to intervene on their behalf in a different form. Private property owners were hamstrung to make their case effectively in a political atmosphere committed to land reform and to elevating ejidos. For example, Miguel Rivera, who lost some of his property in the Hacienda San Diego Pinar to ejidos, requested an inspection by the Forestry Department in November of 1939.[50] In the course of the inspection, Rivera found fifty-five pine stumps, "recently and covertly logged," and he blamed such illegal activity on the ejidatarios. Whether Rivera or ejidatarios harvested the trees is impossible to know, but someone profited at others' expense. Rivera further claimed that because of the activities of the Agrarian Department and the park declaration, he had lost nearly all control over his property in the past two years. Equating the loss of private control and increase in campesinos residence with environmental degradation and chaos, Rivera used the Forestry Department as an intermediary in his critique of campesinos and ejidatarios. He was able to do so because of the larger conception of the problem of forests.

People assessed forest conditions based on their agendas more readily than with an ecological formula. Modern forestry, the discipline Mexican foresters esteemed, lauded a certain type of forest. Foresters preferred a conglomeration of larger tree species with a higher percentage of light filtration and water capture. They generally promoted pine and fir trees but were also likely to call for afforestation with nonnative species, particularly eucalyptus and acacia.[51] When discussing pine trees, Forestry Department employee and forest engineer Ángel Roldán explained, "This woodland tree . . . forms more or less extensive forests that have a great importance from a commercial forestry point of view." Their extended range and ability to withstand intense cold and prolonged drought made the species even more valuable.[52] Roldán's comparative illustrations of "disastrously exploited pine forests and healthy forests" reveal common conceptions. A degraded area involved fewer trees and a notable absence of conformity. It lacked tall trees, but closer to the ground there existed smaller brush. In contrast, Roldán's "healthy forest" retained long, slender trunks with no debris, or even downed wood. The features in a forest that proved valuable to a forester to promote logging—even, uniform, same aged stands—actually degrade its quality for woodland animals and other species of plants. In the foresters' frame of mind, destroying the understory and small brush promoted management while cutting large trees meant destruction.

From the perspective of variety, campesino forests were likely more respectable. Without the vision for a uniform stand of trees or the capacity to use only the larger trees, campesinos relied upon many levels of a forest canopy. From using grass or brush and foliage for fodder, collecting branches for charcoal, and drawing sap from trunks and bark for shingles, campesinos saw value in more of the forest than simply the trunks. This meant they also had a greater interest in protecting its many facets. Campesino forests probably supported far more species than rationally managed forest stands cultivated by modern forestry. Yet campesino views were largely shaded by use and lacked an emphasis on either protection or on production. Some campesinos commented on the ability of the forests to resurge, as one noted that "when you cut one aged tree, ten new grow in its place."[53] And this resiliency provided a buffer for otherwise intrusive exploitation and shaped an idea of forests as reliable and useful.

There proved no agreement on what made up a healthy forest or what exactly conservation meant. Forests are dynamic places where cycles of destruction—like fires and grazing—were followed by periods of resurgence. Although foresters advocated the suppression of fire as a wasteful force, ecologists have come to know that fire can help improve the health of forests over the long term. Quevedo advised Cárdenas on rapid responses to forest fires, arguing that the "fires destroy our natural forest richness" and advocating a system of notification to dispatch brigades into the forest to squash fires that prevented them from regulating brush levels.[54] Foresters were historically locked in a battle with agriculture and similarly raged against domesticated animals. Yet sheep and goats prosper in forests where they can forage on brush and undergrowth. They can complement a forest system that values mixed species, but they will destroy bark and low hanging branches in forests that privilege closely clustered uniform trees.

Although scale and pressure matter, the role of livestock remained a contested issue around forests.[55]

Most foresters agreed Malinche's forests stood degraded; explanations
for how they got that way belied deeper convictions. Two broad approaches
to the problem of forest destruction existed: either the causes were social
or the causes were ecological. In essence, these differing views hinged on
causation. People who approached the issue of forest destruction from a
social or political perspective believed that certain groups lacked access to
sufficient resources because of who they were and how power had been
traditionally distributed within society. This lack of, or perceived lack of,
access to resources then led to antagonisms that resulted in degraded and
destroyed forests. The social problem was one of inequality among citizens, and the consequence was forest destruction. Saving the forests meant
solving the issue of inequality first, which would release the pressure on
forests down the line. In contrast, people who approached the issue of forest destruction from an ecological view believed that protecting the forest
would ameliorate social problems that arose from competition over scarce
resources. In their view, if the condition of the forests were stabilized, the
amount of water available for agriculture would improve, social pressures
would be reduced, and there would be fewer destitute peoples who destroyed the forests out of necessity. For these people, saving the forests
would solve the social issues. Both perspectives had their merits, and in
fact they are difficult to separate, yet by teasing out competing solutions to
the problem of forest destruction, individual orientations toward the cause
become apparent. Such points of concord, rather than merely conflict,
provide a more thorough explanation for how Mexico came to have so
many national parks in this period.

A Social View

Around Malinche, many people discussed the park in terms that reinforced
racial and class distinctions among groups largely through the application
of the law. Some foresters, engineers, and surveyors representing the Forestry and Agrarian Departments saw the problem of forest destruction in
legal terms first and viewed discord in rural communities as a destructive
force. They legitimated their opinions through references to laws created
for administering forests, such as the Forestry Code and the Six-Year Plan.
Although foresters came from different roots, from department heads to inspectors, these officials expressed the importance of formulaic regulations

and backed this with an emphasis on vigilance and enforcement. Miguel Ángel de Quevedo wrote specific codes and then later employed them to justify his department's labors. Surveyors and engineers used laws to authenticate their work. By creating permits, embarking on research, and issuing reports, federal officials demonstrated their desires to keep track of resources. For example, in 1923, Ramón Corral Soto, an engineer with the National Agrarian Commission, responded to a request from his superiors for information about the logging activities of Ixtenco. His response explained simply that understanding the issue required more detailed reports, increased monitoring, and written infractions.[56] Federal workers had a more advantageous position when it came to the law because they had closer access to its formulation. They enacted and then employed a network of laws that created increasing amounts of documentation and identified certain individuals and communities as violators of those laws. Foresters' legal strategy involved creating a traceable written record, and when foresters could legibly see the causes of forest destruction, they saw campesinos as the culprits.

But they also saw that not all campesinos were the same. Whereas some foresters saw campesinos unilaterally as the cause of deforestation, others opined that certain campesinos could be solid stewards. The former believed adequately controlling campesinos would solve the problem of forest destruction. Take engineer Alfonso de la O., for example. His report on the area revealed his contempt for local residents. Besides the irreverent behavior the residents of Zitlaltepec demonstrated toward him, he opined, "the concentration of this indigenous group in the prodigious forests undermines their protection."[57] De la O. claimed that the only activity of the community was the determined misuse of the forests by overharvesting trees and producing charcoal. These unregulated, clandestine activities damaged the little water the community could get from the spring and would soon leave them destitute and force them into lives of crime.[58] He saw community-level mismanagement as detrimental not just to the region, but to society as a whole. He recommended that the municipal president be removed from office for evading the engineer's research and that the forests be placed under strict federal vigilance. The engineer expressed concern for the fate of Zitlaltepec, doomed under poor leadership and hapless to protect their own resources, and above all he expected the federal government to intervene and save this small community from its own fickle local authorities. For de la O., forest degradation was a social and political issue, one that required shaping campesinos' behavior by ensuring proper political leadership.

Zitlaltepec gave other engineers cause to dismiss the efficacy of local resource management. In March of 1938, when the agrarian expert Fernando Nuñez went to the community to undertake an inspection and clear up issues of entitlement to specific parcels, the campesinos who requested him could not be found. After much effort, he succeeded in arranging a village meeting. He hoped to get clarification on the parcels that did not conform to the Agrarian Code but it turned out that rather than the hundred parcels he had been told about when he made the arrangements for the inspection, less than a third of the plots were wrongly delineated.[59] This figure seemed regular or below average, and Nuñez accused the entire village of deception because out of all the complaints he received, only two justified action—that of an inheritance resulting in plot confusion and that of a blind woman whose parcels were completely invaded. He attributed the whole episode to the political ambitions of a local politician, José Maria Peralta, who amplified discord to finagle his way into the role of ejido commissioner. Furthermore, he complained that the ejidatarios had the custom of moving the engineer's boundary markers, which created parcel conflicts and eternal bickering. Nuñez lamented that as long as ejidatarios disrespected the determined boundaries, all of the work of the Agrarian Department would be lost.

Exasperated, Nuñez made a series of assumptions about the community that reflected the frustrations of federal officials in dealing with campesinos. First, he implied that the ejidatarios who removed stakes had no respect for order and needed to be schooled in proper land management techniques. His determination for social order overlooked the lack of environmental context in that markers establishing federal jurisdiction, whether ejidos or parks, rarely took into account ecological variations such as topography or soil quality. Instead they marked social and political authority. Challenges to this authority concerned Nuñez, yet he failed to see the possibility that rather than a political challenge, residents changed the stakes to better meet growing patterns, water flow, vegetation regimes, or other ecological characteristics.[60] He saw ejidatarios only through sociological lenses. Second, Nuñez viewed most of the complaints as at best petty and at worst disingenuous. He distrusted local administrators as manipulative individuals out for their own gain. He assumed that boundaries and plots delineated according to the Agrarian Code provided the best solution for the community because he saw the federal government as the appropriate determinant of resource allocation.

Nuñez's colleague in the Forestry Department, Pedro Segovia, held similar animosity for local authorities and disdain for ejidatarios' ability to manage forests. The ejidal commissioner of Zitlaltepec, Emiliano Mendoza, decided to ignore federal policy and instead provide local permits for cutting forests on the ejido. Mendoza not only authorized the cutting of trees, but he collected fees on the permits, ignoring the federal system already in place. This violated the Forestry Code, which applied to all forests regardless of their status as private, ejidal, or federal. Such disregard for federal policy caused Segovia to write Mendoza and threaten him with prosecution and fines under the forestry law. "You must recognize," Segovia wrote, "that you have no authority to allow the cutting of trees; only the Department of Forestry can give permission."[61] Segovia's paternalistic tone and wielding of the law as the source of his superiority overlooked the possibility that the Forestry Department might have authorized the same cutting, had it been asked. The argument against the community of Zitlaltepec, according to Segovia, was their failure to follow the rules and their disregard for the proper federal authorities. In other words, they ignored their appropriate social status.

That campesinos caused degradation may have been the case, but these officials did not have the authority to forcibly remove residents because of the legal standing given by their ejidal grants. To solve the problem, they advocated that campesinos be restricted from unfettered access to the sources of natural wealth. The ways de la O., Nuñez, and Segovia enacted policies and tried to make sense out of local resource use reveals a rigid view of campesinos as politically and socially incompetent stewards because of scheming local politicians, shortsighted organization, and ignorance to regulations. If the problem was forest destruction, for these men, the cause came in social and political terms—the wrong people had control over the forests.

Yet for other foresters these views sounded altogether too Porfirian. Campesinos, in a revolutionary government, were partners, not problems. Some foresters held more nuanced views that interpreted the problem of forest destruction in ecological terms. Saving the forests for the nation proved futile if the government excluded its citizens from conservation. To determine the causes of forest destruction, they needed to evaluate the conditions of the forests and then differentiate among varying regimes of stewardship. In other words, forest destruction came at the hands of misinformed campesinos, but not all campesinos were misinformed. These foresters admitted that there were campesinos who had provided reliable stewardship for years, and therein lay the hope for the country's remaining forest stands. The right campesinos could be allies in solving the problem of forest destruction by incorporating, rather than excluding, campesinos into Forestry Department plans. These foresters looked at the state of the Malinche forests and saw that the only healthy stands and protected watersheds existed on the lands of Ixtenco and Huamantla, communities chartered in the sixteenth century. This led them to an ecological interpretation based on the condition of resources managed by different groups, rather than a social one that dismissed local management.

An Ecological View

Rather than focusing foremost on social identities, some foresters placed forest dynamics at the forefront of their explanations for problems in Malinche. Mario González's survey of the forests in the national park in early 1939 found that members of Zitlaltepec repeatedly encroached upon not only parklands, but the lands of neighboring communities and private owners.[62] González reported the existence of numerous charcoal ovens, dozens of downed trees, and hundreds of stumps that he believed were caused by the Zitlaltepecos he found with axes, hatchets, and shovels. To this point, González sounds much like his colleagues who blamed the incompetence of ejidatarios as forest managers for the resulting destruction, but then his perspective diverges. González goes on to claim that the new ejido of Zitlaltepec was created by people who had no knowledge of forestry, which of course led them to want to cut the forest to increase their amount of agricultural land. Other communities in the area did not share this recent history; in fact, Zitlaltepec created grave problems for Ixtenco and Huamantla who had lived from the forests for decades and even centuries of stewardship. Not all campesino communities managed the forest the same, and the introduction of new ejidos into well-established forests created an ecological, as well as a social, disruption.

Defenders of campesino forestry, like González, rendered their critiques in the language of justice and aimed them directly at President Cárdenas. In another example, federal employee Román Díaz wrote, "In virtue that the campesinos keep being bothered by the Forestry Department who is reducing their rights to be owners and work in their legitimate forest property, and because they find it indispensable to feed their families . . . I promise you they will be the best guardians in this question of forestry, as you already know that in the cold regions, theirs is the best help."[63] Díaz concludes imploring the president to respect campesinos and explaining that some campesinos are willing to back protection of the forests in consonance with that respect. Emphasizing rights to property in tandem with proven stewardship gave foresters a utilitarian method to advocate conservation without evicting residents. This alternative understanding of conservation as coming from invested campesinos eroded the pernicious impulse to eradicate residents and tempered foresters' strategies.

A sense of frustration toward campesino behavior and resource management also came directly from the Forestry Department inspector, Antonio Sosa. Sosa claimed that the Malinche area represented the most scarred and brutalized forest in the entire country. He attributed the abuse to the lack of appropriate methods for harvesting the products and the greed of the residents who extracted wood beyond sustainable levels. He also lamented the lack of a "forest mentality" among lower-class citizens.[64] The sad condition of the forests, according to Sosa, derived from habits of campesinos and the neglect of the government to teach them better. Yet Sosa did not see campesinos as an intractable problem. The ray of hope that glimmered through the destroyed forests were the communal forests. Sosa explained, "The best surviving forest on the volcano is the communal forest of Huamantla," which survived because of the long standing traditions among the community members who learned to use the forests rather than rely on agriculture. In Sosa's view, communities that had not yet learned those lessons provoked forest destruction, but those that had learned to survive should be seen in a different light. Sosa saw Huamantla, and to a certain extent, Ixtenco, as models for forest recovery.

Sosa previously commented that the mistletoe epidemic on the mountain was the worst in the republic but he also believed that the greatest threat to the area came in the form of a plague of specific campesinos and ejidatarios: those from Zitlaltepec and Francisco Javier Mina, who believed that they could make an easy living out of gathering tree sap and firewood to sell as combustibles.[65] Illegal and not extremely lucrative, this practice proved troublesome to Sosa because it expended the resources allocated to the ejido, and they quickly moved into the surrounding forests to continue extraction. Foresters distinguished among communities' treatment of woodlands and sought out the better of two evils—the community that had the "best" practices in their view should be given more access. Although the political rhetoric of land reform was universalizing, the ecological conditions of that land were worth differentiating, as were specific community practices. Smartly, foresters who could connect their ecological goals to larger processes of social change that extended rights to rural people earned more traction than exclusionists.

Despite their frustration with campesino forestry, foresters enacted several concessions that allowed local residents some recognition and afforded limited use of forest products. Community members that could prove membership in a community within the park were granted the right to extract fallen dead wood on their property to alleviate their economic situation.[66] This reluctance to enforce total exclusion allowed foresters to accrue approval by those seeking justice. In turn, by demonstrating their flexibility, foresters succeeded in getting President Cárdenas to declare that lands in national parks were ineligible for restitution to communities.[67] Making parklands ineligible reduced the number of residents who could legitimately claim ancillary rights, like the concession to gather downed wood.

Within this political atmosphere, foresters felt hampered from regulating park residents in ways park planners in other countries had done. Despite his clear disdain for campesinos, Sosa refrained from calling for their expulsion. In a formal thirty-six-page report addressing the mistletoe crisis during the summer of 1939, Sosa took a measured tone recommending the removal of weakened trees and the allocation of greater resources within the Forestry Department to limit mistletoe's spread.[68] Six months later, writing to Salvador Guerrero, the general secretary for forest conservation, Sosa claimed the reason for the plague was "the misconduct of the local authorities, the inability of owners to exercise control, and the campesinos that protest they are cutting because they are dying of hunger."[69] He then reaches the exasperated conclusion that the only way to save the forests is to call in the military: "For the protection of the park the best thing to do is to order the organization of a group of armed and mounted light cavalry [*monteros*], to constantly maintain surveillance in the forest."[70] Military patrols were standard features of national parks in the United States, but such a recommendation gained little headway with President Cárdenas, who remained reluctant to employ the army to enforce his domestic agenda.

Almost a year later, in April of 1940, Sosa formally proposed the use of armed forces to patrol the park and stamp out illicit extraction. These suggestions were quickly rebuffed by the legislative director Raúl Calderón, who explained, "I do not believe it would be possible to use the armed forces to place a limit on the mentioned deeds, as much because they would not put an end to these irregularities as because one of the desires of the First Magistrate of the Nation has been to avoid frictions between the campesino element and the armed forces."[71] Instead of creating a fortress of conservation patrolled by soldiers, foresters admitted a degree of defeat and advocated reducing the park's size just before Cárdenas left office in 1940.[72]

In late 1940, Sosa recommended reducing the park to better fit the needs of the resident communities and to recognize the ways that ecological dilemmas of the park abutted social needs. The new boundaries reduced the extension of the park, moving the boundary up the volcano's slopes, providing vigilance inside the park while allowing more activities below. By simultaneously giving greater autonomy to the communities that maintained forests and more rigid patrols within the reduced park, Sosa's revised plan credited communities who already served as stewards and elevated them as models for other groups. Rather than arbitrary control, these restrictions reveal attention to the habits of different groups and greater concerns with the ecological ramifications rather than the social dimensions of the forest problem.

For Sosa and his colleagues, ecological issues diffused and disguised social tensions and no one explicitly argued for nature alone. Mistletoe became a way of using the language of ecology to talk about rights of access, methods of resource use, and social power. Forest destruction, when blamed on a parasitic plant, gained an air of impartiality and located a unifying enemy, despite foresters' tendency to use mistletoe as a critique of campesino forest management. Discussions of ecological dilemmas expose the fissures that existed not only among but within social groups affected by a park's creation. National parks exacerbated preexisting tensions over resources, and in most places park promoters proved able to provide tangible alternatives to residents. In Malinche, the park brought about seething conflict because of prior tensions but also because foresters proved unable or unwilling to satisfy competing demands.

Conclusion

Malinche's creation involved complicated legal and regulatory battles over property, resources, and approaches to management from rural residents and federal foresters. Local power brokers, external scientists, and recent ejidatarios competed to determine the fate of their forests. They drew up appeals based on historical legitimacy, legal authority, and political clout to wrangle control over the region and the natural resources within. At the heart of these battles were contested social and ecological interpretations of appropriate use associated with solving the problem of forest destruction. Rather than absorbing federal plans and policies, local residents suffused these debates with their own understandings of conservation and justice. Ejidatarios articulated their moral position through the use of land reform law, but they also physically altered boundaries or strategically ignored federal policies.

This process left a mosaic of land claims reflecting the diversity of resource demands. Observable ecological changes in the landscape increased the tensions of the competing interests, who turned their frustration into accusations and insults. Environmental damage and resource exhaustion were real phenomena, but critiquing the observable changes also became a forum to act out competing interests among humans. Interpretations of forest condition varied and relied on personal, political, and scientific understandings of the environment. Foresters used the eruption of mistletoe as a cry for help in consolidating a park in a socially fragmented area, while members of Ixtenco critiqued their neighbors' activities to justify their own usage.

A national park declaration caused controversy in Malinche because it did not provide viable alternative livelihoods for residents, but other communities rallied around such outside attention. In Tepoztlán, rather than another point of conflict, the park decree confirmed for residents a common bond that tied them directly to the national patrimony. The park there celebrated the community's traditional uses of the forests and highlighted the sacred landscape's contribution to local and national identity formation.

CHAPTER FIVE

Tradition

Community Environmentalism and Naturalized Patrimony in El Tepozteco National Park

President Cárdenas, his brother, and a few officials decided to visit Tepoztlán on a whim. The village, located about ninety kilometers south of Mexico City and twenty-five kilometers northeast of the capital of Morelos, Cuernavaca, was not so different from many Morelos pueblos in that it maintained a population of Nahuatl-speaking Indians and had been a locus of Zapatista fighting. The municipality's forty-four square kilometers contained eight villages (the largest also named Tepoztlán), and it supported a stable population of about 3000 people.[1] But with its gently sloping fields fortified by a forested ridge and punctuated by dramatic rock escarpments, Tepoztlán's natural setting helped set the village apart, and over time the residents themselves earned international fame. Most villagers engaged in agriculture, but harvesting and selling forest products became increasingly common in the 1920s and 1930s.[2] At first, it seemed Tepoztlán had little to attract outsiders except for a railroad stop built on community lands during a 1897 deal with the Mexico-Cuernavaca railroad company.[3] The railroad stop's simple name, "El Parque," portended the importance of the natural world in this community.

When Cárdenas arrived at "El Parque" just before noon on March 23, 1935, his hosts sprang into action.[4] Cárdenas began the descent into the village on foot through the same rocky two-kilometer-long path its residents took to the railroad station, but the excited residents led him on an immediate detour through the mountains to the site of the legendary pre-Columbian pyramid. Unearthed in 1895, the archaeological site contained a stone temple honoring a Tepoztecan deity.[5] Positioned on the top of

President Lázaro Cárdenas (standing, in dark-suit) with a group of villagers on the pyramid in Tepoztlán, 1935.

the steep stairs and surrounded by several generations of Tepoztecan men clamoring to be near him, Cárdenas posed for a picture as his brother sat among the villagers in front of him. The image captured the enthusiasm of a representative male citizenry, mostly muslin-wearing agriculturists with a few uniformed municipal officials and bespectacled professionals. The unexpected visit caused villagers to scramble to impress the president, and many apologized for the humble meal of sausage and bread they offered him while promising a more elaborate dinner and lively fireworks in the evening.[6] Next, the proud Tepoztecans whisked the president through the municipal office building and up to the roof of their sixteenth-century Dominican convent. From here, another photo was taken, this time with the stunning forested hills in the background and the already visited pyramid hidden, but not forgotten, in the natural area on the horizon.

These pictures attested to why the president declared the entire municipality a national park over a year later. In general, Cárdenas's national parks highlighted landscapes with high profiles, like Popo and Izta, or places that boasted accessibility and educational opportunities like Zempoala. Years later, in Malinche, park promoters learned that local conflicts

President Cárdenas (center) with a group of villagers on the roof of a former convent in Tepoztlán. The pyramid is along the ridgeline above them, 1935.

could prevent them from gaining full authority over the management of forests. It was in the founding of Tepoztlán that federal reformers began to recognize the importance of rural traditions as a component of a shared national identity. While each of these parks shared similarities of purpose and content, Tepoztlán went beyond the typical landscapes, the spectacular sites, and the controversial land claims to carve a national space out of the traditional features of a village. The park promoted Cardenista environmental and social policy as part of a common national patrimony, but it also connected nature and culture by recognizing resilient local ties to distinct landscapes.

Nahua and railroads, sandals and cameras, pyramids and fireworks: the interplay between a traditional village and a modern park tugged at the community with increasing reverberations in the 1930s. The railroad station, born of nineteenth-century expansion, brought the outside world closer, although access still demanded physical labor in the hike through a steep ravine. Though the distance was relatively short, the village had no easy connection to Cuernavaca, and villagers rarely made the trek there. On the other hand, outsiders, from politicians to anthropologists, came to the town for its quaint qualities and persistent indigenousness. One of thousands of villages facing similar tensions, Tepoztlán represented to these outsiders "a village in transition" between traditional and modern life.[7] In addition to its exemplary significance, Tepoztlán's history reveals an attribute often overlooked by scholars of the revolution: ecological awareness and the organized defense of common resources.[8] Villagers played an important role in presenting themselves and their landscape to national and international audiences, making this park an example of the adoption of ecological arguments for their own purposes.

Not long after his visit, President Cárdenas approved the building of a road to Cuernavaca. After the road's completion, he decreed a national park around the entire community. The road forced divergent interests to cohere because its construction required local labor and mandated that festering antagonisms be set aside for a common goal.[9] Unlike the open demands for the road, the national park came about in response to the smoldering conflict over charcoal production in the communal woods. Village-level debates over resource management speak to the engagement of rural peoples in the stewardship of communal property. As shown elsewhere, the federal government increasingly usurped decisions about forests, but Tepoztlán's residents' actions demonstrate that by no means were foresters the only citizens who debated resource use. In fact, residents envisaged village politics as the appropriate location for dealing with the issue of forest use. Having managed communal woods for generations, some residents authoritatively promoted conservation while others agitated for expanding charcoal cooperatives. More specifically, powerful caciques advocated charcoal production for their own enrichment while residents (described as socialist-oriented) privileged conservation to retain the forests in the longer term. These contingent prospects remind us that local peoples have no inherent proclivity for destruction or conservation of forests but rather that they make decisions based on available options and changing priorities.

In four interrelated ways, Tepoztlán and its national park demonstrate how environmental concerns shaped identity formation at the local and national level. First, Tepoztlán received a disproportionate amount of outside attention, from academics, politicians, and artists. Status as a "classic village" rendered the place symbolic as an archetypal community intended to illustrate change and continuity to multiple audiences. Such notoriety made Tepoztlán exceptional for its ordinariness and allowed foreigners to contribute to the definition of national spaces. Second, the location, in the central valley's forests, and the contents, including a pre-Columbian pyramid and a Dominican convent, highlighted the fusion of spiritual spaces with the natural world. A national park here represented the sacredness of places that layered history with nature, not an imagined wilderness that divorced them. Third, local struggles over use and conservation in the municipality show how resource decisions never belonged solely to the federal government. Deciding how to appropriately use the communal forests became the orbital axis of local politics shaping the development of a charcoal cooperative, the decline of powerful families, decisions over ejido lands, and debates pitting immediate profit over future preservation. Divisions existed, but the continuation among some residents of a community ecological consciousness, or a sense that local residents deserved final say in how their resources got used, persisted here throughout the twentieth century. Finally, Tepoztlán and its national park captured national tensions over the transition from a traditional society to a modern nation, and this case helps explain how and why parks formed a part of this social transition. As Indians, who made up the ethnic majority of Tepoztlán, became symbols of national rehabilitation, they demanded the retention of prior rights to resource wealth while their incorporation as citizens allowed them to acquire material improvements to their lives. Such identity earned notice from a cadre of outsiders.

A Classic Village

Cárdenas's trip is only one example of how visitors endowed Tepoztlán with a peculiar prestige. Foreign and domestic observers have given this small community an astonishing amount of attention, and it remains a classic case of a community changing, and not changing, from the pressures of modernization. A popular tourist guide now calls the village "something of an international hippie venue" where, nevertheless, "the town retains indigenous traditions."[10] This contradictory reputation as an oasis for enlightened foreigners and a source of authenticity has roots in the patterns of academic research and tourism that unfolded in consonance with revolutionary social reforms.

Tepoztlán gained notoriety among outsiders when anthropologists studied, restudied, reconsidered, analyzed, and celebrated the municipality over the course of the twentieth century. Tepoztlán's location and its ethnic composition made it one of the most studied villages in the country, thus deepening the identification between a classic village and a national culture.[11] Anthropologists asked how the influx of modern technologies altered the culture and how individuals and communities dealt with a changing world around them. Robert Redfield, an anthropologist from Chicago, gathered ethnographic material from the town and surrounding villages in 1926 and 1927. The "ways of the folk" in this rural community interested Redfield, as did the changes residents underwent through contact with urban culture because of the arrival of electricity, mill, and other technology.[12] In addition to scrutinizing holiday festivals, songs and dances, and culinary customs, Redfield made observations about the environmental setting and the importance of the woods and springs to the town.[13] Oscar Lewis, another anthropologist concerned with the rural poor, restudied the village in 1943 and again in 1956–1957, providing the most authoritative chronicle of village life and customs with special attention to relationships among villagers.[14] Redfield and Lewis approached Tepoztlán from different frames of reference and provide distinct, but related, information.

Redfield's thesis, that Tepoztlán's folkways represented "the real Mexico," had resounding influence on the discipline of anthropology in general but also on the crafting of cultural politics nationwide.[15] In contrast to the disciplinary convention of portraying primitive peoples as existing in a timeless state, hermetic and unchanging, Redfield aimed to show subtle transformations, or "the general type of change whereby primitive man becomes civilized man, the rustic becomes the urbanite."[16] His concern with peasants as an "intermediate culture" in the transition from primitive to civilized contributed to the development of theories of modernization that held considerable policy sway worldwide in the mid-twentieth century.

Redfield's high estimation of folk culture came in part from his personal relationship with Manuel Gamio, who convinced him to become an anthropologist.[17] The intellectual architect of the *indigenismo* movement that revered native cultures, Gamio served in the Ministry of Education during the 1920s and held various academic and government positions in the 1930s. His most influential work, *Forjando Patria*, provided a template for an inclusive mestizo nation that could assimilate indigenous peoples through education and modernization.[18] Redfield's discussion of folk culture in Tepoztlán laid the platform for the village's persistent reputation, one that would be challenged and reinforced over time.

In a move then uncharacteristic in anthropology, Lewis elected to restudy the village. He also inquired into the processes of cultural change, and when he arrived fifteen years later, he saw none of the folk harmony portrayed by Redfield. Because he resided in the village for much longer research periods, Lewis and his wife, Ruth Maslow Lewis, a psychologist, often found Tepoztecans at conflict with each other. Lewis hoped to demonstrate the broader historical and social contexts that shaped the village through research into transitional events, like the railroad and highway, economic activities from agriculture to charcoal, and family life and social structures among villagers. This detailed research allowed Lewis to dispute the idea of a transition from a folk culture to an urban civilization as either obligatory or simple. Lewis dismissed Redfield's romanticization of village life, claiming Redfield imposed that value judgment despite the wealth of evidence to the contrary. For Lewis, change in the village had more to do with material dearth, psychological conditions, and government neglect than with influence from city people or technology. Lewis's desire to effect change also caused him to work to produce a study that could inform government policy makers about the needs of rural villagers.[19]

Tepoztlán's significance to academics did not diminish after these studies. Indeed, it continued to provide a template for understanding the struggles between urban and rural culture.[20] An anthropologist from New Mexico, Phillip K. Bock, reconsidered the village in the 1970s, arguing that although Lewis emphasized the community's disillusionment with modernization, the strength of the traditional social system persisted. Claudio Lomnitz, a Mexican anthropologist, examined the town in the 1980s with attention to how the dynamics of power evolved from a Marxist perspective more explicitly dealing with class divisions in the village. Most recently, JoAnn Martin studied the politics of Tepoztlán and the ways that economic crises of the 1980s fostered popular movements with a particular style of political engagement.[21] These detailed examinations of the people and the community provide a wealth of historical data for how the community and culture did (and did not) transform along with or despite the revolution.

Anthropological studies, especially ethnographies, provide two things for a historian interested in Tepoztlán. First, their "thick description" recounts the details and material aspects of daily life in a manner lost in traditional documents. In these minute details come glimpses of the ways villagers manipulated their environment, especially in terms of charcoal production. Second, the studies based largely on interviews give a significant voice to ordinary residents, those without access to a government post or a position of power. Although they certainly have their own biases, such interviews provide a strong counterbalance to juridical documents or ejido solicitations that are framed by particular demands. Despite differing interview techniques, rapport with villagers, and research objectives, the accumulation of these texts in one locale also provides insight into trends over the course of the twentieth century. By looking at the studies cumulatively and combining them with historical evidence, a persistent ecological consciousness emerges in which community control over resources reached beyond agricultural lands. Through interviews with residents, for example, Oscar Lewis details how village politicians debated forest use and conservation.[22]

The depth of study reveals several interpretations of this village relevant to the question of national park creation and community resource stewardship. These studies simultaneously reinforced and ripped apart the notion of a rural village. On the one hand, the more Tepoztlán was chosen as a site for studying typical rural life, the more attention it received and the less it remained typical. Lewis explained that in 1943, "Tepoztlán parallels, to a remarkable degree, many of the characteristics of Mexico as a whole."[23] Greater attention increased the number of outsiders living in the municipality and heightened access to and desires for modern amenities. In none of the studies did the references to national parks figure largely as an influential change, but in all of them the writers revealed a pride by the locals in the beauty of their setting and the bounty of the resources nature provided. The accumulation of studies also illustrates a far-reaching fascination with this town tied directly to its landscape. Just as park planners viewed the concordance of natural and cultural elements as a reason to create a national park, in subsequent years, anthropologists, artists, hippies, and tourists flocked to the site because of this same combination of natural and cultural elements.

The cumulative effect of anthropological study in Tepoztlán was to create a heightened sense of place in the village and among national and international visitors. The residents received the full attention of the academics, but the studies validated the community in a broader sense. The fame Redfield afforded to Tepoztlán as the "real Mexico" in the late 1920s opened the door for a national designation that confirmed the village's uniqueness. After the park's declaration, the number of researchers continued to mount, challenging and confirming their predecessors but always ensuring that the classic village retained its status as an illustrious example of a common national patrimony.

Local Resource Struggles

Beyond a place in the collective imaginary, Tepoztlán had large reserves of communal land that were worked and allocated in an organized, if informal, fashion. Villages within the municipality maintained what Lewis called "moral boundaries" to differentiate property rights. Although communal land (excluding the ejido) was legally owned by the municipality, the lands within a particular village were in practice worked by residents. This standard generally proved adequate except with charcoal production. In this case, "moral boundaries" lapsed when lucrative opportunities arose. The village of San Juan, where the railroad station El Parque sat, had little agricultural land but ample forests. The proximity of the forests and the existence of a railroad station gave San Juan two advantages over the rest of the municipality that served as incentives for creating a cooperative. As a result, San Juanicos organized a forestry cooperative in 1926, the first in the state of Morelos and one of the first nationwide to respond to the Forestry Law of 1926.[24] The cooperative was not the only communal property in Tepoztlán. The municipality received one ejido from the federal government, in 1929, which included 2100 hectares out of the municipality's 23,800 and made up a relatively minor portion of the village's communal lands.[25] Local debates about how to use the lands, including arguments by vocal advocates of conservation, reached a climax before Cárdenas's visit and subsequent declaration of the national park.

The cooperative's main enterprise was charcoal. Charcoal burns longer and can be transported further for less expense than sticks and branches. Conventionally, villagers produced charcoal by roasting several kilos of wood into briquettes of dense fuel. San Juan's charcoal was then transported on the railroad for sale mostly in the southern Federal District. Charcoal production involves burning wood in a enclosed space, usually a partially underground oven, and then removing nearly all of the oxygen from the fire long enough to carbonize the wood but not so long as to let the fuel expire. This delicate process required considerable attention and skill to which the cooperative added organization. The cooperative served as a centralized distribution center that collected charcoal from its members, kept records of the quantity, dispersed payments, and, most important, dealt with the federal foresters. Members saw the cooperative as a success despite recurrent suspicions of mismanagement. For example, accusations sprang up when the cooperative secretary deducted fees and expenses from the compensation of its members. In 1929, several members denounced the secretary, Demetrio Moreno, for charging the cooperative thirty-eight pesos for a forestry inspection that the denunciates complained never occurred. The dispute was taken to the municipal authorities who then gained greater awareness of the cooperative's lucrative activities.[26]

After several years of profitability, municipal authorities challenged the right of San Juan residents to cut municipal trees to benefit the single village. The dispute was partially settled by federal authorities, who ruled the municipality had legal title to the lands being logged.[27] The resolution involved organizing a new and more expansive cooperative in 1930, one that included San Juan and residents in other villages of the municipality. The new cooperative had 500 members at its peak, more than 15 percent of the entire population. Although a large constituency remained opposed to forest use altogether, the cooperative became a receptacle for local economic and political aspirations.

The anthropological studies provide glimpses into an important event that involved the cooperative in 1935: the violent culmination of a village controversy over forest resources. Like many communities in the revolution, internal struggles for power from different groups characterized Tepoztecan politics in the 1920s. Two major factions vying for municipal power, known as the Bolshevikis and the Centrales, diverged on the larger question of whether they should seek improvement from outside or inside the community.[28] In the early 1930s, this question came down to a material debate asking this: should the commercial exploitation of wood be used to improve the livelihoods of Tepoztecans immediately, or should the forests be preserved to secure future subsistence for the community? The Bolshevikis, so named by critics who saw them as socialists, were led primarily by former Zapatistas. Their slogans included "Conserve the Communal Resources" and "Stop the Exploitation of the Forests."[29] They claimed a platform promoting internal equality for the community, and they defended common property by demanding an end to logging in the forests to maintain stability for future generations by keeping extraction at traditional levels. The Centrales were made up largely of sons of former *caciques* who wanted to promote immediate methods out of poverty, and from their perspective, the logical way to do so was by intense exploitation of forest products.[30] The Bolshevikis maintained power from 1922 to 1928 until a violent shoot-out during Carnaval celebrations on February 26, 1928, which left twenty-two dead and put an end to Bolsheviki rule.[31] This was not the only local power struggle that erupted in a violent conflagration, and such events were tied to the charcoal industry's context.

Charcoal production may have been considered by some a "traditional" activity and source of income, but during the cooperative's peak period the intensity and ubiquity of it reached an unprecedented scale taking a traditional activity into mainstream village life. Lomnitz noted that before the cooperative, charcoal making had a social stigma attached to it; it was marginally profitable but production required men to stay away from home for several days at a time watching the ovens. This time away made the occupation a last resort for the very poor. After the creation of the cooperative, this stigma no longer held because many villagers wanted to convert the forests to cash. The release of some of the social stigma, the organization of transport to market, and the visible profitability invited increased activity. One villager remarked, "The whole village became charcoal burners. We practically cut down the forests at that time."[32]

Juan Hidalgo, a Centrales leader, emerged out of the 1928 carnival shoot-out as a powerful figure, and he became municipal president and later cooperative head. Hidalgo, from a poor family in the central barrio of Santo Domingo, guided the cooperative to be a powerful force in the village. In these positions, Hidalgo oversaw the industry and retained control over nearly all opportunities for credit in the village. Some residents criticized Hidalgo for his dictatorial role, while others applauded the entrepreneurial industry that required little federal intervention and functioned effectively, providing security and economic stability for those involved. The proximity of Tepoztlán to the markets of Mexico City and even the smaller markets of Cuernavaca and Cuautla produced steady demand, and the thick forests of the municipality provided a solid supply of timber. After six years of production, at the cooperative's peak in 1934, they produced 1,209,430 kilos of charcoal for the year.[33] The community proved it could support a new industry, organized on a large scale, with high demand and equally high returns.

The scale of production was matched by the extent of money involved. The cooperative bought charcoal from its members starting at a price of thirty five pesos per ton, or twenty-five centavos a sackful. A skilled charcoal producer with a well-located kiln could manufacture enough charcoal to bring home fifty to sixty pesos a week. Hidalgo's cooperative retained a monopoly on transport through an arrangement with the railroad, but it allowed residents an opportunity to make up to sixty pesos a week when the average laborer made two.[34] The cooperative had expenses, and so it deducted fees for handling, a tax to the Forestry Department, a salary for the secretary, and the costs of office equipment. Hidalgo used the cooperative funds for public works, including repairing the municipal building, constructing public toilets in the court house, and building several schools. These works increased the reputation of the cooperative and Hidalgo's popularity. The cooperative also functioned as a credit union for those in good standing with Hidalgo. The profitability of charcoal brought outsiders with fraternal connections to Hidalgo from as far away as Toluca. The appearance of noncommunity members arriving to benefit from their woods stirred resentment among groups who reluctantly logged the forests.[35]

Behind a strong leader, Tepoztecans organized into a community group that took advantage of their collective resources, human and natural, and produced wealth for themselves, shared semi-equitably. Hidalgo rose into the position of a cacique, but his mode of organizing labor and redistributing wealth made his power exceptional. Members of the authoritarian cooperative retained incentives to participate in the exploitation of lands in which they owned a stake. Cooperatives marked alternative organizational methods that allowed collective labor and resources to provide communities with an economy of a scale profitable in ways individual production had historically eluded them.[36] Yet the difference between how Juan Hidalgo came to run Tepoztlán's cooperative and the manner in which Cardenistas envisioned cooperatives had one stark distinction: Hidalgo's cooperative had no need for the revolutionary state. It functioned nearly autonomously for almost five years until disagreements and jealousy decapitated it.

In 1935, tensions the over excess destruction of forests, unequal lending practices, and personal enrichment came to a violent resolution when Hidalgo was dragged from his home, shot, and killed, likely by the former cooperative leaders.[37] This, and another political assassination, put an end to the charcoal cooperative as a local entity. Subsequently, the forest was converted from communal woods to national forest, which ended the locally run, commercial exploitation of the forest. Charcoal production in 1935 barely reached 137,400 kilos.[38] After Hidalgo's death, the remnants of the Bolshevikis placed many obstacles in the way of the cooperative's productivity and obstructed logging.[39] Ensuing cooperative presidents were accused of financial irregularities and illegal logging, and they were charged with negligence. After investigation, the cooperative was fined and then went into bankruptcy and collapsed in 1937.

Suspiciously, the disintegration of a solid local industry occurred in tandem with the creation of the national park.[40] State involvement regularly favors some local constituents over others, but rarely has this included local measures to conserve environmental resources. In place of the cooperative came a national park aligned more closely with the desires of the Bolshevikis. The park conserved the woods first and allowed for minimal clearing determined on a case-by-case basis. The park discouraged outsiders from taking advantage of the opportunities to produce charcoal and reoriented village use once again. Bolshevikis were concerned about the environmental and social costs of long-term exploitation of the forests for charcoal.[41] They defended the forests as a symbol of social justice and intergenerational equity, and the insertion of the revolutionary state as a carrier of these ends proved plausible. Despite the combative village opinions over how the forests should be used, the arrival of Cárdenas in their village created rapport with his administration. The park, created on the heels of the disintegration of the charcoal cooperative, took steps to heal the wounds of that fracas. Tepoztecans accepted a degree of federal administration as the idea of a national park aligned with preexisting conservation norms (at least of the Bolshevikis).

As the charcoal cooperative fell apart, individuals continued production on a less obtrusive and less profitable scale. Federal officials offered certain concessions and leniency to residents for other usage. For example, Daniel Galicia allowed residents to use oyamel trees and branches to repair their houses, conceding that locals could use forests in temporary and low impact ways.[42] Locals abstained from large-scale use, but they also spoke up when outsiders sought to profit from their conservation. For example, in 1942, forty-six locals complained against Marcelino Romero, a forest guard in the national park who made charcoal along with his brothers and shipped it by railroad to Cuernavaca. This violated the logging ban, and the location of the charcoal production also polluted the springs that gave residents water. Residents further accused Romero of extracting firewood for his personal use within the national park, an act they knew carried a minimum fifty-peso fine.[43] Others besides Romero illegally extracted charcoal and firewood from the park; in fact, investigators made yearly accusations against users.[44] What made Romero different, in the eyes of the residents, was his authority to enforce the rules as the park and forest guard. When he violated the ban, he not only committed a legal offense, he proved disloyal and corrupt thus deserving punishment.

Localized Nature Becomes National Culture

At some point, national merges with local. For Tepoztlán, a national agenda tangibly abutted local circumstances when the president arrived in town. When Cárdenas arrived, he saw a space that integrated culture and nature. The village had the basic elements of most villages—humble homes, hardscrabble fields, and worn government buildings. But it also boasted a recently unearthed pyramid, a centuries-old convent, and ample forests. One of these attributes alone might have earned attention from the Forestry Department or the SEP, but all three, intertwined in a place still accessible for a day trip from the capital, piqued the aspirations of park planners. The presidential visit occurred at the climax of swirling local tensions over forest use and set in motion a series of wide-reaching changes that marked the entry of the federal government into custodianship of community resources. The natural and cultural attributes of the location, combined with persistent outside interest and vocal internal discord, wove national parks into the negotiations between divergent and unequal sources of power that played out in concert with struggles for natural resource control.

Tepoztecans saw themselves included in a national story stretching back before the arrival of the Spanish. Several residents studied village history with particular attention to the intertwined Indian, Spanish, and revolutionary elements. The history they preserved included tidbits of famed national events involving residents who participated in the Zapatista movement and prestigious village politicians, several who became governors. Occasionally, there were more formal articulations of local pride, such as when a group of schoolchildren from the primary school in Cuernavaca took a field trip to Tepoztlán in 1922.[45] Their teacher, Mariano Rojas, who was born and raised in Tepoztlán and previously directed the school, guided their trip. The trip sought local interpretations of Tepoztlán's historical import as it relied upon interpretations by village intellectuals like Dr. Miguel Salinas and Valentín Conde, and conversations with the elder Don Estanislao. The men described how the ancient pyramid provided residence to the deity Ometochtli, also known as Tepoztecatl, who was feared for his ferocity and at one point oversaw a trade network reaching all the way to Guatemala. Rojas was deeply interested in the Nahua language, publishing books of its orthography and delivering speeches for several academies on the language's history. This reverence for the indigenous heritage of the village did not prevent the teacher from leading the students in singing the national hymn during their excursion.[46] Although anthropologists noted that Tepoztecans viewed themselves as villagers first, during the 1930s and 1940s identification between local sources of pride and the Mexican nation coincided.[47]

In the 1920s, visits to the pueblo increased for several reasons. In 1920, Jesús Conde Rodríguez penned a small pamphlet on the history of Tepoztlán that included directions on how to reach the village via the El Parque railroad stop.[48] As the resident expert, Conde also served as the coordinator for Redfield and his family's visit to the village, deeply shaping their experience.[49] The pamphlet advertised the benign climate, the beautiful vistas, and the recently revived village traditions like the celebration of Carnaval. Families from Mexico City took advantage of this trip, especially for Sunday excursions. Visitors would arrive on Sunday mornings around ten and could visit the pyramid and pueblo and return in time to catch the train home in the late afternoon. Visitors of all different professions, including modest factory workers, bathed in the springs and calmed their nerves in the pleasant atmosphere. The round-trip fare cost less than three pesos, and many visitors purchased boxes of plums in the fall. President Cárdenas was not the first revolutionary leader to appear in the village; President Abelardo Rodríguez and former president Plutarco Elías Calles came to town to visit one of the many thermal springs, in 1933.[50] Visitors, from school groups and humble families to presidents, reinforced the position of the village as a worthy and important site, and such tourism stirred interest in the village, which led to deeper justifications of the site's historic importance.[51]

The identification of broad national history with a specific natural setting intensified as foresters visited the park and promoted its significance. Antonio Sosa, an engineer with the Forestry Department who became embroiled in conflicts in Malinche, saw the village as nearing sophistication. He described the pre-Columbian legends in a 1938 newspaper article, making multiple references to the ancient Greeks by comparing the pyramid to an acropolis and the deities to Greek polytheism.[52] Sosa drew on these comparisons to embellish the cultural patrimony of the site. Sosa explained that the end of the Tepoztecatl cult came with the Dominican friars who worked to convert the Indians to Catholicism by performing baptisms at the base of the pyramid. He then explained that Charles V granted the dominion of Tepoztlán to Hernán Cortés, who later passed it to his son, Martin.

Sosa raved about the site, claiming that nowhere in the country compared to the legendary beauty of the Tepoztlán range. He claimed that the only place dignified enough to merit a close comparison to Tepoztlán's landscape was Montserrat, Spain. At the highest peak in the range resided the pyramid of Tepoztlán, which dated from the twelfth or thirteenth century, and stood as a "beautiful archeological gem whose value for the history of our disappeared races is incalculable." Sosa's choice of words, including *beauty*, *value*, and *race*, reveal just how he sought to reclaim the past. By invoking the remnants of a culture 800 years past as part of "our history," Sosa reinforced the importance of the space and the inclusion of that heritage into the national patrimony. Revolutionaries regularly glorified indigenous roots but the larger expanse of his statement justified the glory of nature as well and the appropriation of a historic space for current, and future, ends.[53] Although he naturalized the human remnants in the park, Sosa also made an effort to humanize nature and pull both into the national patrimony. He pointed out that one of the pillars on the northern ridge was known as Tlacatepetl, or the Hill of Man. In his description of the various peaks and hills that writhed their way across the ridge, he likened them to a crumbling wall, deteriorating with the ravages of time, but in his view, the wall—just like the village—persisted and survived with a resilience that rendered it exceptional.

Sosa chose to include these prestigious and religious events within his description of the national park for strategic reasons. The existence of a distant religious cult adorned the park, as did the presence of Catholic priests and a heritage that could claim residence of the first symbolic Mexican, the child of La Malinche and Hernán Cortés. As a representative of the revolutionary government, Sosa selectively claimed the past as part of the revolution. By marking the territory, he took the sacred space of Tepoztlán and forged it into a physical national symbol, a park. While this history set the stage, the majority of Sosa's comments focused on the wealth of flora and topography in the area. With the combination of historic and natural attributes, Sosa could easily justify a park there. Like his superiors, Quevedo and Cárdenas, Sosa merged the cultural and the natural patrimony in promoting this park.[54] Sosa and Quevedo investigated filming a movie at Tepoztlán, recognizing that the area contained vast importance to the nation because of its natural, geological, botanical, archeological, and folkloric elements. The movie contained the picturesque valley and the "holy" (*santísima*) Tepoztlán Ridge. Sosa explained that the vast basalt pillars of the ridge made a colossal mural of towers and peaks produced by erosion. These men sought state control over the natural resources of the area, but they also appropriated the place's past and shaped it into a narrative that proved their revolutionary righteousness.

Sosa was not the only forester to articulate reasons for lauding Tepoztlán. The site contained several features that the forestry employee Roberto Quirós Martínez noted as worthy of a park: large and healthy stands of forests, dramatic geologic relief, and captivating vistas. He did not differentiate between past human edifices and the natural world because both held importance for park creation. When Quirós noted the variety of parks established by 1939, he did not separate attributes into categories of historic or natural, cultural or biological. For him, each park had its own particular importance, sometimes because of the picturesque springs or beautiful forests, other times because of the ruins of old monasteries, the

lava rock formations, or the snowy peaks. Pre-Columbian pyramids, archeological relics, or stalactites and stalagmites each provided justification
for a park. Quirós noted that with comfortable roads, lodging, benches,
running water, and bathrooms, these sites would easily wake great interest
in tourism and offer unforgettable memories to travelers.[55] The "forestry
spirit" that Quirós hoped the Forestry Department would foster merged
the natural and historic aspects of his native land and embraced the embel-
lishment and enjoyment of such places with modern amenities. National
parks indicated a particular convergence of the natural, the historic, and
the spiritual that made a place both beautiful and revolutionary. These
lands were not productive in a traditional sense, but a proactive federal
designation could make them so through tourism.

Local resident Esperanza Martínez might have agreed with Quirós's
assessment that forests were oases. She saw the woods as a physical security blanket around the village.[56] Many villagers noted that they cared
for and respected the forest because it provided free firewood from fallen
branches, curative herbs that grew in its shade, and a site of relaxation and
recreation.[57] In fact, many villagers saw forests as crucial refuges that had
provided sanctuary for villagers and rebels who fled into the surrounding
trees and caves during revolutionary fighting.[58] After they ceased being
physical safe havens, the existence of the woods provided security to residents by supplementing their agricultural produce. While the place of
Tepoztlán in history reinforced the import of the forests, it was also the
material elements of the trees that continually buttressed their protection.
Parks encompassed living resources and living communities who aimed to
use those resources for their livelihoods. Although forestry officials were
amenable to small usage, they also recognized that cutting down trees in a
park sacrificed some of the beauty they aimed to protect.

The Cárdenas government sought to solidify the unity of cultural and
natural patrimony by declaring a national park around the mountains,
Pre-Columbian relics, and the village of Tepoztlán. In the 1930s, deciding
who would administer pyramids, either the SEP or the Forestry Department, involved plenty of bureaucratic wrangling along unclear divisions
between culture and nature.[59] The compartmentalization of archeological
sites happened later, when the park administration moved into the Ministry of Agriculture and the National Institute for Anthropology and History
(INAH) took charge of pyramids, colonial churches, and other historic
sites. The division of the natural from the cultural never appeared inevitable, nor was it part of the social project of the revolution that promoted
resource management.

Picturing Sacred Nationalism

Cárdenas, Quevedo, and Sosa saw that the region became a national park because they admired the geologic, botanical, and archeological aspects.[60] In making this appeal heard, revolutionaries tugged at the aesthetic sensibilities of their literate audience and the imaginations of their readers. Sosa, Quirós, and other park promoters repeatedly referred to the beauty of the parks to justify their conservation agenda. Within the context of declaring national parks, natural beauty described attributes of curious or particular originality but also those that represented important aspects of Mexicanness. Calling rural or provincial spaces beautiful elevated them. Every park declaration in the 1930s used beauty as a justification for the park.[61] By calling the landscape beautiful and conceptualizing it as wondrous, foresters tried to unify the country under a cultural patrimony of pride. Before the creation of the Forestry Department, Forester Gilberto Serrato outlined the relationship that parks should have with cultural monuments by advocating "an autonomous commission constituted by specialists in natural science and fine arts to take charge of the conservation and administration of our national parks so that they are preserved from mistreatment and respected as they should be as monuments or living museums to nature, sacred temples of natural beauty and exhibits of the regional flora and fauna that they conserve."[62]

The rhetoric of beauty tended to gender natural spaces feminine and reinforce the need for paternalistic state control over those spaces. A beautiful space merited protection, the rationalization implied, and the best protector was the fatherly state. Within this schema, beauty was a gift recognized by the patriarch, a process that protected a hierarchy at the same time that it fostered ideas of inclusion. Yet a corollary of this gendered component was a deep persistence of ideas about beauty. Idolizing the beauty of nature was not a revolutionary invention; Spanish explorers astounded at the landscapes of New Spain, and nineteenth-century landscape artists reproduced nature's aesthetic.[63] Revolutionaries seized the beauty of the landscape as a worthy attribute, mirroring what others before them had done. Magnificent landscapes appeared readily in cultural renderings of the territorial nation, but how the revolutionaries promoted the beauty of nature intoned inclusion and national prestige in new ways. The majesty and endowment of nature served as an indisputable point upon which every citizen could agree; irreverent detractors that ruined nature for self-serving purposes then deserved punishment. Natural beauty served as a resource, ripe for the promotion of the nation and the unification of disparate peoples.

On another level, parks like Tepoztlán included a spiritual side of nature adoration. Conflicts over religion had not been resolved by the time the Cárdenas government created national parks. The revolution abolished Catholicism, in theory, which sparked some of the most vehement counterrevolutionary activity, especially the Cristero Rebellion.[64] Scholars have noted the persistence of popular religion throughout the decades of social revolution and the concessions by the federal government to local belief structures.[65] The existence of local spirituality formed an area of weakness for Cárdenas in regions from Sonora to the Yucatán, particularly where it coincided with entrenched local political interests. With this in mind, the recognition by the Forestry Department of churches within and around national parks holds significant symbolism. Federal officials naturalized Catholic churches, many still in heavy use, as national spaces, and simultaneously monumentalized them as relics of the past alongside pre-Columbian temples.

The language employed by both Sosa and Quirós implied a sense of sacredness in addition to beauty. Churches proved sacred because of their role as sites of worship, but pre-Columbian pyramids also deemed respect because of their past importance (although that did not protect them from the reconstructions of archaeologists or the trampling of curious tourists).[66] High volcanic peaks held a degree of sacredness because of their place in the collective imagination, the sheer difficulty of ascending them, and the awe sparked by their presence. Climbers marked nearly all high peaks, not with geological survey markers but with crosses or shrines. A place like Tepoztlán encompassed the church, the Aztec temple, the forest, and the struggles over the imposition and embrace of modernity. In this way, Tepoztlán blurred the categories of religion, history, and the natural world, combining all of them within a space deemed national.

In addition to verbal descriptions of the park as a religious site, several photos reveal the likenesses between the natural form and the built environment. The professional photographer Hugo Brehme saw the mountains as the appropriate parallel to the religious buildings. In Brehme's image, the moss-covered spires of the church rooftop mirrored the ridge behind it, naturalizing the building and marking the mountain as sacred. Because Brehme displayed only the upper level of the church, he emphasized the height of both the geologic and the human-built landscape. The sliver of sky at the top places the ridge at the culmination. The blending of the natural and the spiritual unify this image.

National parks were not the only way to appropriate the benefits of mixing nature with culture. Many foresters embraced this mixture in their

The roof of the former convent in Tepoztlán, with a forested ridge behind, 1930.

personal lives. Although foresters were men of science, many were also men of God. Quevedo, for example, was a practicing Catholic his entire life, and he extended his religiosity into his vocational calling. He explained, "The forestry question is for me like a religion" in one of his final years.[67] Quevedo, always the forestry leader, also provides a suitable example for the overlap between science and religion in Mexico. Deemed the "Apostle of the Tree" by his peers, Quevedo maintained his own personal Catholic faith despite his role in the revolutionary government and the conflicts between the church and the state. He attended mass every Sunday, and his church sponsored a special religious mass to celebrate his fifty years of professional service in 1937. Family members invited President Cárdenas to this public recognition of Quevedo's faith.[68] In addition to his personal convictions, Quevedo drew larger parallels between religion and forestry—he saw saving the nation's forests as a moral mission. Speaking to the first class of the reopened Forestry School, Quevedo implored them to take up this high mission of forest conservation, not just for the *patria* but for the good of all humanity.[69] This speech typified Quevedo's belief in a higher calling for young professionals to strive for the protection of nature's wealth. The apostle spread the word about this calling and spoke often of the infinite moral force he believed drove the struggle to protect the forests against the abuses inflicted by unenlightened people. Other foresters took up this discourse of religiosity to describe conservation work. Sosa referred to the French foresters who taught at the first forestry school as missionaries. In Sosa's mind, they appeared to help Mexicans "realize their destiny."[70]

Discourse alone does not attest to spirituality within the paradigm of national park creation. The actual park designations honored religious spaces by appropriating already sacred landscapes. The shrine to the Virgin of Los Remedios became a national park, as did the forested hills around the holy site where the Virgin of Guadalupe appeared. The first national park protected a Carmelite monastery nestled into the woods above the capital city. Sacromonte, outside of Amecameca and across the valley from Popo and Izta, protected a sacred hill with its church and cemetery. In one sense, these parks merely vindicated preexisting relationships between religion and nature. Followers had constructed convents and monasteries in the austerity of the wilderness to allow people to be closer to God and further from worldly temptations. Just as expensive and elaborate designs adorned the architecture of churches and shrines, the magnificence of nature decorated the holy grounds. Park designers latched on to spaces that already held cultural resonance and spiritual importance by declaring these spaces part of the national project. This process did not create the meaning, but it symbolically altered the relationship of authority and management.

Once a holy site became a national park, administrators assumed the power to regulate use of that space. For example, they imposed a system of permitting in Los Remedios National Park, which required preapproval for vendors on festival days.[71] In Sacromonte National Park, administrators regulated forest use around the shrines, undertook reforestation programs, and hired peons to alter the landscape according to their designs. Rather than creating an agnostic park in a sacred space, one impervious to religious zealots, administrators redirected the behavior they disliked and appropriated the dedication of believers to their own revolutionary project. Through discourse and action, parks became a palpable part of the national patrimony. The urgency of social reform in the 1920s and 1930s penetrated society, from education to art, from law to industry. By grounding reforms directly into the control of natural resources, Cardenista reformers solidly placed their political system in a position that would allow it to last.

Gradually, certainly by the 1950s, villagers who had compromised with federal authority began to reassert their authority against large projects.

Objections were aimed beyond just the Forestry Department. Residents rejected other state projects proposed in the area because of the lack of congruity with community-defined environmental integrity. For example, six ejidatarios wrote to President Manuel Ávila Camacho in April of 1945. These men did not request money, land, or infrastructure from the federal government; instead, they protested the introduction of a dam above their community. The construction of this dam, they maintained, would deprive them of the elemental necessities for the sustenance of their families, flooding their fields, and destroying their homes. In fact, they claimed the preparations for the dam constituted a criminal act violating their right to survive. The ejidatarios claimed that reworking the small drains and aqueducts (*atarjeas*) would provide less costly and more efficient irrigation to the surrounding fields than a large, expensive, unsanitary dam.[72] The dam was never built. In this case, residents relied on their own expertise to reject a large piece of infrastructure in favor of their customary use systems.

At least some individuals in the community of Tepoztlán continued to take the protection of their region seriously. Around 1960, locals and federal officials encouraged a recuperation plan for the park.[73] By 1963, residents formed a local committee to protect the natural beauty of the region because of its value as national patrimony and to maintain the integrity of the pre-Columbian monuments. They feared for the landscape because of the development of a modern communication tower and a proposal for more construction. These activists appealed to the director of national parks for help protecting this local site of national patrimony.[74] The formation of these committees two decades after the boom in park creation attests to the depth of the "forestry spirit" in some citizens and their reluctance to let the adoration of nature fall completely away. More challenges surfaced in the subsequent decades.

In 1994, the Mexican owner of the company Kladt-Sobrino (Grupo KS) chose Tepoztlán and its surrounding park as the site for a new luxury golf course. The proposed tourist complex included a course designed by Jack Nicklaus, 700 luxury condos, a pool, a clubhouse, restaurants, and a heliport. A technology park, with a thirty-million-peso computer center, would accompany the luxury resort. The project maintained support from major federal departments, including the Federal Electricity Commission, the Office of the Secretary of Communication and Transport, the National Water Commission, and the Office of the Secretary of Public Works. Various state-level secretariats in Morelos also endorsed the golf course, citing the wealth of development and tourist money such a project would bring. The last remaining federal obstacle was that the company lacked the certification of land transfer authority from the secretary of agrarian reform. Thanks to the Constitution of 1917, this was necessary to proceed with the development plans.[75]

Although they did not ask, Kladt-Sobrino also lacked the support of a group of environmentally conscious actors who ultimately prevented the entire complex. These fierce and adamant competitors were not Greenpeace or even Mexico's leading environmental activists in El Grupo de los Cien (The Group of One Hundred); they were the residents of Tepoztlán. The project could not proceed without authorization by Tepoztlán's municipal government to transfer the soil rights of their communal forests to the developmental corporation. Despite a widespread publicity campaign and promises of jobs as gardeners, plumbers, electricians, and laborers, Tepoztecans refused to relinquish their rights. As they did so, they drew on a long history of environmental awareness and solid community conservation.

In late 1995, activists in Tepoztlán escalated their objections to the golf course. In a series of events vaguely reminiscent of the charcoal cooperative conflict, politicized residents joined together and demanded the mayor's resignation. They replaced the mayor who had allowed the project with a seven-member council and rallied to prevent a golf course inside their national park.[76] Tepoztlán's protestors contained a mixed alliance of wealthy residents who desired to preserve the quaint atmosphere of their town and campesinos who resented the possible intrusion into their resources. Several surveys of residents show that these mixed groups represented the overwhelming sentiments of residents who cited adverse ecological effects as their main objections to the project.[77] The famed town had grown into an oasis for wealthy Mexico City dwellers, although it also retained longstanding ejido-owning families. The village that anthropologists chose as a site to examine the progressive change from traditional to modern retained vestiges of both, as it always had. These local residents maintained that there would be no development, modern or otherwise, if the resources necessary for their survival—namely, forests and waters—were compromised by granting their use to outside private interests. Individual opportunities associated with the golf course tempted many residents, as they were offered the right to lead tourists up to the pyramid or to sell their vegetables to the new restaurants. Yet a group of elders, teachers, ejidatarios, and social activists began to ask important questions: When did communal land become eligible for resale? Isn't Tepozteco a national park? Where would the water for the golf course and the gardens come from? What would the fertilizers and pesticides do to our crops?[78] These questions and the unresolved issues they revealed began to unite the community around the cause of their common future.

Angry villagers who ousted the municipal president for rubber-stamping the plans aroused the attention of the *New York Times*. This newspaper, along with many others, claimed that the golf course rejection exemplified how the residents "cling to the village's peasant traditions."[79] Reporters noted attributes that signified antiquity, such as the "ancient Nahuatl language still heard in the marketplace" or the rocks and barbed wire they used as weapons, but they overlooked the fibers of an environmental and moral authority stretching back to specific moments in national history.[80] The residents did not, as their competitors claimed, reject modernity or refuse to participate in their nation's march toward development and entry into the first world. The residents were not grasping desperately for the past or ignoring progress, but indeed they were drawing on an important tradition of environmental activism that had characterized their village since at least the 1920s. Portraying residents as relics of an imagined time when Indians lived in harmony with the land gave Tepoztecans little credit for advocating experience-based conservation or developing their own plans to utilize the benefits of their natural resources.

Although Tepoztecans bore no innate environmentalism, they did have a past that empowered them to recognize environmental issues. The forest remaining in 1995 stood because of the convergence of ideas about conservation that found expression in a national park declaration in the 1930s. Local ideas became enveloped by federal policy, with neither local nor federal interests imposing complete authority. Defense of the forest against a golf course belonged to a larger tradition of residents claiming power over their future—not clinging to the distant past. Tepoztlán represents an ecologically activist community with various experiences of organizing against threats to local ideas about a proper, sustainable, livable environment. Activists, campesinos, vendors, politicians, ex-patriots, and others spoke out about the loss of control of their resources and defended their national park, or, more specifically in their minds, their community's resident nature. This defense took the form of pushing out nonlocal intrusions, and it also meant locals explained to the federal government how they intended to use their resources, and not always to preserve them. The golf course development complex was cancelled and the federal permissions revoked in 1997.[81] Certainly divisions existed and not all residents agreed on issues of conservation, but strikingly, some degree of conservation repeatedly won out. This ecological consciousness does not characterize all communities that received parks, but it reveals, in a certain context, how local people appreciated the natural wealth of their community and thought it worthy of defense against intrusion.

Conclusion

The declaration of El Tepozteco National Park in 1937 made the entire municipality a park.[82] Such a designation may seem idiosyncratic and absurd—how could eight villages be inside a national park? Upon closer inspection, such inclusion reveals important facets of Mexican national park ideology. Primarily, national parks did not mean permanent abstention from resource use. National parks included people because nature and culture intertwined and shaped new ideas about the nation. And, finally, in this inclusive vision, villages maintained traditions and represented desires for a modern future. Parks could contain cultural attributes because the Mexican national park model deviated from notions of parks as impervious reserves and thus placed nature behind social justice. The villages served as symbols of resilience and rehabilitation that tied into the national image of reconstruction promoted during the Cárdenas era.

This community faced decisions over forest use well before federal intervention, and residents consistently defended their right to decide how resources would be allocated and utilized. Villagers overwhelmingly desired a road in 1935 as a means of facilitating trade and travel, but they refused a funicular tramway in the 1960s and detested the idea of a golf course in 1994. Resource disputes unfolded in many ways—they are not merely a story of local versus federal agendas. The cooperative boss Hidalgo, like the national foresters, knew that by controlling a village's resources, one could also control the fate of the village and its politics, at least for a time. Cárdenas's political party, the PNR, and its future incarnation, the PRI, learned this lesson well and used direct state control over land, water, oil, and forests to add to its longevity. As in Lagunas de Zempoala, Popo and Izta, and Malinche, the existence of local conflict often signaled deep-seated opinions about the environment, not merely resistance to a federal designation. The national park neither started nor solved resource disputes; instead, it served as a point of federalizing conflict and diffusing local confrontation.

Tepoztlán's park captures facets of Cárdenas's revolutionary agenda that came to redefine the national patrimony with attention to nature and culture. The village contained a beautiful natural landscape populated by rural people. The location boasted remnants of reputable past events important for a national version of its history that over time became layered into the present. The park, and even the cooperative before it, gave symbolic presence to federal control while most decisions remained local. All of these attributes lined attention to the environment alongside social and political dynamics. Despite the fact that villagers never referred to themselves as environmentalists, they organized the defense of resources they saw as their own and repeatedly offered claims to the effectiveness of their stewardship. In doing so, they devised a sense of local sustainability and a persistent notion of traditional life.

If Tepoztlán represented the classic village, as proposed by the studies of Redfield, Lewis, Lomnitz, Martin, and others, then local variations of environmentalism merit greater attention. Some classic villagers held environmental opinions, opposed outside control, and engaged in internal infighting and disagreement. Little formal education did not exclude this community from recognizing the natural wealth of their surroundings (or from squandering that wealth at opportune moments). Charcoaleros saw they could produce rapid profits but also quickly erode the landscape. Agrarians and villagers refused a dam and a golf course that would have benefited nonlocal interests more than the community itself. These acts had clear aims to protect the natural resources of the community and maintain those resources intact for the future generations. Part of the reason for such strident environmentalism came from the site's sacred value. The coordination of natural, indigenous, and Catholic spirituality inside this park formed a particularly moving symbiosis.

Yet this story of village-level conservation, of ecological awareness, and even of federal conservation meeting local needs would be lost in many recent histories that claim that parks largely create refugees. In Mexico, some communities accommodated national parks while others rejected them. Certain parks captured highly regarded sacred spaces, whereas others marked virtually unknown places. The actions of individuals, from the foresters Quirós and Sosa, intellectuals Redfield and Lewis, and cooperative members Hidalgo and Moreno, reinforced a widespread identification with natural surroundings. The frequent surfacing of conservation ideas and the physical integrity of the forests of Tepoztlán attest to the popularity of conservation that went far beyond federal designations. In their 1994 golf course protest, Tepoztecans drew on a history of conservation but reacted to the contemporary challenges of globalization.

Environmental literature tends to regard incidents like Tepoztlán's golf course protests as assertions for environmental justice, not environmentalism.[83] The distinction reinforces the idea that environmentalism, with tenets of conservation and sustainable resource use, is reserved for privileged, educated, white citizens from North America and Europe. This segregates the battles of the poor, the nonwhite, and often the feminine into a category of resistance that denigrates the range of their awareness, reduces the strength and sophistication of their value systems, and retains an elitist monopoly over environmental issues. Time and again campesino activists in Tepoztlán sought to protect their resources out of a reverence for and pride in their home and a sense of moral responsibility to present and future generations. These acts of ecological resistance were not remnants of a pre-Columbian past or denials of modernity; they were deliberate and conscious measures undertaken by informed and diligent citizens who demanded protection of what they saw as rightly theirs. Although they may not have designed or requested Tepoztlán's national park, over time, the park became a rallying point and a symbol of a community of people who regarded their survival as linked to their natural and cultural surroundings.

Conclusion

Just Parks? A Silent Failure with Enduring Lessons

In March of 1939, three campesinos, Firso Espinosa, Guadalupe Rosas, and Salomé Romero, wrote to President Cárdenas and asked him to dismiss the head of the Department of Forestry: "We request that because of his advanced age and demonstrated incompetence, Miguel Ángel de Quevedo be removed from his current post." In his place Cárdenas should name someone of "verifiable capabilities" who would "attend to the necessities of the people who make a living from the forest."[1] Espinosa, Rosas, and Romero claimed that Quevedo failed to do these things and condemned his mismanagement. The authors invoked their status as rural people who earned their living from the forests to convey their sense of justice. In this expression, these citizens did not ask the federal government to abstain completely from involvement in their lives; instead, they requested input on the attributes of Quevedo's replacement because they wanted a say in what the government did and whom that replacement would serve. A series of similar requests and a rapidly changing context erased the institutional tools for radical conservation just as they reached full form.[2] President Cárdenas removed Quevedo in January of 1940, and, rather than select a replacement from the ranks of rural forestry, Cárdenas returned the Forestry Department to the Ministry of Agriculture. The move was swift and did not address the larger complaints about the management of parks and forests but foretold the challenges ahead.[3]

After this change and a shifted political climate, many of the compromises that had emerged from years of proposing and contesting conservation receded as rural production slipped into industrial development. The

149

An automobile on the road through the pass between Popocatépetl and Iztaccíhuatl, the peak shown in the photo, ca. 1945.

window of opportunity for conservation projects rapidly closed, and forestry reforms fell further from governmental priorities. Cárdenas nationalized the oil fields, which increased strain on the federal treasury forcing fiscal cuts elsewhere.[4] A second Six-Year Plan reflected the shift toward rapid urban industrialization by relying on cheap agricultural products. Forestry goods did not directly contribute to the diets of urban workers, nor did they create enough capital to justify long-term investments in sawmills or machinery to develop forest industries. This reality scattered foresters' ambitions and dissolved the tapestry of rural incorporation and creative use.[5] Bureaucrats who administered forests shifted their vision to more profitable large-scale logging development over the less lucrative social values in recreation or conservation. As the population increased, more and more people left the fields and forests for opportunities in the cities and squatter settlements while highways took over the same hillsides around the capital that foresters had hoped to conserve.[6]

On a global level, the worldwide economic depression allowed Cárdenas some room to maneuver national projects toward domestic development. The onset of war in Europe distracted the British from immediate retaliation over the nationalized oil fields, but investors still withdrew their money and helped destabilize Mexico's economy. In order to make progress toward economic goals, Cárdenas and his successors looked toward wartime opportunities. Mexico's role as a supplier of raw materials promoted increased extraction of wood products like mahogany, and farm labor programs encouraged workers to enter the United States. This migration helped disrupt newly forged forest plans, producers' cooperatives, and even park tourism, all of which threatened fledgling parks.

The slow and silent failure of this revolutionary model of conservation arose in part because of the flexibility of the park program. More than other Cardenista reforms, the park administration promoted a style that offered a common cultural patrimony of nature as a vision of how humans could live softly in their natural environment. This vision relied on a landscape dotted with community enterprises and supported by federal programs with a degree of democratic acceptance and a clear sense of scale. Even in places where locals rejected a park, such as Malinche, the political atmosphere that recognized their right to do so hampered federal administrators from authoritarian land seizures and placed ecological dilemmas in a new light. This system of conservation, predicated on the radical combination of social justice, revolutionary nationalism, government responsibility, and contemporary science, lost its champion when Cárdenas left office.

At no point since the Cárdenas era have federal conservation efforts placed the forests around the capital as highest priority. The decades of industrial expansion and economic growth between 1946 and 1972, known as the "Mexican Miracle," took place at the expense of the environment and fundamentally transformed the Valley of Mexico. Forest management considerations were ignored or reformed to permit destructive clearcutting. Parks lost their funding and their support as educational activities dwindled. Soils eroded, or were poisoned, and developers tapped aquifers to near depletion.[7] As Oscar Lewis chronicled, promises of a productive rural life gave way to opportunities that drew families into the urban experience at increasing rates.[8] Air became toxic to breathe as Mexico City transformed from a city known for its clean air to the archetype of urban pollution.[9] Gradually, Cárdenas's political heirs in the PRI strangled the last vestiges of democratic rule at the same time that the institutionalized revolution became a visible environmental catastrophe.

Yet by the 1980s, a period similar to the 1930s in terms of its intense social and economic restructuring, federal bureaucrats again turned toward conserving nature as part of their broad plan for reorganizing the means of ownership, production, and labor. The federal government looked to conservation anew when the temptations of neoliberal reforms and foreign tourism became appealing.[10] The new sites of natural value lay far from the temperate forests esteemed by the earlier foresters. These reserves protected examples of rare biological value, such as coral reefs, gray whale habitats, and tropical forests coveted by the "rainforest" tourism of North Americans and Europeans. Hippies, hikers, college students, retirees, and resort goers replaced peasants, workers, nationalists, and foresters as the main constituents of protected areas. Global fascination with tropical nature echoed developments in conservation biology and amplified attention on tropical countries as incidental stewards of these areas. Neoliberal biosphere reserves provided a fresh green stamp for a country with a blackened environmental record. Over the decades during which capricious development proceeded unchecked, protected natural areas lost their attachment to programs of social change and visions of revolutionary justice.

How and why the elaborately quilted landscape of rural production and nature conservation eroded into a threadbare patchwork of increasingly alienated political subjects deserves more attention than can be afforded here. Instead, this conclusion reconsiders the rise of revolutionary environmentalism to suggest some of the attributes worth recovering from the legacies of these early national parks. Next, it addresses the many critiques of the parks that emerged as concern for tropical nature materialized. Then, it briefly recollects the ways parks arose as artifacts of a certain context, one with a particular commitment to political incorporation. Finally, it examines lessons from the Mexican experience relevant to park makers everywhere.

Just Parks

In considering the collapse of the Cardenista park movement, it is worth remembering that these were just parks in two senses. First, they were parks for justice in that they recognized preexisting ownership and use, honored rural traditions, and envisioned public parks as part of revolutionary social reforms. This elevated the human and political aspects of nature protection over understandings of nature's function and independent value. They were also just parks in the sense they were only parks, fragile places subject to the whims of budgets and preferences of a fickle populace. These park designers never claimed that they controlled nature or created wilderness; their aims were social. Such attributes set Mexican parks apart and help explain why they've been overlooked and misunderstood.

Foreigners and Mexicans alike today assume that little tradition of conservation exists because of widespread problems of air pollution, waste disposal, drought, and deforestation. Journalist Joel Simon maintained that "environmentalism in Mexico has shallow roots," and John Terborgh, a leading conservation ecologist, agrees. "As a conservation prospect, Mexico is disappointing."[11] The historian Warren Dean makes a similar claim about all of Latin America: "It cannot be said that conservationism, an appreciation of nature, or a cult of the wilderness were either widely diffused or profoundly nourished in Latin American societies, not, at least in its Europeanized sectors."[12] I do not dispute these assessments, yet missing from laments over the lack of strict nature protection is attention to alternative types of environmentalism, especially the ways that valid reasons for protecting nature arose in a revolutionary context. In particular, Mexico's early experiment with conservation proved radical because its proponents tried to mediate local demands with conservation objectives, a concept that has more recently become vogue.

The early creation of Mexican parks suggests that observers interested in environmental issues should refrain from asking why Mexican national parks are not more like those in the United States with answers already set in their minds. Presuming a single standard of conservation well before one existed writes alternative conceptions out of the story.[13] More fruitful historical questions might be, what made these early parks special, or in what different ways did Mexicans come to define environmentalism? In Mexico's national parks, foresters attempted to make conservation sustainable by conceding to the requests of local residents. Concern for designing an inclusive patrimony of nature meant incorporating local demands as much as scenery preservation and wildlife protection into park creation. The park system that emerged aimed to preserve a rural way of life and tried to put parks and local residents on the same side of conservation debates by restricting larger forces of land conversion, such as logging. The way that Mexican officials complied with democratic demands of the period—for example, by refusing to send in the army and by making legal exceptions for the destitute—ultimately weakened their ability to protect natural areas from overuse as rural populations increased and development priorities changed.

These decisions raise the profile of a revolutionary type of environmentalism and expose a gulf that exists among understandings of environmentalism, the environmentalism of the poor, and environmental justice. Historians have long attributed the rise of environmentalism to early conservation movements in the United States and later popular concerns over industrial wastes, signified eloquently by Rachel Carson's book *Silent Spring*.[14] The rise of popular concern over environmental degradation came about in the 1960s, but by the 1970s critiques began to point to the racial and class inequalities rampant among the siting of hazardous waste facilities and uneven exposure to toxic risks. These calls for environmental justice often came from suffering communities with little sympathy for symbols that resonated with environmentalists, like wilderness areas and charismatic megafauna. Two decades ago, Ramachandra Guha claimed that environmentalism does not have elite origins but that the poor are often the ones who most intimately know the need for environmental conservation.[15] These divergent socioeconomic realms of environmental activism give environmental issues added legitimacy. They also offer an artificial conundrum—why isn't environmentalism always about justice?

The creation of national parks in Mexico before these competing international environmentalisms emerged exposes difficult lessons for those concerned with both protecting the environment and ensuring socially just governance. More than other countries, the revolutionary context and the insistence by reformers on inclusion forged a democratic environmentalism. In contrast to U.S. park origins, Mexico's establishment of natural parks near the main centers of business, government, and industry proved more radical than establishing a park in the least populated part of the country.[16] Creating parks within citizens' immediate reach boosted efforts of equality more than making parks to bolster wealthy railroad businesses.[17] And building social change on a platform of natural resource management that maintained access for all sectors of society provided an ambitious goal when segregation dominated elsewhere. The focus on inclusive management in parks also left open the door for their destruction. These democratic parks disappeared faster than those in countries that excluded residents and patrolled with soldiers. It is worth considering the critiques of the parks that developed in Mexico as tropical nature became a higher priority.

A Silent Failure

In tandem with the changing political and economic context of the mid-twentieth century came a transformation in scientific understandings and popular imaginings of parks. In many ways, this became a critical noose around the neck of the Mexican national parks that slowly but effectively strangled their successes and withered their recognition. Critiques of the parks first came from within; the dismissal of early conservation movements paralleled shifts away from the tenets of the revolution. At the same time, worldwide interest in wilderness ideas expanded with the formal articulation of the U.S. Wilderness Act of 1964 and with the genesis of conservation biology as a discipline in the 1980s.[18] New scientific notions of value, such as biodiversity, allowed a hierarchy of protection to elevate large expanses of remote nature and write off bureaucratically weak parks that were created under an older scientific paradigm like Mexico's. This redefinition erased the fiercely contested compromises such parks constructed, sacrificing important constituents in the process.

The 1960s and 1970s proved the chronological transition of ideas of park value from temperate to tropical, from domestic to foreign, and from inclusive to exclusive. In 1962, the International Union for the Conservation of Nature (IUCN) held its first conference on national parks. The Mexican representative, Enrique Beltrán, at the time serving as director of the Institute of Renewable Natural Resources and a sub-secretary of agriculture, spoke with an inside perspective on the innovations, legacies, and flaws of Mexican parks created decades earlier. He gave a talk entitled "Use and Conservation: Two Conflicting Principles," in which he pointed out that national parks always reflected social values. Beltrán explored the contradictory mandates to both protect and enjoy parks, claiming, "I realize the enormous value of areas in which human action has not disturbed nature and which therefore lend themselves to studies of their native flora, fauna, and ecology. But, at the same time, I am not able to avoid considering the social questions that oblige us to create national parks."[19] Beltrán noted the trajectory of Mexican park establishment, which entailed a trickle of parks until the boom of 1935 to 1942 and then few subsequent parks. He did not hesitate to critique the parks, remarking both that "legislation with respect to national parks was notoriously deficient, which made it difficult to manage the parks properly" and that many of the parks were consequently too small. Beltrán learned early lessons from concrete experiences, and he went on to explain that compromises between use and conservation would be better managed by establishing zones of differentiated use, with the strictest for purely scientific studies, followed by intermediate zones without either easy access or rigid restrictions, and then general zones for the majority of the public's use with visitor services. In later years, the idea of zoning became standard in protected areas of tropical countries. Trained as a biologist, Beltrán understood the scientific value of parks, yet, influenced by his experiences in Mexico, he also felt obliged to respect the spirit of parks as social spaces.

Although he reflected back on this initial period of park creation, Beltrán represented a new generation of Mexican conservationists. He could see the aspirations of the originators and the mistakes during subsequent decades. His moderation represented an ambivalence toward conservation that came to replace the revolutionary alliance of justice and action. On the one hand, he promoted many of the same scientific principles that brought parks to the forefront. On the other, he dismissed the revolutionary context as irrelevant to the process of park creation. Such dismissal would help to bury the radical nature of nature protection as Mexicans strove to emphasize the maturity and stability of their government. Despite such ambivalence, his and others' observations deepened the critique throughout the twentieth century until the national and international publics scarcely knew Mexico had once led the world in park creation.

The national parks had serious flaws, many of which initial park planners anticipated and some they could not have imagined. Beltrán's measured critiques pointed to some of the greatest unfolding pressures, including rapid population growth and increasing demands on the land. He identified two factors of great concern specific to Mexico—the devolution of an independent Forestry Department and the subsequent pairing of forestry with agriculture—that subverted conservation management goals to mandates for rapid production. More specifically, he critiqued the fact that a large part of the land included in the national parks never officially belonged to the nation. "As a consequence," Beltrán explained, "there exists within the parks some communal property—especially in the peculiar form that Mexican law calls 'common property' and even some small villages. Such a condition . . . greatly complicates planning for the proper use and management of our parks."[20] The quandary that property acquisition created for the government proved nearly insurmountable and led critics to dismiss the parks as lacking substance or significance even though this inclusion proved central to the parks' original design.

Largely because of these internal critiques, during the genesis of international conservation networks, Mexican participation dwindled. Beltrán, accompanied by Daniel Galicia, was a leading speaker at the first IUCN conference on national parks, but by the second in 1972, Mexicans had no central role.[21] Their park systems represented an older model with less resonance among growing notions of environmental degradation that embraced the concepts of wilderness and biodiversity. Although aspects of their broad conservation program, such as the educational apparatus, earned praise, the very contents of the parks became an issue.[22] By 1971, the increasing standardization of national parks excluded many Mexican parks from the IUCN's lists: at least thirty-five were not included. Most of them did not fulfill the size requirements, and four were excluded for doubts about their effectiveness.[23] Common IUCN standards for parks introduced criteria for recognition and possibly funding, but the excision of national spaces from international definitions dismissed the parks' novel origins and ignored increasingly relevant lessons from this model. This voided the history of parks that predated these guidelines and originated in a different scientific context in symbiosis with land reform and cooperatives. More important, recent critiques of parks as exclusionary miss the lessons from the Mexican case that show how people-centered parks can lead to degradation, making some parks hardly park-like at all.[24]

New international definitions for parks grew out of a rising cultural affinity for wilderness among the citizens of industrialized nations. Although the wilderness idea dates much earlier, sympathies for expanses of wild nature, first within and soon outside of these countries, grew exponentially in the second half of the twentieth century at the same time that such places evaporated in the face of development. Wilderness advocates argued compellingly that nature had its own value outside and separate from humanity, an idea solidified most firmly when the U.S. Congress passed the Wilderness Act on September 3, 1964: "A wilderness, in contrast with those areas where man and his own works dominate the landscape, is hereby recognized as an area where the earth and its community of life are untrammeled by man, where man himself is a visitor who does not remain."[25] The act goes on to clarify that wilderness areas have opportunities for solitude or primitive recreation, that the imprint of man's work should be unnoticeable, and that the designated area should be at least 2023 hectares in size. Historian Roderick Nash points out that the Wilderness Act marked an innovation in changing popular conceptions of nature in part because it triggered offensive moves supporting nature rather than merely defensive stances against development.[26] Once set, the legislation led to the tightening of values about uninhabited nature around the globe. That Mexico's early parks lack wilderness stems from their creation during a time when different cultural values (especially values that promoted social justice) shaped conservation, and the lack of a concept of or specific criteria for wilderness. These parks conserved a lot of things—rural traditions, national landscapes, and political compromises—but wilderness was never part of their design, nor did it later come to exist within these parks.

For the next three decades, the elevation of wilderness gathered strength worldwide (despite ongoing resistance by indigenous peoples), and in the process, an ethic of wilderness permeated the work of international conservation organizations and government planners. In the 1970s, protected areas doubled and international conferences and congresses on conservation expanded.[27] By some estimates, 86 percent of Latin American protected areas had inhabitants.[28] By the 1990s, the cumulative examples of exclusion became too blatant to ignore. Critiques echoing Guha's sentiments came from the tropics and soon also from industrialized nations, including William Cronon's provocative essay, "The Trouble with Wilderness, or Getting Back to the Wrong Nature."[29] Such critiques raised important questions of restoration. If wilderness is the appropriate state of nature, what state of wild was original and worthy of preservation or of going back to? What about the areas where humans modified nature and created a sublime that, after centuries of colonial encounters, now stood uninhabited? Some old-growth forests adored by environmentalists may date their origins to the catastrophic postcontact deaths of millions of indigenous peoples. Wildlands with open fields and varied meadows conducive to wildlife, like those on the Serengeti, may have anthropogenic origins especially tied to the role of fire.[30] These critics suggested that where wilderness dominated, labor, largely of indigenous peoples or those without access to structures of social power, is erroneously lumped alongside large-scale destructive forces like logging.

Many of these critiques found strength in their claims of justice, in their concern for rural peoples, and in their recognition of the compromises asked of protected areas, which were all issues Mexican revolutionaries confronted decades earlier. Indeed, in the Mexican case, claims of external interference hardly hold up: it was revolutionaries themselves who initially gave up on their park program, and a changing transnational scientific paradigm kept it from reemerging. Revolutionary Mexicans expanded social justice to local groups in and around parks, prioritized rural peoples' livelihoods over those of urbanites (for a time), and extended access to social power in unprecedented ways. As the example at the start of the chapter illustrates, Mexicans themselves argued for changes that led to an abandonment of such carefully balanced resource management. The results gradually compromised nature within the parks and withered the innovations of a socially just system of nature protection.

Conversations about a wilderness idea have been more muted within Mexico. Beltrán, like Quevedo and Cárdenas before him, never idealized wilderness.[31] His vision advocated more of an ethical human place in nature—a position now widely regarded as an ethic of sustainability—rather than an isolated oasis of wild land. Mexican ethnobotanist Arturo Gómez-Pompa and American anthropologist Andrea Kaus point out that the idea of untouched wilderness is an urban perception and that rural inhabitants have different views. They remind us that "throughout the world, communally held resources have been managed and conserved by diverse human societies via cultural mechanisms that attach symbolic and social significance to land and resources beyond their immediate extractive value."[32]

Despite the advice of Beltrán, or the work of Cardenistas, Mexican nature at the end of the twentieth century came to be valued for the exotic, wild, and tropical nature that the country lagged to conserve. Few people, including few Mexicans, remembered that they had forged a compromise reflecting the nearness of nature and the necessities of humans in their forests. Indeed, the trouble with wilderness was not that there was too much of it but that too many people became troubled by wilderness to the detriment of a wider array of conservation objectives, many of which had been tried in Mexico.

In Mexico, the delisting of certain parks and the rise of wilderness ideals worked to shift perceptions of value from central dry forests to distant rain forest reserves. Areas in the north and south had been overlooked by earlier protections, and the rationales for new reserves did not aim to compensate for these oversights within the older paradigm. For good reason, concern over habitat conversion and species extinctions gained dramatic social and cultural influence among scientists, governmental leaders, and concerned citizens. Understandings of biodiversity struck a popular chord because they allowed rigorous science to be translated into lay understandings of natural functions based on these transparent values. Such developments brought the tropics into focus for a new generation of scientific educators and ordinary people. Mexico is consistently lauded among the world's most biodiverse countries because such a range of species exists in constant interaction and flux.[33] Although affinities for the central pine, fir, and oak forests remained widespread, recognition of the value of the tropics has largely been a foreign enterprise, which has implied that residents of tropical countries have neglected to care for or protect nature. This neglect is undeniable, but it is also irremediable without a more accurate understanding of how societies come to conserve nature and why they do not. Although the initial abandonment of Mexican conservation work midcentury came when Mexicans themselves gave up the project, the historical context of recent scientific understandings has created a dichotomy in the legacies of protected areas where temperate countries, with less biodiversity, are acknowledged as leaders, and tropical countries, with more "valuable" nature, lag precariously behind.[34]

The conservation efforts of tropical countries have been critiqued in many ways, but the notion of "paper parks" has proved a particularly compelling mechanism for dismissing domestic efforts. The phrase, common among biologists and international conservation organizations, refers to "parks that have not been implemented in any serious way and that enjoy only a virtual existence as lines drawn on official maps."[35] Undeniably, there are protected areas with little scientific substance, parks indistinguishable from nonparks, and reserves severely neglected both economically and culturally. That "paper parks" occur due to political expediency, manipulative public relations, or gradual decline is not a question but a reality. However, lumping parks of national origins into such a category has troubling effects, in particular on parks with domestic roots designed originally to serve collective functions. When tracing the historical origins of conservation areas, a distinction should be made in terms of intentionality. In certain cases, such as early Mexico, administrators and designers fully intended to create parks that worked to preserve nature and rural communities nearby. That their actions did not remain in the longer term had more to do with available knowledge, experience, and the ways their work was not honored later. Initially, the intent to conserve was there. Other parks are designed with no intention of enforcing or enacting measures to protect nature within; in other words, they are designed at best as unfunded mandates and at worst as deceitful symbols. Conflating both intentionalities as paper parks obscures the lessons of the first.

The "paper parks" concept arose as a means to bring awareness to the lack of effective conservation in tropical areas, but the accusatory term severs failed conservation projects from their historical roots that in Mexico's case supported environmental protection and social justice in an unexpected landscape. The dismissal of domestic recognitions of nature and the elevation of wilderness validated by the international scientific community and by foreigners—despite their often altruistic concerns— exacerbates already sensitive issues of sovereignty. Deracinating these parks allows conservation to be redefined in exclusive and exclusionary ways, unnecessarily creating animosity among potential supporters.

Several problems remain with conventional histories of protected areas. To start, affluent temperate countries such as the United States have applied a retroactive standard that implies their parks are grounded in an allegiance to transcendent scientific principles.[36] Yet the scientific principles that might have justified the creation of Yellowstone as a sizable habitat for wolves or grizzly bears did not yet exist. Some advocates claimed the park would provide habitat to prevent bison extinction, but an understanding of the size needed for such a function came later. In other words, that the size of U.S. parks proved large enough for ecosystem conservation had more to do with the relative accessibility of large expanses of land than with adherence to scientific principles for species range. Even early biologists who worried about the decline of large mammals in the parks in the 1930s made up a small minority within the National Park Service.[37] More commonly, park advocates spoke of the touristy and tributary functions of the park.[38] In the United States, wilderness was set aside to protect national and natural heritage, which incidentally perpetuated biologically sound areas for wild nature to remain. The science that would confirm that size was crucial to the integrity of ecosystems came decades after initial U.S. park designs.

If science did not ordain park history, culture certainly guided it. Scholars have shown that rather than a benevolent scientific enterprise, the construction of U.S. parks was predicated on the exclusion of people already living within park areas. Indigenous people did occupy the landscapes that became U.S. parks, and cultural conceptions of property, ownership, and citizenship—not of science—excluded them. Indeed, Yellowstone became the world's first national park (rather than another state or provincial park) in part because of the culturally constructed fact that it resided within the Wyoming territory (not a state) and because it provided a new area for capital enterprise on the frontier. Beyond the exclusion of inhabitants, resource managers proved extremely influential in shaping ecosystem functions within the parks. Multiple management strategies—from feeding bears to the suppression of fire—influenced natural patterns and demonstrate that no perfect park model ever existed, but as scientific understandings and management policies change, they affect protected areas.[39]

These critiques are not intended to dispute the value of tropical nature, scientifically, culturally, or philosophically. The work of judiciously and sensitively defending tropical nature and advocating for the sovereignty of peoples that call it home proves a difficult and necessary endeavor. At issue here is the unfortunate trend of holding tropical countries hostage to a changing model of conservation that they could not possibly replicate. The result is that tropical countries are paralyzed from realizing a vigorous defense of their own patrimony and subjected to a standard that industrialized countries themselves base on a fallacious understanding of their own past. Future park protection requires the contextualization of history.

For instance, the discourse of biodiversity allows tropical nature to stand for the entirety of a country, despite the fact that a country like Mexico is diverse because of the existence of tropical *and* temperate regions. Conflating all of nature in tropical countries into an idea of the "rainforest" collapses diversity into an exotic vision.[40] Views of tropical nature as superior and corollary critiques of "paper parks" erase historical actions and deny the agency and legitimacy of domestic conservation efforts.[41] The dismissal of historical park programs by foreign and domestic audiences contributes to a hegemonic grasp on conservation's goals, its definitions, and its ultimate content. It also inhibits international conservation organizations from genuinely requesting and receiving support from countries that remain the sovereign stewards of valuable natural areas. How can an organization ask for cooperation when it devalues a government's prior contributions or dismisses them altogether? Denunciations of "paper parks" deny Mexicans an association with past visions of conservation, perpetuating the idea that conservation is foreign, that parks are colonial, and that citizens must choose between the economy and the environment. These are not fair approximations of choices that national governments can make. A paradigm of imposed conservation does not have to be the contested nature of conservation. Without a shift in social values, all the science in the world does not result in conservation.

My aim is to point out that parks, with or without residents, do not exist independent of people. Parks are never natural designations but always cultural constructions, and by constructing them, humans shape the subsequent conditions of the natural areas. Some human actions are more intrusive than others, and it would serve park proponents and objectors alike if conservationists gave more focus to large-scale land conversion enterprises, the lack of economic alternatives for impoverished people, and climate change as the largest threats to wild nature. By pitting scientists against local people, polarizing debates over conservation detract from the larger possibilities that come with parks. Rather than accepting this division, for conservation to move forward the antecedents of the current debates must be unpacked with attention to the ways societies have articulated claims to their natural patrimony.

Cultural Artifacts and Critical Context

This history contends that despite their current condition, Mexico's first parks were more than vestiges of paper. But if Mexican national parks were not wilderness, what were they? They, too, were cultural artifacts that provide a testament to a vision of conservation that balanced the work of rural people with the goals of protecting the national patrimony. That national parks can have a revolutionary—rather than an authoritarian or colonial—origin provides much hope for once again bridging the aims of social justice with environmental protection. Mexican parks were exceptional in at least three ways. First, the design of Mexican national parks strengthened, rather than eroded, common property structures. As part of the land reform process, parks were one of a spectrum of strategies used to keep rural people on the land. In this way, parks helped to root rural people in nature rather than evict them. This tradition contributes to the reality that Mexico still maintains one of the highest percentages of community-run forests in the world.[42] Second, Mexican parks pulled nature into the national patrimony in a way that merged human and nonhuman relics of the past. The close proximity of parks to seats of governance, historical sites, and productive enterprises speaks to a larger vision of how parks fit into the definition of the nation. Third, the timing of the parks during the vast set of revolutionary social reforms reveals the symmetry of a view of nationalizing nature and extending the benefits of citizenship to the popular classes. In this historical moment, revolutionary governments had options beyond exploiting people or exploiting nature. Rather than the later revolutionary agendas worldwide, such as China's "war on nature" or Cuba's "conquering nature," Mexico's conservation agenda supported the integrity of natural spaces and the dignity of revolutionary citizens.[43]

Although the history of national parks in Mexico pushes back the chronological understandings of conservation's global history, it does not revise current interpretations of the revolution's trajectory or the Cárdenas period except by deepening the scope of change. While retaining the timeline, park creation does enhance the interpretation of the revolution's aims because the environment can no longer be excluded from discussions of revolutionary goals. Attention to nature undergirded policy as an understanding of the land, its contents, and its potential informed decisions about what value lands contained. Park creation became wrapped up in the same aims for political longevity that shaped the national peasant congresses, indigenous committees, and federally run unions. Rural residents altered resource management plans by denouncing intransigent regulations, negotiating park boundaries, and objecting to certain leaders. Ordinary citizens restrained experts' actions because the political atmosphere permitted—indeed, encouraged—their participation. In a regime that privileged a sense of revolutionary nationalism, campesinos could not be sacrificed to scientific objectives. Justice demanded their inclusion.

However exceptional, local peoples are not the romantic heroes of Mexican conservation but simply participants in the process that made social justice a component of park creation. Communities of rural people were as likely to object to protecting the forest, as the ejidatarios of Zitlaltepec did, as they were to advocate for it, as did Tepoztlán's Bolshevikis. Knee-jerk deference to local peoples' resource demands out of moral principle defeats larger aims of protection by clouding the reality that although some were excellent stewards, others proved eager to rapidly exploit resources afforded to them. There is no guarantee that the rural poor will look out for their long-term interests through careful stewardship or that they can inherently manage fragile natural areas. To argue otherwise ignores the historical record and naively overlooks human desires. What made revolutionary environmentalism radical was the manner in which its proponents aimed to mediate local demands and conservation objectives without assuming the superiority—or the immutability—of either.

Despite their existence in an unexpected place, national parks remain cultural artifacts based on a narrow interpretation of nature. They capture a vision of nature as valuable and a particular set of justifications for that value. Mexico's revolutionary vision—one of firs and pines, lakes and rivers, volcanoes and mountains, pyramids and villages—emerged in a particular moment, one that no longer meets the prevailing conservation standards within or outside of the country. Although the importance of forests for mediating the climate and preventing erosion readily emerged as justifications in the 1930s, the foresters lacked an understanding of biodiversity, species interaction, and other principles that shape conservation areas today. Instead, the cultural context that permitted—indeed, called for—the creation of these parks around the nation's capital combined forest plans, social goals, and commitments to political justice. This fine balance resulted in a swath of parks that appear quite similar, and in many ways unspectacular. This, too, is part of the resonance of these spaces with the people who had the power to mark them in perpetuity. Despite their natural façade, parks cannot escape their social and cultural context.

Lessons and Laments

The institutional heritage and traditions of a country are vital to making conservation effective. National culture provides the key to sustainable conservation projects because private conservation can be a catalyst only as it remains subject to government regulations and cultural shifts. If humanity is to protect what remains of the natural world, it must rely upon the work of governments and the support of citizens in honoring everything from wilderness to just parks. To this end, several lessons can be drawn from the successes and failures of Mexico's early experiment with conservation.

First, local people's opinions, desires, and activities must be included in conservation planning. In parks like Zempoala, where local peoples were given priority in vending enterprises or provided jobs in vigilance, they became park defenders. When parks planners made enemies or did not present suitable alternative livelihoods, like in Malinche, residents retaliated with obstruction. Local residents must be included, but this does not mean they have final or supreme authority. Local groups cannot be expected to choose what is better for their own livelihoods or for conservation in the long term. Indeed, part of the reason Cárdenas demoted the Forestry Department was because of campesinos' complaints, even though their relationship with forest management would likely have been more advantageous if the department remained. Sensitivity to local rights cannot triumph over larger national and global purposes; each must be balanced in a continual effort to find a sustainable middle ground. The Mexican case demonstrates that there are institutional ways of mediating these differences.

Second, although historians in other countries have critiqued strict exclusion, in Mexico, park planners' reluctance to utilize more authoritarian actions contributed to the deterioration of the parks. Mexican parks lapsed because claims to social justice and recent memories of violence made the public suspicious of prohibitions and patrols. As populations increased, this promoted lawlessness and haphazard harvesting of forest products in parks, both of which degraded community lands. Although uncomfortable, this should be a lesson that parks with deeply democratic origins but few mechanisms to prohibit gradual encroachment or clandestine extraction ceased to be democratic. Parks without enforcement are hardly parks at all; indeed, they unintentionally become "paper parks." Although parks may restrict individual activities, their long-term existence means more for democracy than do immediate authoritarian restrictions. In other areas, such as child protection or consumer safety, the state reserves authority to protect the vulnerable. Within parks, the vulnerable assets are nonhuman species, and a state's reluctance to undertake responsibility for nature's protection degrades the landscape and the larger environment for all.

Third, parks find public resonance when they are integrated into a nexus of social policies. The opportunity for parks arose at a time when systems of governance and access to state benefits in general were restructured. This essential atmosphere of reform suggests that parks should be nested within reforms that address other social issues—from poverty to property rights—rather than tacked on as afterthoughts. Interpreting parks as privileges of the rich or out of sync with social needs wrongly disconnects human and environmental policy. Mexican parks came about as inclusive reserves, and although that inclusiveness partially eroded their strength, it is easy to envision how, with a material commitment, resiliency could be built into parks if their design coincided with social policies.

Fourth, conservationists cannot assume that certain societies are unable to plan for the environment despite chaotic political pasts or violent revolutions. The creation of record numbers of parks on the heels of Mexico's revolution should serve as an inspiration to look for opportunities in unlikely places. Healthy institutions and greater public responsibility can be cultivated following periods of crisis, and cultural values are reformulated in these times of flux.

Finally, conservationists must remember that in most cases, park promoters and local people are on the same side pitted against the political and economic forces that support large-scale land conversion and that push wild nature and indigenous peoples into the last refuges of undeveloped land. It is unreasonable to accept that they are "terribly at odds with one another," because these groups have more in common than in conflict.[44] Concluding that the most pressing struggles facing conservation are the disputes between conservationists and local people largely underestimates the rapaciousness of the corporations and consumers that rapidly degrade both. If the choice for conservation were simply one between parks and people, it might be an easier plight. Instead, the real issues are open land versus highways, indigenous hunters versus soybean fields, and a fossil-fueled industrial society versus abundant flora and fauna. In each of these examples, the cars, crops, and consumers push aside both parks and people, further impoverishing the world as a result. Critiques of the tepid relationship between conservation organizations and local residents smokescreen the genuine threats to both.

Today, Lagunas de Zempoala, Malinche, Popo and Izta, and Tepozteco National Parks still exist in and around an incredibly urbanized country with an industrial reality. Nearly all the vestiges of green found throughout the Valley of Mexico have their roots in Cardenista environmental plans. The rampant deforestation and wanton disregard for ecosystem integrity that dominate displaced commitments to conservation. The shift from a rural to an urban country, the solidification of a one-party state that allocated patronage in the form of resources, the rapid increase in population, the promotion of industrialization and economic growth above all else, and shifts in the global economy all contributed to the decimation of communities and forests. Such degradation did not occur out of a fatalistic or antienvironmental ethic. As economic and political choices moved the country further from solidarity and toward authoritarian rule, both national culture and national nature became objects of domination rather than agents of inclusion. The early national parks demonstrate that a different path once existed and may exist again.

Appendix A

National Park Declarations and Contents, 1935–1941

Table A.1. Declaration Date, Size, and Property Status for the National Parks

National Park	Date[a]	Hectares	Property[b]
Alejandro de Humboldt	18 September 1936	NA	Expropriate
Barranca del Cupatitzio	2 November 1938	452	Not noted
Benito Juárez	30 December 1937	2737	Remain
Bosencheve	1 August 1940	15,000	Remain
Cañón del Río Blanco	22 March 1938	55,690	Remain
Cerro de Garnica	5 September 1936	968	Expropriate
Cerro de la Estrella	24 August 1938	1,100	Remain
Cerro de las Campanas	7 July 1937	58	Expropriate
Cofre de Perote	4 May 1937	11,700	Remain
Cumbres de Ajusco	23 September 1936	920	Expropriate
Cumbres de Majalca	1 September 1939	4,772	Remain
Cumbres de Monterrey	24 November 1939	246,500	Remain
El Histórico Coyoacán	26 September 1938	584	Remain
El Potosí	15 September 1936	2,000	Expropriate
El Sabinal	25 August 1938	8	Remain
El Tepeyac	18 February 1937	302	Expropriate
El Tepozteco	22 January 1937	24,000	Remain
Fuentes Brotantes	28 September 1936	129	Expropriate
Gogorrón	22 September 1936	25,000	Expropriate
Grutas de Cacahuamilpa	23 April 1936	1,600	Expropriate
Insurgente José María Morelos	22 February 1939	4,325	Remain
Insurgente Miguel Hidalgo	18 September 1936	1,750	Expropriate
Iztaccíhuatl and Popocatépetl	8 November 1935	25,679	Expropriate

(continued)

167

Table A.1. (Continued)

National Park	Date[a]	Hectares	Property[b]
Lago de Camecuáro	8 March 1941	9	Not noted
La Malinche, Matlalcueyatl	6 October 1938	45,711	Remain
Lagunas de Chacahua	9 July 1937	14,187	Remain
Lagunas de Zempoala	27 November 1936	4,669	Expropriate
Lomas de Padierna	22 April 1939	670	Not noted
Los Mármoles	8 September 1936	23,150	Expropriate
Los Novillos	18 June 1940	42	Remain
Los Remedios	15 April 1938	400	Remain
Molino de Flores Netzahualcóyotl	5 November 1937	55	Expropriate
Nevado de Colima	5 September 1936	22,200	Expropriate
Nevado de Toluca	25 January 1936	51,100	Expropriate
Pico de Orizaba	4 January 1937	19,750	Expropriate
Pico de Tancítaro	27 July 1940	29,316	Remain
Sacromonte	29 August 1939	45	Not noted
Xicotencatl	17 November 1937	680	Remain
Zoquiapan y Anexas	13 March 1937	19,418	Remain

[a] Date of publication in *Diario Oficial*, which made the park legally constituted.

[b] The declaration's recommendation for property holdings within the park boundary to remain with current owners or expropriate for the federal government.

Table A.2. National Park Natural and Cultural Contents Mentioned in Declarations

National Park	Forests	Water	Mountains	Historical figure	Historic site
Alejandro de Humboldt	Yes	Yes	No	Yes	No
Barranca del Cupatitzio	Yes	Yes	No	No	No
Benito Juárez	Yes	Yes	No	Yes	No
Bosencheve	Yes	Yes	No	No	No
Cañón del Rio Blanco	Yes	Yes	Yes	No	No
Cerro de Garnica	Yes	Yes	Yes	No	No
Cerro de la Estrella	Yes	No	No	No	Yes
Cerro de las Campanas	No	No	No	No	Yes
Cofre de Perote	Yes	Yes	Yes	No	No
Cumbres de Ajusco	Yes	Yes	Yes	No	No
Cumbres de Majalca	Yes	Yes	No	No	No
Cumbres de Monterrey	Yes	Yes	Yes	No	No
El Histórico Coyoacán	No	No	No	Yes	Yes
El Potosí	Yes	Yes	Yes	No	No
El Sabinal	Yes	No	No	No	No
El Tepeyac	Yes	No	No	Yes	Yes
El Tepozteco	Yes	Yes	No	Yes	Yes
Fuentes Brotantes	Yes	Yes	No	No	Yes
Gogorrón	Yes	Yes	No	No	Yes
Grutas de Cacahuamilpa	No	Yes	No	No	No
Insurgente José María Morelos	Yes	Yes	No	Yes	No
Insurgente Miguel Hidalgo	Yes	Yes	No	Yes	No
Iztaccíhuatl and Popocatépetl	Yes	Yes	Yes	Yes	No
Lago de Camecuáro	Yes	Yes	No	No	No
Lagunas de Chacahua	No	Yes	No	Yes	No
Lagunas de Zempoala	Yes	Yes	No	No	No
La Malinche o Matlalcueyatl	Yes	Yes	Yes	Yes	No
Lomas de Padierna	Yes	No	Yes	Yes	Yes
Los Mármoles	Yes	Yes	No	No	No
Los Novillos	Yes	Yes	No	No	No
Los Remedios	Yes	Yes	No	No	Yes
Molino de Flores Netzahualcóyotl	No	Yes	No	No	Yes
Nevado de Colima	Yes	Yes	Yes	No	No
Nevado de Toluca	Yes	Yes	Yes	No	No
Pico de Orizaba	Yes	Yes	Yes	No	No
Pico de Tancítaro	Yes	Yes	Yes	No	No
Sacromonte	Yes	No	No	No	Yes
Xicotencatl	Yes	No	No	No	Yes
Zoquiapan y Anexas	Yes	No	No	No	No

Table A.3. National Park Contents and Objectives Mentioned in Declarations

National Park	Highway	Tree nursery	Beauty	Education
Alejandro de Humboldt	No	No	Yes	No
Barranca del Cupatitzio	No	No	Yes	No
Benito Juárez	No	No	Yes	No
Bosencheve	Yes	No	Yes	No
Cañón del Rio Blanco	No	No	Yes	No
Cerro de Garnica	Yes	No	Yes	No
Cerro de la Estrella	No	No	Yes	No
Cerro de las Campanas	Yes	No	Yes	No
Cofre de Perote	No	No	Yes	No
Cumbres de Ajusco	Yes	No	Yes	No
Cumbres de Majalca	No	No	Yes	No
Cumbres de Monterrey	Yes	No	Yes	No
El Histórico Coyoacán	Yes	Yes	Yes	Yes
El Potosí	No	No	Yes	No
El Sabinal	No	Yes	Yes	No
El Tepeyac	No	No	Yes	Yes
El Tepozteco	No	No	Yes	Yes
Fuentes Brotantes de Tlalpan	No	Yes	Yes	Yes
Gogorrón	No	Yes	Yes	Yes
Grutas de Cacahuamilpa	No	No	Yes	No
Insurgente José María Morelos	Yes	Yes	Yes	No
Insurgente Miguel Hidalgo	Yes	No	Yes	Yes
Iztaccíhuatl and Popocatépetl	Yes	No	Yes	No
Lago de Camecuáro	No	No	Yes	No
Lagunas de Chacahua	No	No	Yes	Yes
Lagunas de Zempoala	Yes	No	Yes	Yes
La Malinche o Matlalcueyatl	No	Yes	Yes	No
Lomas de Padierna	No	Yes	Yes	Yes
Los Mármoles	Yes	No	Yes	No
Los Novillos	No	No	Yes	No
Los Remedios	No	No	Yes	No
Molino de Flores Netzahualcóyotl	No	No	Yes	Yes
Nevado de Colima	No	No	Yes	No
Nevado de Toluca	No	No	Yes	No
Pico de Orizaba	No	No	Yes	No
Pico de Tancítaro	No	No	Yes	No
Sacromonte	No	No	Yes	No
Xicotencatl	No	No	Yes	Yes
Zoquiapan y Anexas	No	No	No	No

Table A.4. National Park Contents and Administrators Mentioned in Declarations

National park	Tourism[a]	Six-Year Plan	Recommended administrators[b]
Alejandro de Humboldt	Yes	No	DFCP, SHCP
Barranca del Cupatitzio	Yes	No	DFCP, SHCP
Benito Juárez	Yes	No	DFCP, SHCP
Bosencheve	Yes	No	DFCP, SHCP
Cañón del Río Blanco	Yes	Yes	DFCP, SHCP
Cerro de Garnica	Yes	No	DFCP, SHCP
Cerro de la Estrella	Yes	No	DFCP, SEP, SHCP
Cerro de las Campanas	Yes	No	DFCP, SEP, SHCP
Cofre de Perote	Yes	No	DFCP, SHCP
Cumbres de Ajusco	Yes	No	DFCP, SHCP
Cumbres de Majalca	Yes	No	DFCP, local, SHCP
Cumbres de Monterrey	Yes	No	com, DFCP, SCOP, SPF
El Histórico Coyoacán	Yes	No	DFCP, SEP, SHCP
El Potosí	Yes	No	DFCP, SHCP
El Sabinal	Yes	No	DFCP, local
El Tepeyac	Yes	Yes	DDF, DFCP
El Tepozteco	Yes	No	com, DFCP
Fuentes Brotantes de Tlalpan	Yes	No	DFCP, SHCP
Gogorrón	Yes	No	DFCP, SAF, SHCP
Grutas de Cacahuamilpa	Yes	Yes	DFCP, SHCP
Insurgente José María Morelos	Yes	No	DFCP, local, SHCP
Insurgente Miguel Hidalgo	Yes	No	DFCP, SHCP
Iztaccíhuatl and Popocatépetl	Yes	No	DFCP, SHCP
Lago de Camecuáro	Yes	No	local, SAF
Lagunas de Chacahua	Yes	No	DFCP, SHCP
Lagunas de Zempoala	Yes	Yes	DFCP, SHCP
La Malinche o Matlalcueyatl	Yes	No	DFCP, local, SHCP
Lomas de Padierna	Yes	No	DDF, DFCP, SDN, SEP
Los Mármoles	Yes	No	DFCP, SHCP
Los Novillos	Yes	No	com, SAF
Los Remedios	Yes	No	DDF, DFCP, local
Molino de Flores Netzahualcóyotl	Yes	No	local, DFCP, SEP, SHCP
Nevado de Colima	Yes	No	DFCP, SHCP
Nevado de Toluca	Yes	No	DFCP, SHCP
Pico de Orizaba	Yes	No	local, DFCP, SHCP
Pico de Tancítaro	Yes	No	SAF, SHCP
Sacromonte	Yes	No	DFCP, SEP, SHCP
Xicotencatl	Yes	Yes	DFCP, SHCP
Zoquiapan y Anexas	No	No	DFCP, SHCP

[a]Tourism refers to mention in the declaration of opportunities for tourism.

[b]Abbrebiations

com	committee of mixed membership	SDN	Secretaría de Defensa Nacional
DFCP	Departamento Forestal y de Caza y Pesca	SEP	Secretaría de Educación Pública
local	local residents or managers	SHCP	Secretaría de Hacienda y Crédito Público
SAF	Secretaría de Agricultura y Fomento		

Appendix B

Lagunas de Zempoala Sample Entries in Visitor Log, August 1938

Car	City or State	Occupation	Comments	Companions
1	California	Consular	Very pretty	6
2	Cuernavaca	Employee	Pretty	6
3	Cuernavaca	Engineer	Lovely place	5
4	Cuernavaca	Road employee	Very good	5
5	Dallas, TX	Musician	Beautiful	4
6	Denton, TX	Student	Pretty	5
7	Mexico City	Accountant	Marvelous	7
8	Mexico City	Accountant	Precious	6
9	Mexico City	Architect	[Illegible]	16
10	Mexico City	Architect	Very interesting	4
11	Mexico City	Businessman	A unique place	2
12	Mexico City	Capitalist	Unique	4
13	Mexico City	Chauffeur	Magnificent	7
14	Mexico City	Chemist	Marvelous	9
15	Mexico City	Chemist	Very pretty	5
16	Mexico City	Cotton worker	Interesting	7
17	Mexico City	Dentist	Unique	5
18	Mexico City	Legislator	Beautiful	5
19	Mexico City	Doctor	Very good	3
20	Mexico City	Electrician	Magnificent	6
21	Mexico City	Electrician	Very interesting	9
22	Mexico City	Employee	Beautiful	7
23	Mexico City	Employee	Excellent	11
24	Mexico City	Employee	Extra pretty	7
25	Mexico City	Employee	Good	5

(continued)

Car	City or State	Occupation	Comments	Companions
26	Mexico City	Employee	[Illegible]	8
27	Mexico City	Employee	Magnificent	6
28	Mexico City	Employee	Magnificent	6
29	Mexico City	Employee	Magnificent	9
30	Mexico City	Employee	Magnificent	17
31	Mexico City	Employee	picturesque	2
32	Mexico City	Employee	Precious	6
33	Mexico City	Employee	Precious	8
34	Mexico City	Employee	Pretty	4
35	Mexico City	Employee	Unique	3
36	Mexico City	Employee	Unique	5
37	Mexico City	Employee	Very beautiful	7
38	Mexico City	Employee	Very good	7
39	Mexico City	Employee	Very pretty	4
40	Mexico City	Employee	Very pretty	6
41	Mexico City	Employee	Very pretty	6
42	Mexico City	Employee	[Illegible]	4
43	Mexico City	Engineer	Interesting, pretty	5
44	Mexico City	Engineer	Magnificent	3
45	Mexico City	Engineer	Marvelous	2
46	Mexico City	Federal employee	Magnificent	14
47	Mexico City	[Illegible]	Beautiful	10
48	Mexico City	[Illegible]	[Illegible]	2
49	Mexico City	[Illegible]	Very pretty	6
50	Mexico City	Industrialist	Marvelous	5
51	Mexico City	Industrialist	Precious	3
52	Mexico City	Industrialist	Precious	13
53	Mexico City	Industrialist	Very pretty	8
54	Mexico City	Jeweler	So pretty	6
55	Mexico City	Lawyer	Precious	6
56	Mexico City	Lawyer	Pretty	2
57	Mexico City	Lawyer	Regular	2
58	Mexico City	Licenciado	Fantastic	4
59	Mexico City	Licenciado	Marvelous	6
60	Mexico City	Mechanic	Majestic	5
61	Mexico City	Medical surgeon	Very beautiful	8
62	Mexico City	Medical surgeon	Very beautiful	8
63	Mexico City	Merchant	Enchanted	4
64	Mexico City	Merchant	Enchanted	5
65	Mexico City	Merchant	Excellent, pretty	5
66	Mexico City	Merchant	Good	4
67	Mexico City	Merchant	Picturesque	2
68	Mexico City	Merchant	Precious	4
69	Mexico City	Merchant	Pretty	2

(continued)

Car	City or State	Occupation	Comments	Companions
70	Mexico City	Merchant	Pretty	2
71	Mexico City	Merchant	Very beautiful	4
72	Mexico City	Merchant	Very beautiful	4
73	Mexico City	Merchant	Very pretty	5
74	Mexico City	Merchant	Very pretty	5
75	Mexico City	Merchant	Very pretty	5
76	Mexico City	Merchant	Very pretty	6
77	Mexico City	Nurse	So beautiful	4
78	Mexico City	Pemex administrator	A marvel	8
79	Mexico City	Pharmacies	Pretty	9
80	Mexico City	Photographer	Enchanted	8
81	Mexico City	Professor	Picturesque	30
82	Mexico City	Reporter	[Illegible]	4
83	Mexico City	[Illegible]	Quite good	25
84	Mexico City	Student	Fix the cave	4
85	Mexico City	Student	Picturesque	7
86	Mexico City	Student	Precious	22
87	Mexico City	Student	Pretty	4
88	Mexico City	Telephone operator	Ideal	4
89	Mexico City	Writer	Magnificent	6
90	Monterey, CA	Student	Precious	5
91	Monterrey	Employee	Pretty	6
92	Monterrey	Vagabond	Very pretty	10
93	Tacubaya	Mason	Very pretty	8
94	Toluca	Engineer	[Illegible]	8
95	Toncon	Student	Very pretty	7
96	Torreón	Pemex employee	Very pretty	5
Total	11 locations	33 jobs	26 comments	623 visitors

Appendix C

Classifications of Number of Entries for Occupations with More than One Visitor for Lagunas de Zempoala, 1938

Occupation category	Occupations included	Visitors
Agriculturists	Agricultor, algodonero (agriculturalist, cotton worker)	14
Artisans	Electricista, herrero, carpintero, sastre (electrician, blacksmith, carpenter, tailor)	15
Artists	Artista, dibujante, pintor, fotógrafo, cinematógrafo, productor de películas, joyero, cantante (artist, sketch artist, painter, photographer, cinematographer, movie producer, jeweler, singer)	27
Business professionals	Comerciante, abogado, propietario, banquero, arquitecto, capitalista, empleador (businessman, lawyer, owner, banker, architect, capitalist, employer)	428
Business workers	Contador, agente, oficinista, empleado administrador, contratista, comisionista, profesionista, cobrador, pagador, cajero (accountant, agent, secretary, administrative employee, contractor, commissioner, professional, collector, payment collector, cashier)	80
Domestic workers	Domestica (domestic worker)	18
Educators and students	Estudiante, profesor, licenciado, maestro, bibliotecario, director escuela (student, professor, official with diploma, teacher, librarian, school director)	138

(*continued*)

Occupation category	Occupations included	Visitors
Health-care providers	Medico, dentista (doctor, dentist)	93
Media workers	Periodista, escritor, tipógrafo, publicista, radio operador, telefonista (journalist, writer, typist, publicist, radio operator, telephone operator)	27
Public employees	Empleado público, militar, SCOP, diputado, representativa (public employee, military, employee of the Secretariat of Communication and Public Works, diplomat, representative)	50
Scientists	Ingeniero, químico (engineer, chemist)	131
Tourists	Excursionista, alpinista, turista, vago, guía de turistas, viajero, retiran (sightseer, mountaineer, tourist, vagabond, tourist guide, traveler, retiree)	80
Transport workers	Chofer, camionero, aviador, ferrocarrilero, motociclista (chauffeur, truck driver, aviator, railroad worker, motorcyclist)	85
Workers	Empleado, industrial, mecánico, obrero, constructor, petrolero (employee, industrial worker, mechanic, worker, construction worker, petroleum worker)	388
Total		1,574

Notes

Introduction

1. Because some parks were reduced from their original sizes to accommodate land reform parcels and communities, Mexican administrators did not always know the sizes. In 1941, various government documents listed the size of the parks as 827,093 hectares, 830,195 hectares, and 840,220 hectares. Miguel Ángel de Quevedo to Secretaría de Hacienda y Crédito Público, 3 February 1939, Archivo General de la Nación (hereafter AGN): Secretaría de Agricultura y Recursos Hidráulicos (hereafter SARH) 1434, 1/2007; Programa de Trabajos, AGN: SARH 1425, 1/1609, 2; Relación de Parques Nacionales, 5 August 1941, AGN: SARH 1434, 1/2007. For comparison, the total of the parks is less than the size of Yellowstone National Park in the United States at 898,317 hectares and greater than the Adirondack Forest Preserve of upper New York State, at 619,395 hectares, Karl Jacoby, *Crimes against Nature: Squatters, Poachers, Thieves, and the Hidden History of American Conservation* (Berkeley: University of California Press, 2001), 46.

2. Eucario Leon to Quevedo, 29 December 1938, AGN: SARH 1434, 21/2007.

3. Quevedo to Secretaría de Hacienda y Crédito Público, 3 February 1939, AGN: SARH 1434, 1/2007, 2.

4. Ibid.

5. Reformers did not use this term yet their intentions convey this sentiment. Notably absent is a rationale for parks reliant upon ideas of wilderness. See Arturo Gómez-Pompa and Andrea Kaus, "Taming the Wilderness Myth," *BioScience* 42:4 (1992): 271–279.

6. Arturo Gómez-Pompa and Andrea Kaus, "From Pre-Hispanic to Future Conservation Alternatives: Lessons from Mexico," *Proceedings of the National Academy of Sciences of the United States of America* 96:11 (1999): 5982–5986. Their concern is largely with forest stewardship of the Yucatecan Maya of southern Mexico, but the lessons they draw resonate with earlier federal conservation programs. For more on

177

the relationship between conservation and agriculture in tropical regions, see Ivette Perfecto, John Vandermeer, and Angus Wright, *Nature's Matrix: Linking Agriculture, Conservation, and Food Sovereignty* (London: Earthscan, 2009).

7. José V. Cardoso, "Presupuesto para el departamento autónomo forestal y de caza y pesca," n.d., AGN: Ramo Presidentes, Lázaro Cárdenas del Rio (hereafter LCR), 554, 501.1/1.

8. My use of the word *patrimony* involves more than an implied inheritance or estate endowment but instead signifies a cumulative process by which material, cultural, and social values shape the understandings of a collective past. This definition draws from aspects outlined by Enrique Florescano, including the ways that each era rescues the past in distinct ways, how dominant social groups shape the selection of the past that is included in the patrimony, the manner in which the government identifies the patrimony in contradistinction from the universal and the personal, and the ways patrimony is constructed to balance distinct social and political interests, see Florescano, "El patrimonio nacional. Valores, usos, estudio y difusión," in *El Patrimonio Nacional de México I: Biblioteca Mexicana*, ed. Enrique Florescano, 15–27 (Mexico City: CONACULTA, Fondo de Cultura Económica, 1997).

9. The standard classification system comes from the entity that began in 1948 as the International Union for the Protection of Nature (IUPN) and became the International Union for the Conservation of Nature (IUCN) in 1956. Today, it has six broad categories (and two subcategories) with national parks under the second strictest protections. Nigel Dudley, *Guidelines for Applying Protected Area Management Categories* (Gland, Switzerland: IUCN, 2008), 11.

10. The first attempt to clarify protected area terms came at the 1933 International Conference for the Protection of Fauna and Flora in London and was attended by representatives of Belgium, Egypt, France, Italy, Portugal, South Africa, Spain, Sudan, and the United Kingdom. P. van Heijnsbergen, *International Legal Protection of Wild Fauna and Flora* (Amsterdam: IOS Press, 1997), 16. The Western Hemisphere Convention on Nature Protection and Wildlife Preservation held in Washington DC and ratified in 1942 laid out four categories: national parks, national reserves, nature monuments, and strict wilderness reserves, Dudley, *Guidelines*, 3. Recognition of these categories took much longer.

11. Mark Dowie, *Conservation Refugees: The Hundred-Year Conflict between Global Conservation and Native Peoples* (Cambridge, MA: MIT Press, 2009), xx.

12. Dudley, *Guidelines*, 4.

13. John Muir, *Our National Parks* (Boston: Houghton Mifflin, 1901); Roderick Nash, *Wilderness and the American Mind* (New Haven: Yale University, 1967); Alfred Runte, *National Parks: The American Experience* (Lincoln: University of Nebraska Press, 1979); Samuel Hays, *Conservation and the Gospel of Efficiency: The Progressive Conservation Movement, 1890–1920* (Cambridge, MA: Harvard University Press, 1959); Ronald Foresta, *America's National Parks and Their Keepers* (Washington DC: Resources for the Future and Johns Hopkins Press, 1984); Joseph Sax, *Mountains without Handrails* (Ann Arbor: University of Michigan Press, 1980).

14. David G. Anderson and Eeva K. Berglund, eds., *Ethnographies of Conservation: Environmentalism and the Distribution of Privilege* (London: Berghahn Books, 2003); William Cronon, "The Trouble with Wilderness; or, Getting Back to the Wrong Nature," in *Uncommon Ground: Rethinking the Human Place in Nature*, ed. William Cronon, 69–90 (New York: W. W. Norton, 1995).

15. Such assumptions overlooked the consumptive capacity of modern societies that has quickly degraded the possibility of this happening. David Harmon, "Cultural Diversity, Human Subsistence, and the National Park Ideal," *Environmental Ethics* 9 (1987): 147–158; Hays, *Conservation*; Richard W. Judd recently revisited the idea the U.S. conservation movement was elitist, *Common Lands, Common People: The Origins of Conservation in Northern New England* (Cambridge, MA: Harvard University Press, 1997).

16. This has been called the "Yellowstone Model" or "fortress model" of conservation in many critiques of parks in the developing world. See Patrick. C. West and Steven. R. Brechin, eds., *Resident Peoples and National Parks Social Dilemmas and Strategies in International Conservation* (Tucson: University of Arizona Press, 1991), and John Shelhas, "The USA National Parks in International Perspective: Have We Learned the Wrong Lesson?" *Environmental Conservation* 28 (2001): 300–304. Recent scholarship, such as Judith Meyer, "Re-packing the Yellowstone Model: Historical Geography and the Transnational Transfer of an Ideal," paper presented at "Civilizing Nature: Toward a Global Perspective of National Parks" conference, German Historical Institute, June 2008, points out how the idea of a Yellowstone model inaccurately portrays the way Yellowstone has been historically open to change.

17. Roderick Neumann, *Imposing Wilderness: Struggles over Livelihood and Nature Preservation in Africa* (Berkeley: University of California Press, 1998), and "Nature-State-Territory: Toward a Critical Theorization of Conservation Enclosure," in *Liberation Ecologies: Environment, Development, Social Movements*, ed. Richard Peet and Michael Watts, 195–217 (New York: Routledge, 2004); Jane Carruthers, *Kruger National Park: A Social and Political History* (Pietermaritzburg, South Africa: University of Natal Press, 1995); Nancy J. Jacobs, *Environment, Power, and Injustice: A South African History* (Cambridge: Cambridge University Press, 2003); Dan Brockington, *Fortress Conservation: The Preservation of the Mkomazi Game Preserve* (Bloomington: Indiana University Press, 2002); Mark Spence, *Dispossessing the Wilderness: Indian Removal and the Making of the National Parks* (New York: Oxford University Press, 1999); Jacoby, *Crimes against Nature*; Louis Warren, *The Hunters Game: Poachers and Conservationists in Twentieth Century America* (New Haven: Yale University Press, 1997); Theodore Binneman and Melanie Niemi, "'Let the Line Be Drawn Now': Wilderness, Conservation, and the Exclusion of Aboriginal People from Banff National Park in Canada," *Environmental History* 11 (October 2006): 724–750; Katrina Z. S. Schwartz, *Nature and National Identity after Communism: Globalizing the Ethnoscape* (Pittsburgh: University of Pittsburgh Press, 2006). For important perspective on scientific preserves and the intricacies of environmental activism in the USSR, see Douglas R. Weiner, *Models of Nature: Ecology, Conservation, and Cultural Revolution in Soviet Russia* (Pittsburgh: University of Pittsburgh Press, 1989), and *A Little Corner of Freedom: Russian Nature Protection from Stalin to Gorbachev* (Pittsburgh: University of Pittsburgh Press, 1999).

18. Ramachandra Guha, "Radical American Environmentalism and Wilderness Preservation: A Third World Critique," *Environmental Ethics* 11 (1989): 71–83.

19. José Augusto Drummond's *Devastação e preservação ambiental: os parques nacionais do Estado do Rio de Janeiro* (Rio de Janeiro: Editora da Universidade Federal Fluminense, 1997); and "The Garden in the Machine: Rio de Janeiro's Tijuca Forest," *Environmental History* 1:1 (1996): 83–104. See also Shawn Miller, *Fruitless Trees: Portuguese Conservation and Brazil's Colonial Timber* (Stanford: Stanford University

Press, 2000); José Pádua, *Um sopro de destruição: pensamento politico e crítica ambiental no brasil excravista (1786–1888)* (Rio de Janeiro: Jorge Zahar, 2002), and the recent articles by José Luiz de Andrade Franco and José Augusto Drummond, "Wilderness and the Brazilian Mind (I): Nation and Nature in Brazil from the 1920s to the 1940s," *Environmental History* 13:4 (2008): 724–750; and "Wilderness and the Brazilian Mind (II): The First Brazilian Conference on Nature Protection (Rio de Janeiro, 1934)," *Environmental History* 14:1 (2009): 82–102. For historiographic overviews of environmental history of Latin America, see Guillermo Castro Herrera, "The Environmental Crisis and the Tasks of History in Latin America," *Environment and History* 3 (1997): 1–17; Joan Martinez-Alier, "Ecology and the Poor: A Neglected Dimension of Latin American History," *Journal of Latin American Studies*, 23 (1991): 621–639; Warren Dean, "The Tasks of Latin American Environmental History," in *Changing Tropical Forests: Historical Perspectives on Today's Challenges in Central and South America*, ed. Harold K. Steen and Richard P. Tucker, 5–15 (Durham: Forest History Society, 1992); Sterling Evans, "Historiografía verde: Estado de la historia sobre la conservación de la naturaleza en América Latina," in *Naturaleza en declive: miradas a la historia ambiental de América Latina y el Caribe*, ed. Reinaldo Funes Monzote, 81–96 (Valencia, Spain: Centro Francisco Tomás y Valiente UNED Alzira-Valencia/ Fundación Instituto de Historia Social, 2008); and Mark Carey, "Latin American Environmental History: Current Trends, Interdisciplinary Insights, and Future Directions," *Environmental History* 14:2 (2009): 221–252.

20. Lane Simonian, *Defending the Land of the Jaguar* (Austin: University of Texas, 1995); Ambrosio González and Víctor Manuel Sánchez L., *Los parques nacionales de México: situación actual y problemas* (Mexico City: Instituto Mexicano de Recursos Naturales Renovables, 1961); For early ideas about nature, see also, Jorge Ruedas de la Serna, *Los orígenes de la visión paradisiaca de la naturaleza Mexicana* (Mexico City: Universidad Nacional Autónoma de México, Colección Posgrado, 1987).

21. Fernando Ortiz Monasterio, *Tierra profanada: historia ambiental de México* (Mexico City: INAH and Secretaría de Desarrollo Urbano y Ecología, 1987); Joel Simon, *Endangered Mexico: An Environment on the Edge* (San Francisco: Sierra Club Books, 1997).

22. Alan Weisman, *Gaviotas: A Village to Reinvent the World* (White River Junction, VT: Chelsea Green, 1998); Sterling Evans, *The Green Republic: A Conservation History of Costa Rica* (Austin: University of Texas Press, 1999).

23. Benjamin S. Orlove, *Lines in the Water: Nature and Culture at Lake Titicaca* (Berkeley: University of California Press, 2002), 190.

24. Susana Hecht and Alexander Cockburn, *The Fate of the Forest Developers, Destroyers, and Defenders of the Amazon* (New York: Harper Perennial, 1990), 228.

25. The Brundtland Commission, named after the prime minister of Norway, Gro Harlem Brundtland, is the common name for the United Nations' World Commission on Environment and Development that published its report, *Our Common Future*, in 1987.

26. Patrick C. West and Steven R. Brechin, eds., *Resident Peoples and National Parks: Social Dilemmas and Strategies in International Conservation* (Tucson: University of Arizona Press, 1991); Charles Zerner, ed. *People, Plants, and Justice: The Politics of Nature Conservation* (New York: Columbia University Press, 2000); and Stephan Amend and Thora Amend, eds., *Espacios sin habitantes? Parques nacionales*

de América del Sur (Caracas, Venezuela, and Gland, Switzerland: UICN and Nueva Sociedad, 1992).

27. The pendulum of interpretations of the revolution has gone from unabashed praise of the radical changes, such as Frank Tannenbaum, *The Mexican Agrarian Revolution* (New York: Macmillan, 1929), to harsh criticism of an increasingly authoritarian government starting in the late 1960s, for example, Adolfo Gilly, *La revolución interrumpida* (México City: Ediciones El Caballito, 1971). See also Alan Knight, *The Mexican Revolution*, 2 vols. (Cambridge: Cambridge University Press, 1986); John M. Hart, *Revolutionary Mexico: The Coming and Process of the Mexican Revolution* (Berkeley: University of California Press, 1987); Mary Kay Vaughan, *Cultural Politics of Revolution Teachers, Peasants, and Schools in Mexico, 1930–1940* (Tucson: University of Arizona, 1997); Guillermo Palacios, *La pluma y el arado los intelectuales pedagogos y la construcción sociocultural del "problema campesino" en México, 1932–1934* (Mexico City: El Colegio de México Centro de Investigación y Docencia Económica, 1999); Gilbert Joseph and Daniel Nugent, eds., *Everyday Forms of State Formation Revolution and the Negotiation of Rule in Modern Mexico* (Durham: Duke University Press, 1994).

28. The PNR underwent two subsequent name changes, to the Party of the Mexican Revolution (PRM) in 1938 and the Institutional Party of Revolution (PRI) in 1946. The party remained in power until 2000.

29. In addition to those works in footnotes 26, see Alan Knight, "Cardenismo: Juggernaut or Jalopy?" *Journal of Latin American Studies*, 26:1 (1994): 73–107; Moisés González Navarro, "La obra social de Lázaro Cárdenas," *Historia Mexicana* 34:2 (1984): 353–374; Alexander Dawson, *Indian and Nation in Revolutionary Mexico* (Tucson: University of Arizona Press, 2004); Adrian Banjes, *As if Jesus Walked on Earth: Cardenismo, Sonora, and the Mexican Revolution* (Wilmington, DE: Scholarly Resources Books, 1998); Ben Fallaw, *Cárdenas Compromised: The Failure of Reform in Postrevolutionary Yucatán* (Durham: Duke University Press, 2004); Jocelyn Olcott, *Revolutionary Women in Postrevolutionary Mexico* (Durham: Duke University Press, 2005).

30. Import-substituting industrialization refers to the style of development promoted by Latin American countries that tried to limit foreign dependency by producing at home products once imported. It is largely associated with the work of Raúl Prebisch and Celso Furtado from the United Nations Economic Commission for Latin American and the Caribbean (ECLAC).

31. Ilene V. O'Malley, *The Myth of the Revolution Hero Cults and the Institutionalization of the Mexican State, 1920–1940* (New York: Greenwood Press, 1986); Jean Franco, *Plotting Women: Gender and Representation in Mexico* (New York: Columbia University Press, 1989); Thomas Benjamin, *La Revolución: Mexico's Great Revolution as Memory, Myth, and History* (Austin: University of Texas Press, 2000); and Eric Zolov's discussion of the "Revolutionary family" in *Refried Elvis: The Rise of Mexican Counterculture* (Berkeley: University of California Press, 1999).

32. Christopher R. Boyer, *Becoming Campesinos: Politics, Identity, and Agrarian Struggle in Postrevolutionary Michoacán, 1920–1935* (Stanford: Stanford University, 2003).

33. Lázaro Cárdenas, "Mensaje del C. Presidente de la República, General Lázaro Cárdenas, radiado al pueblo mexicano el 10. de enero de 1935 en lo concerniente a la creación del Departamento Autónomo Forestal y de Caza y Pesca," *Boletín DFCP*, 1:1 (1935): 36–38.

34. Christopher R. Boyer and Emily Wakild, "Social Landscaping Forests of Mexico: An Environmental Interpretation of Cardenismo, 1934–1940," *Hispanic American Historical Review*, 92:1 (2012).

35. Jesús Silva Herzog, *El agrarismo mexicano y la reforma agraria: exposición y crítica* (Mexico City: Fondo de Cultura Económica, 1964); David Rodfeldt, *Atencingo: The Politics of Agrarian Struggle in a Mexican Ejido* (Stanford: Stanford University Press, 1973); Ann L. Craig, *The First Agraristas: An Oral History of Mexican Agrarian Reform* (Berkeley: University of California Press, 1983); Dana Markiewicz, *The Mexican Revolution and the Limits of Agrarian Reform, 1915–1946* (Boulder, CO: Lynne Reinner, 1993); Iván Restrepo and Salamón Eckstein, *La agricultura colectiva en México: La experiencia de La Laguna* (México City: Siglo XXI, 1971); Raymond Wilkie, *San Miguel: A Mexican Collective Ejido* (Stanford: Stanford University Press, 1971); William K. Meyers, *Forge of Progress, Crucible of Revolt: Origins of the Mexican Revolution in La Comarca Lagunera, 1880–1911* (Albuquerque: University of New Mexico Press, 1994); Nora Hamilton, "Mexico: The Limits of State Autonomy" *Latin American Perspectives* 2:2 (1975): 81–108. For comparative literature, see William Thiesenhusen's *Broken Promises: Agrarian Reform and the Latin American Campesino* (Boulder, CO: Westview Press, 1995); T. Lynn Smith, ed., *Agrarian Reform in Latin America* (New York: Alfred Knopf, 1965); Peter Dorner, *Latin American Land Reform in Theory and Practice* (Madison: University of Wisconsin Press, 1992); Alain DeJanvry, *The Agrarian Question and Reformism in Latin America* (Baltimore: Johns Hopkins University Press, 1981).

36. In addition to authors above, see Susan Walsh Sanderson, *Land Reform in Mexico, 1910–1980* (Florida: Academic Press, 1984); Alan Knight, "Land and Society in Revolutionary Mexico: The Destruction of the Great Haciendas," *Mexican Studies/Estudios Mexicanos* 7:1 (1991): 73–104.

37. Myrna I. Santiago, *The Ecology of Oil: Environment, Labor, and the Mexican Revolution, 1900–1938* (Cambridge: Cambridge University Press, 2006); Christopher R. Boyer, "Contested Terrain: Forestry Regimes and Community Responses in Northeastern Michoacán, 1940–2000," in *The Community Forests of Mexico: Managing for Sustainable Landscapes*, ed. David Barton Bray, Leticia Merino-Pérez, and Deborah Barry, 27–48 (Austin: University of Texas Press, 2005), and "Revolución y paternalismo ecológico: Miguel Ángel de Quevedo y la política forestal, 1926–1940," *Historia Mexicana* 57:1 (2007): 91–138; Luis Aboites, *El agua de la nación: Una historia política de México (1888–1946)* (Mexico City: Centro Investigaciones y Estudios Superiores Antropología Social, 1998); Alejandro Tortolero Villaseñor, ed., *Entre lagos y volcanes. Chalco, Amecameca: pasado y presente*, vol. 1 (Mexico City: El Colegio Mexiquense, 1993), and *Tierra, agua, y bosques: Historia y medio ambiente en el México central* (Mexico City: Centre Français d'études Mexicaines et Centraméricaines, Instituto Mora, Potrerillos Editores, Universidad de Guadalajara, 1996); Víctor Manuel Toledo, *Naturaleza, producción, cultura: Ensayos de ecología política* (Mexico City: Universidad Veracruzana, 1989), and "Modernidad y ecología. La nueva crisis planetaria," in *Sociedad y medio ambiente en México*, ed. Gustavo López Castro, 19–42 (Mexico City: El Colegio de Michoacán, 1997).

38. Between 1977 and 2002, the federal government declared ninety-seven reserves with an average area of 160,000 hectares, or more than four times the size of the earlier parks. During this period, politicians increased the amount of protected land nearly

tenfold. Park dates and sizes are compiled from *Diario Oficial* decrees and CONANP figures found here: http://www.conanp.gob.mx. These include national parks, natural monuments, areas of natural resource protection, areas of flora and fauna protection, biosphere reserves, and sanctuaries.

39. A few studies take up the transformation of productive landscapes into conservation areas in this latter period: Nora Haenn, *Fields of Power, Forests of Discontent Culture, Conservation, and the State in Mexico* (Tucson: University of Arizona Press, 2005); Lydia A. Breunig, "Conservation in Context Establishing Natural Protected Areas during Mexico's Neoliberal Reformation," Ph.D. diss., University of Arizona, 2006.

40. These results have much in concord with John Terborgh's predictions for Manu National Park, see *Requiem for Nature* (Washington DC: Island Press, 1999), especially chapter 4.

41. Shepard Krech III, *The Ecological Indian: Myth and History* (New York: W. W. Norton, 1999); Roger Bartra, "Paradise Subverted: The Invention of Mexican Character," in *Primitivism and Identity in Latin America: Essays on Art, Literature, and Culture*, ed. Erik Camayd-Freixas and José Eduardo González, trans. Christopher J. Hall, 3–22 (Tucson: University of Arizona Press, 2000), 4.

42. International Union for Conservation of Nature, *First World Conference on National Parks* (Washington DC: National Park Service, 1962), 427–432.

43. Emilio Kourí, "Interpreting the Expropriation of Indian Pueblo Lands in Porfirian Mexico: The Unexamined Legacies of Andres Molina Enriquez," *Hispanic American Historical Review* 82:1 (2002): 69–117; Alejandro Tortolero Villaseñor, *Notarios y agricultores: Crecimiento y atraso en el campo mexicano, 1780–1920* (Mexico City: Universidad Autónoma Metropolitana, Iztapalapa, Siglo XXI editores, 2008).

Chapter 1. Science

1. Felipe Ruiz Velasco, "Bosques y manantiales del estado de Morelos y apéndice sintético sobre su potencialidad agrícola e industrial," in *Fuentes Geográficas y Estadísticas del Estado de Morelos*, ed. Valentín López González, 10–37 (Cuernavaca, Morelos, Mexico: Cuadernos Históricos Morelenses, [1925] 2004), 11.

2. Despite their occurrence south of the Tropic of Cancer and the rainy and dry seasons, Mexican geographers routinely classified the pine, fir, and oak forests occurring in the high plateau and mountain ranges of the Sierra Madre as *bosque templado* (temperate forest) or alternatively part of the *región fria y forestal* (cold forest region). I follow their use of the general term *temperate* to differentiate these coniferous and broad leaf forests from the tropical rain and cloud forests known as the *regiones tórridas* (torrid zones) found in the southern, eastern, and western lowlands. Abel Gamiz, *Geografía Nacional de México* (Mexico City: Compañia Nacional Editora Aguilas, S.A., 1926), 35–37. The scientific standards for classifying forests came after these parks were created; today they would be subtropical dry forests, see Leslie R. Holdridge, "Determination of World Plant Formations from Simple Climatic Data," *Science* 105:2727 (1947): 367–368.

3. Ruiz Velasco, "Bosques," 12. Scholars of North and West Africa have questioned the trope of forest destruction as a mechanism to expand colonial rule and circumscribe traditional uses. The Mexican conversation differs because of the way the revolution

mediated science with social goals. This study does not measure forest destruction to validate Ruiz Velasco's claims but instead uses them as a rhetorical illustration of the arguments put forth for greater government management of central forests. See Melissa Leach and James Fairhead, "Challenging Neo-Malthusian Deforestation Analyses in West Africa's Dynamic Forest Landscapes," *Population and Development Review* 26:1 (2000): 17–43; Diana K. Davis, *Resurrecting the Granaries of Rome: Environmental History and French Colonial Expansion in North Africa* (Athens: Ohio University Press, 2007); and Caroline Ford, "Reforestation, Landscape Conservation, and the Anxieties of Empire in French Colonial Algeria," *American Historical Review*, 113:2 (2008): 341–362.

4. The F. A. Hampson Company alone logged nearly 17,000 trees in the area around the village of Tlalnepantla in 1910. Ruiz Velasco, "Bosques," 25.

5. For a study that examines some problems with desiccation theory as an explanation for the relationship between forest clearing and degraded water sources, see Andrew S. Mathews, "Unlikely Alliances: Encounters between State Science, Nature Spirits, and Indigenous Industrial Forestry in Mexico, 1926–2008," *Current Anthropology* 50:1 (2009): 75–101.

6. See appendix A, declarations.

7. I borrow this term from Jacoby, who notes the agrarian fantasies for the United States involved the pastoral and the primitive. Mexico's revolution and different history also elevated the agrarian but in markedly different ways. *Crimes against Nature*, 19.

8. Simonian, *Defending the Land*; Ruedas de la Serna, *Los orígenes*.

9. Cárdenas, "Mensaje," 36.

10. Principle eleven of eighteen principles listed in Mexican Forestry Society's journal, *México Forestal* 4:5–6 (1926): 45–46.

11. Geographically, the area surrounding Mexico City is more of a basin (at one time full of lakes) than a valley, but it is near universally called the Valley of Mexico. Bernardo García Martínez, "Regiones y paisajes de la geografía mexicana," in *Historia general de México*, 29–37 (Mexico City: Colegio de México, Centro Estudios Históricos, 2000). Containing the waters of the valley from intruding on urban life inspired a vast and technical drainage project, one that became the largest fiscal expenditure of the Porfirian period. Manuel Perló Cohen, *El paradigma Porfiriano: Historia del Desagüe del Valle de México* (Mexico City: Instituto de Investigaciones Sociales, Miguel Ángel Porrúa, 1999), 29.

12. Secretaría de Agricultura y Fomento: Dirección Estudios, Geográficos y Climatológicos, "Republica Mexicana Servicio Meteorológico: Estudio Preliminar de climas," Archivo Histórico del Instituto Nacional de Antropología e Historia (hereafter AH-INAH) Biblioteca: Mapoteca, 206:E1.

13. They were also bankers, financiers, and commercial farmers, see William D. Raat, "Ideas and Society in Don Porfirio's Mexico," *Americas* 30:1 (1973): 32–53, 34.

14. Laura Angélica Moya López, *La nación como organismo: México su evolución social 1900–1902* (Mexico City: Universidad Autónoma Metropolitana Azcapotzalco, 2003), 11; Moisés González Navarro, "Las ideas raciales de los científicos, 1890–1910," *Historia Mexicana*, 37:4 (1988): 565–583.

15. Hart, *Empire and Revolution*; Kourí, "Interpreting the Expropriation."

16. Deforestation did occur in southern states, see Jan de Vos, *Oro Verde: La conquista de la Selva Lacandona por los madereros tabasqueños, 1822–1949* (Mexico City: Fondo de Cultura Económica, 1988).

17. Carlos Sevilla Serdán, "El consumo de durmientes por los ferrocarriles nacionales de México," *Mexico Forestal* 11:1 (1933): 10–17.

18. José Juan Juárez Flores, "Malintzin Matlalcuéyetl: Bosques, alumbrado público y conflicto social en la desarticulación de un etorno ecológico (Puebla-Tlaxcala, 1760–1870)" (M.A. thesis, Universidad Autónoma Metropolitana, Iztapalapa, January 2005); Herman Konrad, "Tropical Forest Policy and Practice during the Mexican Porfiriato, 1876–1910," in *Changing Tropical Forests: Historical Perspectives on Today's Challenges in Central and South America*, ed. Harold K. Steen and Richard P. Tucker, 123–143 (Durham: Forest History Society, 1992). For Chiapas, see de Vos, *Oro verde*.

19. Miguel Ángel de Quevedo, "Proyecto de Plan Sexenal 1934–40 en lo relativo a la Protección Forestal del Territorio," *Boletín DFCP* 1:1 (1935): 5–29.

20. Robert H. Holden, *Mexico and the Survey of Public Lands: The Management of Modernization 1876–1911* (DeKalb: Northern Illinois University Press, 1994), 10, 16.

21. Quevedo, "Espacios libres y reservas forestales de las ciudades: su adaptación á jardines, parques y lugares de juego, aplicación á la Ciudad de México" (Mexico City: Gomar y Busson, 1911), 18.

22. Wakild, "Naturalizing Modernity," 105; Pérez Bertruy, "Parques y jardines públicos," 110–115.

23. Manuel M. Villada, "Relación de un viaje á la caverna de Cacahuamilpa," *La Naturaleza*, 2:1 (1910): 148–155. These observations come from an analysis of the complete set of journals, covering the years 1870–1911.

24. Gabriel Alcocer, "El Bosque de Chapultepec," *La Naturaleza* 1:7 (1887): 317.

25. Jesús Sánchez, "Museo nacional de historia natural," *La Naturaleza* 3:1 (1923), 1–6.

26. The society drew its name from a prominent and prolific Mexico City eighteenth-century naturalist, José Antonio de Alzate y Ramírez (1737–1799). The society became the Mexican Academy of Sciences.

27. Antonio Sosa, "Cincuentenario de la Enseñanza," *El Universal*, 27 December 1960; Enrique Rodiles Maniau, 9 February 1937, AGN: SARH 1468, 21/4325; Julio Prado, *El apóstol del árbol*, vol. 1 (Mexico City: Emilio Pardo e Hijos, Legión de Divulgación Cultural "Hijos del estado de Michoacán," 1936).

28. He is recognized, in subway stops, major avenues, and in popular forestry. Simonian, *Defending the Land*; Wakild, "It Is to Preserve Life, to Work for the Trees: The Steward of Mexican Forests, Miguel Ángel de Quevedo, 1862–1948," *Forest History Today* (Spring/Fall 2006): 4–14; Boyer, "Revolución y paternalismo ecológico: Miguel Ángel de Quevedo y la política forestal, 1926-1940," *Historia Mexicana* 57:1 (2007), 91–138.

29. Miguel Ángel de Quevedo, *Relato de mi vida* (México City: n.p., 1942); Simonian, *Defending the Land*, 81.

30. Revolutionary demands that refused to separate the social and ecological were not isolated to the Mexican case and drew on a broader set of ideas identifying the radical nature of environmental autonomy beyond campesino identity. See John Bellamy Foster, *Marx's Ecology: Materialism and Nature* (New York: Monthly Review Press, 2000) especially chapter 2.

31. Paul Hart, *Bitter Harvest: The Social Transformation of Morelos, Mexico and the Origins of the Zapatista Rebellion, 1840–1910* (Albuquerque: University of New Mexico Press, 2007).

32. John Womack, *Zapata and the Mexican Revolution* (New York, Knopf, 1969), provides a translation of the Plan de Ayala, 393–404; quote, 402.

33. Larger plans included topics historians have long since paid attention to such as education and labor reforms. See Vaughan, *Cultural Politics*; Héctor Aguilar Camín and Lorenzo Meyer, *In the Shadows of the Mexican Revolution: Contemporary Mexican History 1910–1989*, trans. Luis Alberto Fierro (Austin: University of Texas Press, 1993).

34. E. V. Niemeyer Jr. *Revolution at Querétaro The Mexican Constitutional Convention of 1916–1917* (Austin: University of Texas Press, 1974), 22–27; 140, 144.

35. Ibid, 158.

36. Simonian, *Defending the Land*, 79.

37. "Es preservar la vida trabajar por el árbol: Principios de conservación forestal para todo bien ciudadano y que norman las labores de la Sociedad Forestal Mexicana," *México Forestal* 4:5–6 (1926): 45–49.

38. Niemeyer, *Revolution at Querétaro*, 22–27; Gilberto Serrato, "Algunos antecedentes acerca de la campaña de protección forestal en México y breve relato de las actividades desarrolladas por la Sociedad Forestal México, C.L.," *México Forestal* 17:7–12 (1939): 62–66. All national park decrees in the 1935–1940 period refer to the 1926 Forest Law, mostly articles 22, 31, and 41.

39. Secretaría de Agricultura y Fomento, *Ley forestal y su reglamento* (Mexico City: Talleres Gráficos de la Secretaría de Agricultura y Fomento, 1930), 6.

40. Edmundo Bournet, 6 June 1936, AGN: SARH 1425, 1609, 3.

41. Debates about use or conservation have played a significant role in forestry management in other countries, most famously in the tensions in the United States between the U.S. Forest Service and National Park Service or among the ideas of John Muir and Gifford Pinchot. See Hays, *Conservation*; James G. Lewis, *The Forest Service and the Greatest Good: A Centennial History* (Durham: Forest History Society, 2005). While there were exchanges, Mexican attitudes did not derive from these foreign debates but arose as in reaction to local circumstances.

42. Carranza, Obregón, and Calles saw *ejidos* as merely a stop-gap measure for fixing agrarian problems; this opinion helps account for their lack of implementation. One famous proponent of a private land tenure solution was Andrés Molina Enríquez, *Los grandes problemas nacionales* (Mexico City: Imprenta de A. Carranza e hijos, 1909), who called for a nation of small-holding farmers.

43. John Tutino, *From Insurrection to Revolution in Mexico: Social Bases of Agrarian Violence, 1750–1940* (Princeton: Princeton University Press, 1989), 8.

44. Stephen Haber, Armando Razo, and Noel Maurer, *The Politics of Property Rights: Political Instability, Credible Commitments, and Economic Growth in Mexico, 1876–1929* (Cambridge: Cambridge University Press, 2003), 307–313.

45. The Soviet Union's five-year plans are the best known, but Sweden, Italy, and China enacted them as well. Not called a plan, Franklin Roosevelt's New Deal had similar characteristics.

46. *Plan Sexenal del P.N.R.* (Mexico City: 1934); Gilberto Bosques, *The National Revolutionary Party of Mexico and the Six-Year Plan* (Mexico City: National Revolutionary Party, 1937). For the record of the convention where the plan was approved, see *Memoria, Segunda Convención Nacional del Partido Nacional Revolucionario* (Mexico City: PNR, 1934), 63. The areas addressed included agriculture (and forestry within that), labor, economy, communications and public works, health, education,

governance, army, foreign relations, finances and public credit, and community promotion. See also Ángel Bassols Batalla, *Recursos naturales: Climas, agua, suelos, teoría y uso* (Mexico City: Editorial Nuestro Tiempo, 1967), 32; Fernando Saúl Alanís Enciso, *El Gobierno del General Lázaro Cárdenas 1934–1940: Una visión revisionista* (Mexico City: Colegio de San Luis, 2000), 11.

47. Simonian, *Defending the Land*, 86.

48. Knight, "Juggernaut"; Fallaw, *Cárdenas Compromised*; Bantjes, *As if Jesus Walked*; Gilly, *El Cardenismo: Una utopía Mexicana* (Mexico City: Cal y Arena, 1994); Amelia M. Kiddle and María L. O. Muñoz, *Populism in Revolutionary Mexico: The Presidencies of Lázaro Cárdenas and Luis Echeverría* (Tucson: University of Arizona Press, 2010).

49. Lázaro Cárdenas, *Apuntes*, vol. 1 (Mexico City: Universidad Nacional Autónoma de Mexico, Dirección General de Publicaciones, 1972), 5.

50. Armando R. Pareyon Axpeitia, *Cárdenas ante el mundo: Defensor de la republica espanola, eitiopia, finlandia, africa, luchas populares de asia* (Mexico City: La Prensa, 1971). His son Cuauhtémoc accepted the post as subsecretary of forestry and wildlife in the Ministry of Agriculture in 1976.

51. José V. Cardoso, Report on Forestry Division, n.d., AGN: LCR 554, 501.1/1.

52. Quevedo to Cárdenas, 1 December 1934, AGN: LCR 554, 501.1/1.

53. The Agrarian Department, in charge of land reform, was itself freed from the Ministry of Agriculture in January of 1934, only a year prior to the creation of the Forestry Department. Arturo Warman, *"We Come to Object": The Peasants of Morelos and the National State*, trans. Stephen K. Ault (Baltimore: Johns Hopkins University Press, 1980), 167.

54. Cárdenas, "Mensaje."

55. James D. Cockcroft, *Intellectual Precursors of the Mexican Revolution, 1900–1913* (Austin: University of Texas, 1968), 4–6.

56. Emilio Alanís Patiño, "Síntesis del Ciclo de Conferencias sobre "Los Problemas Agrícolas de México," *Los Problemas Agrícolas de México* 1:2 (1934): 669–739, 711.

57. John Sherman contends that Cárdenas was increasingly threatened by the unity of the right which shaped his decisions, see "Reassessing Cardenismo: The Mexican Right and the Failure of a Revolutionary Regime, 1934–1940," *The Americas* 54:3 (1998): 357–378.

58. Boyer, "Revolución y paternalismo," 118.

59. Cardoso, Report; Dirección General Forestal y de Caza, organizational chart, AGN: SARH, 1425 1/1609. For most of the period, Daniel Galicia was the director of the national parks section.

60. When the Forestry Department resumed its former position within the secretary of agriculture in 1940, the number of divisions was expanded and divided, spreading the work of conservation out among numerous divisions and ultimately weakening its effectiveness. Cardoso, Report; Dirección General Forestal y de Caza, chart.

61. Edmundo Bournet, 6 June 1936, AGN: SARH 1425, 1609, 3.

62. Carlos Treviño Saldana, 1941, AGN: SARH 1425, 1/1609.

63. Olegario Pérez et al. to Cárdenas, 15 November 1939, AGN: LCR 896: 545.3/252.

64. Antonio Sosa, "Cincuentenario de la Enseñanza," *El Universal*, December 27, 1960; Quevedo, *Relato*.

65. "Plan de estudios en vigor para la escuela de guardería forestal y de caza y pesca," *Boletín DFCP* 2:2 (1936), 214–216.
66. Sosa, "Cincuentenario de la Enseñanza."
67. Forestry managed by government agents originated in France and Germany in the early eighteenth century. Donald Worster, *Nature's Economy: A History of Ecological Ideas* (Cambridge: Cambridge University Press, [1977] 1994), 3–56; Nancy Lee Peluso, *Rich Forests, Poor People: Resource Control and Resistance in Java* (Berkeley: University of California Press, 1992), 7–8; James C. Scott, *Seeing Like a State: How Certain Schemes to Improve the Human Condition Have Failed* (New Haven: Yale University Press, 1998), 11–22.
68. Quevedo trained in France, but not as a forester. He studied mathematics at the *Institute Polytechnique* in Paris and later graduated from the *École Supérieure des Ponts et Chaussees* as a civil engineer. Quevedo, *Relato*, 4. U.S. conservationists like Gifford Pinchot trained in Europe, and others like Bernhard Fernow and Carl Schenk were themselves from forestry schools in Prussia and Saxony.
69. Gifford Pinchot, *Breaking New Ground* (Washington DC: Island Press, 1998), 361–372. The other Mexican representatives were Romulo Escobar and Carlos Sellerier. For the League of Nations, see Quevedo, "La creación de los parques nacionales y sus ventajas," *Boletín DFCP* 4:14 (1939): 62.
70. Emily Wakild, "Border Chasm: International Boundary Parks and Mexican Conservation 1935–1945," *Environmental History* 14:3 (2009): 453–475.
71. Octavio Benavides, "Conociendo a nuestro México: El Parque Nacional "Popocatépetl—Iztaccíhuatl," *Protección a la Naturaleza* 3:7 (1939): 14–19.
72. Ángel Roldán, "Informe sucinto acerca de los Parques Nacionales de Europa presentado al C. Jefe del Departamento Forestal por el Ing. Forestal Ángel Roldán, Delegado al Congreso de Silvicultura de Brúcelas," *Boletín DFCP* 2:1 (1936): 281–285.
73. Antonio H. Sosa, "Un viaje a Guatemala: Segunda Parte," *Protección a la Naturaleza* 3:14 (1938): 4–15.
74. "Viaje al Japón de pescadores Mexicanos," *Protección a la Naturaleza* 2:6 (1937): 13–15.
75. Gilberto Serrato to Galicia, 12 February 1937, AGN: SARH 1384, 1/157, tomo 1.
76. *México Forestal*, September 1936 through July 1938.
77. AGN: SARH 1434, 1/2007, tomo 1. Many of the Latin American countries rejected the translated article in English, stating that it is their policy not to publish in foreign languages!
78. For Peru, AGN: SARH 1479, 1/6835. For avocado tree, "Un justo homenaje al aguacate," *Protección a la Naturaleza* 2:7 (1938): 3.
79. Dan Klooster, "Campesinos and Mexican Forestry Policy during the Twentieth Century," *Latin American Research Review* 38:2 (2003): 94–126; 98–99.
80. Scholars of regions distant from central Mexico have challenged the relevance of land reform as a break with the past; Daniel Nugent, *Spent Cartridges of Revolution: An Anthropological History of Namiquipa, Chihuahua* (Chicago: University of Chicago Press, 1993), and Fallaw, *Cárdenas Compromised*, and others have confirmed land reform's importance in deepening divisions between property owning foreigners and dispossessed rural workers; Timothy Henderson, *The Worm in the Wheat: Rosalie*

Evans and Agrarian Struggle in the Puebla-Tlaxcala Valley of Mexico, 1906–1927 (Durham: Duke University Press, 1998).

81. Arun Agrawal, *Environmentality Technologies of Government and the Making of Subjects* (Durham: Duke University Press, 2005), 8, 12.

82. John Tutino, "The Revolutionary Capacity of Rural Communities Ecological Autonomy and Its Demise," in *Cycles of Conflict, Centuries of Change: Crisis, Reform, and Revolution in Mexico*, ed. Elisa Servín, Leticia Reina, and John Tutino, 211–268 (Durham: Duke University Press, 2007), 214.

83. Christopher Boyer has argued that as revolutionary policies developed, they subverted these identities to the larger political category "campesinos" that sought to erase these distinguishing rural identities by linking campesinos to the state unilaterally, *Becoming Campesinos*, 20–21.

84. Types of common property produce a literal and linguistic maze. *Ejidos, comunidades, monte comunal, tierras comunales*, and the more rare *bienes comunales* have sometimes overlapping jurisdictions making generalizations difficult. An ejido might be made out of tierra comunal, but it also might not include all of it. A community might then have communal land and an ejido. These distinctions among varieties of communal property are important, but they are not the main issue here. Hereafter, I use the terms *common property, communal property*, and *commons* to refer to lands held in common by a community. I will use the term *ejido* only to refer to a portion of communal property legally sanctioned by a specific federal decree and approved to be administered as an ejido.

85. Tutino, *From Insurrection to Revolution*, 8.

86. Sanderson, *Land Reform*, 38–49; Raymond Craib, *Cartographic Mexico: A History of State Fixations and Fugitive Landscapes* (Durham: Duke University Press, 2004), 243.

87. Frank Tannenbaum, *Peace by Revolution: Mexico after 1910* (New York: Columbia University Press, [1933]1968), 198–218; John Dwyer, *The Agrarian Dispute: The Expropriation of American-Owned Rural Land in Postrevolutionary Mexico* (Durham: Duke University Press, 2008), 19–23; Henderson, *The Worm in the Wheat*.

88. An exception came in the late 1970s and 1980s in Campeche. See Haenn, *Fields of Power*.

89. Sanderson, *Land Reform*, 5–8 and 44–49. María Rosa Gudiño and Guillermo Palacios, "Peticiones de tierras y estrategias discursivas campesinos: procesos, contenidos y problemas metodológicos," in *Estudios campesinos en el Archivo General Agrario*, ed. Antonio Escobar Ohmstede et al., 75–118 (Mexico City: Centro de Investigaciones y Estudios Superiores en Antropología Social, 1998).

90. Quevedo, 8 February 1937, AGN: LCR 309, 404.1/8535.

91. For an exception, see Comite Pro-Parque Nacional, Teziutlan, Puebla to Cárdenas, 4 September 1936, AGN: LCR 559, 501.2/297.

92. Edmundo Bournet, 6 June 1936, AGN: SARH 1425, 1609, 3.

93. For example, in Cárdenas's meeting with the village of Huitzilac near Zempoala, the residents asked for fruit trees and improvements to the road to bring tourists to the park. Presidente Municipal to Cárdenas, 19 January 1938, AGN: SARH 1384, 1, 1/157 and chapter 2.

94. Cárdenas to Director of Departamento Forestal y de Caza y Pesca, 30 June 1937, Archivo Histórico Municipal de Amecameca (hereafter AHMA), vol. 15, 22.

95. Departamento Forestal y de Caza y Pesca, "Decreto que reforma el Artículo 87 de la Ley Forestal," *Diario Oficial*, 21 January 1938. See also the suggestions for changes to local authorities, Delegado Forestal Toluca to Presidente Municipal, 12 July 1937, AHMA, vol. 159, 22. For correspondence on issue of releasing destitute campesinos from taxes, see AHMA, vol. 155, 33. See further discussion in chapter 4.

96. Salvador Guerrero, 21 April 1937, AGN: SARH 1421, 1/1472. Guerrero explains that in Acuerdo 208, Cárdenas excluded restitution of ejidal land in national parks but not in forest reserves, demonstrating his astute manner of reaching compromises. Restitution of these lands remained legal, but Quevedo and the Forestry Department vehemently objected to the distribution of forest lands to communities that had no prior experience with forests and intended only to clear the forest for their fields.

97. Exceptions include ejidos given to repatriated Mexicans. Sanderson, *Land Reform*, 44.

98. Florescano, "El patrimonio nacional," 17. These issues have earned attention by prominent intellectuals. Guillermo Bonfil Batalla, "Nuestro patrimonio cultural: un laberinto de significados," in *El Patrimonio Nacional de México I: Biblioteca Mexicana*, ed. Enrique Florescano, 34–36 (Mexico City: CONACULTA, Fondo de Cultura Económica, 1997), and Néstor García Canclini, "El patrimonio cultural de México y la construcción imaginaria de lo nacional," in *El Patrimonio Nacional de México I: Biblioteca Mexicana*, ed. Enrique Florescano, 85–86 (Mexico City: CONACULTA, Fondo de Cultura Económica, 1997).

99. Vaughan, *Cultural Politics*, 20–24; Dawson, *Indian and Nation*, xvii; Olcott, *Revolutionary Women*, 11.

Chapter 2. Education

1. Bournet to Quevedo, 28 March 1936, AGN: SARH 1384, 1, 1/157.

2. José Peralta, Marcelo Rodríguez, Teofilo Vazquez to Cárdenas, 2 April 1936, AGN: SARH 1384, 1, 1/157.

3. See the ejidal resolution in the *Diario Oficial*, 7 November 1929, or in Archivo General Agraria (hereafter AGA): Huitzilac 24/3120, 6. Two other communities, Tres Marías and Xalatlaco, existed slightly more distant from the park boundaries and conflicted repeatedly with Huitzilac over ejido boundaries. Alfonso Ruíz Guillen to Delegado Departamento Agrario en Cuernavaca, 4 November 1941, AGA: Huitzilac 24/3120, 5. Tres Marías was sometimes called Santa María.

4. Miguel Dehesa to Quevedo, 28 January 1936, AGN: SARH 1384, 1, 1/157.

5. The declaration of Zempoala as a piece of natural patrimony occurred in stages, and its designation persisted over time. The largest lake was declared national property in 1926 as it met the requirements for nationalizing water sources. Domingo Diez to Director de Aguas, Tierra, y Colonización, 5 July 1926, Archivo Histórico del Agua: Aprovechamientos Superficiales (hereafter AHA: AS) 1699: 24969.

6. On Treasury Department, see J. Manuel Corona, 20 May 1938, AGN: SARH 1384, 1/157, tomo 1. For the camp, Alfredo G. Basurto's report 1 June 1938, AGN: SARH 1384, 1/157, tomo 1.

7. Miguel Dehesa to Quevedo, 14 May 1936, AGN: SARH 1384, 1, 1/157. See also denied request by Luis Rivera Melo from the Federal District, 14 October 1938, AGN: SARH 1384, 1, 1/157.

8. Dehesa to Quevedo, 21 February 1936, AGN: SARH 1384, 1/1/157; Dehesa to Quevedo, n.d., AGN: SARH 1430, 21/1871.

9. Cárdenas, interview with Huitzilac, 9 January 1938, AGN: SARH 1384, 1, 1/157.

10. Quevedo to Cárdenas, 12 January 1938, AGN: SARH 1384, 1/157.

11. Eduardo Madero to Galicia, 12 December 1938, AGN: SARH 1384, 1/157 and Galicia to Eduardo Madero, 9 January 1939, AGN: SARH 1384, 1/157.

12. Eduardo Madero to Galicia, 11 November, 1938, AGN: SARH 1384, 1/157.

13. J. Manuel Corona to Quevedo, 27 May 1937, AGN: SARH 1430, 21/1872, 2.

14. J. Manuel Corona to Delegate Cuernavaca, 17 May 1937, AGN: SARH 1384, 1/157.

15. Claudio Díaz to Department of Forestry, 11 November 1938, AGN: SARH 1384, 1/157.

16. Dina Berger, *The Development of Mexico's Tourism Industry: Pyramids by Day, Martinis by Night* (New York: Palgrave Macmillan, 2006).

17. Ron Mader, "Conversation with Hector Ceballos-Lascurain," http://www.planeta .com/ecotravel/weaving/hectorceballos.html. Hector Ceballos-Lascurain, *Tourism, Ecotourism, and Protected Areas* (Geneva: World Conservation Union (IUCN), 1996); Martha Honey, "Giving a Grade to Costa Rica's Green Tourism" *NACLA Report on the Americas*, 36:6 (2003): 39–46.

18. Ecotourism Society definition, quoted in Martha Honey, *Ecotourism and Sustainable Development: Who Owns Paradise?* (Washington DC: Island Press, 1999), 6.

19. In other contexts, roads are classic symbols of progress and also harbingers of environmental destruction. Roadless areas have provided a rallying point for wilderness advocates. Leopold, "Wilderness as a Form of Land Use" [originally published in 1925], in *The Great New Wilderness Debate*, ed. J. Baird Callicott and Michael P. Nelson, 75–84 (Athens: University of Georgia Press, 1998).

20. Salvador Guerrero to Secretaría de Comunicación y Obras Públicas, División General de Caminos, 13 May 1937, AGN: SARH 1384, 1/157.

21. Segundo Gómez Moreno to Galicia, 31 May 1938, AGN: SARH 1384, 1/157; Daniel Galicia to Quevedo, 12 May 1938, AGN: SARH 1384, 1/157.

22. See appendix B for more from the visitor logs from 1938. The months included were February, March, April, July, August, September, October, November, and an incomplete log for June. Subsequent figures refer to these logs.

23. Zempoala Visitor Log, November 1938.

24. One hundred and two women appear in this set of visitor logs either as signatories or included in Sr. and Sra. (Mr. and Mrs.) entrants, although it is likely many more visited but are unaccounted for in the logs.

25. See appendix C for listings of occupational categories.

26. Zempoala visitor logs, March, April, May 1938, AGN: SARH 1384, 1/157.

27. Maurice Cummskeep to Forest Department, 19 January 1937, AGN: SARH 1437, 21/2100.

28. Pedro Pérez to Director Forestal, 29 November 1945, AGN: SARH 1487, 21/7461. Notably, his critique dates to the post-Cárdenas period.

29. "El resultado de la campaña pro-turismo," *El Nacional*, 23 April 1939, 8.

30. Park signs, parking lots, benches, and picnic tables were the most common adornments in the parks during the 1930s, although some buildings, such as the Tequihua Boy Scout cabin and alpine refuges, were constructed on the higher volcanoes.

See Quevedo's approval for an alpine hut on Ajusco, Quevedo to Forest Delegate in Cuernavaca, 3 February 1938, AGN: SARH 1430, 21/1872, tomo 2. It was not until several decades later, in the 1950s and 1960s, when visitor centers were designed. Galicia to Delegado Administrativo, 10 May 1952, AGN: SARH 1466, 21/3779, tomo 1.

31. While it was common for the Forestry Department to authorize the use of park wood for constructing signs around the park, using forest resources for unauthorized firewood was not condoned. Francisco Alvarado Pérez to Galicia, 10 February 1937, AGN: SARH 1384, 1/157, 1.

32. "Hay 30 Parques de la Nación," *El Nacional*, 16 May 1938, 8.

33. "Existen en el país 32 Parques Nacionales," *El Universal*, 2 April 1939.

34. José Sánchez, Gabriel Reyes to Galicia, 15 September 1938, AGN: SARH 1384, 1 1/157.

35. Quevedo, "Las fiestas del árbol, su significado y finalidades en México," *México Forestal*, 15:3–4 (1937): 19–22.

36. José U. Escobar, *Las tribus de exploradores mexicanos* (Mexico City: Secretaría de Educación Pública, 1929), 4.

37. Actividades de las tribus de exploradores Mexicanos, May 1928, SEP, *Boletín de la Secretaría de Educación Pública*, 7:5 (1928): 48.

38. Observador, "Editorial: Actuación de la juventud," "Un Teocali perdido en la cumbre de una montaña," and "Labor del Departamento Forestal y de Caza y Pesca," *Cumbre: Organo del "Grupo Viejos Tequihuas,"* n.d., AGN: SARH 1430, 21/1872, tomo 2.

39. Ibid.

40. "Labor del Departamento Forestal y de Caza y Pesca," *Cumbre: Órgano del "Grupo Viejos Tequihuas,"* n.d., AGN: SARH 1430, 21/1872, tomo 2.

41. Ibid.

42. Grupo Viejos Tequihuas Revolucionarios to Salvador Guerrero, 25 March 1938, AGN: SARH 1430, 21/1872, tomo 2.

43. Alfredo G. Basurto to Departamento de Enseñanza Agrícola y Normal Rural, Informe: Primera Colonia Escolar Campestre, 18 May 1938, AGN: SARH, 1384, 1/157. References to the camp in subsequent paragraphs all come from Basurto's twenty-two page report.

44. Galicia to Alfredo Basurto, 1 June 1938, AGN: SARH 1384, 1, 1/157.

45. Basurto, Informe.

46. Beezley, Martin, and French, *Rituals of Rule, Rituals of Resistance: Public Celebrations and Popular Culture in Mexico* (Wilmington, DE: Scholarly Resources, 1994), xvii-xviii.

47. Quevedo, "Las fiestas del árbol: Su significación y finalidad en México," *Protección a la Naturaleza*, 2:2 (1937).

48. Ibid, 19–22.

49. Ignacio Ruiz Martínez, to Cárdenas,7 December 1938, AGN: LCR 554, 501.1/1.

50. Quevedo, "Informe sobre parques nacionales y reservas forestales en el Valle de México," *México Forestal* 11:1 (1933): 1–6.

51. Quevedo, "Labor activo del Departamento Forestal de México," *Boletín de la Unión Panamericana,"* Washington DC, 1939.

52. "El Ahuehuete o Sabino: El Árbol Nacional," *México Forestal* 1:9,10 (1923): 1–4.

53. "Resoluciones aprobada por la Convención del Partido Nacional Revoluciona-rio celebrada en Querétaro, en relación con la riqueza forestal del Territorio, dentro del Plan Sexenal 1934–40," *Boletín DFCP* 1:1 (1935): 30–32.

54. "El bimestre de reforestación," *Protección a la Naturaleza* 2:3 (1937): 3–5.

55. Julia Piñedo de Rojas to Quevedo, 14 December 1935, AGN: SARH 1433, 21/1962, tomo 1; Julia Piñedo de Rojas to DFCP, 7 February 1936, AGN: SARH 1433, 21/1962, tomo 1; Quevedo to Gabino Vasquez, 1 June 1937, AGN: SARH 1433, 21/1962. Francisco Vasquez to Fernando Romero Quintana, 7 February 1942, AGN: SARH 1433, 21/1962.

56. Felipe B. Berriozabal to Oficial Mayor, Pesca Interior, 18 May 1937, AGN: SARH 1384, 1/157.

57. Felipe B. Berriozabal to Departamento, 26 January 1939, AGN: SARH 1384, 1/157.

58. Roberto Barrena to Director of Forestry and Hunting, 2 June 1943, AGN: SARH 1385, 1/157, 3.

59. Vaughan, *Cultural Politics*, 3.

60. Scott, *Seeing Like a State*, 4.

61. Quevedo to Cárdenas, 20 April 1936, AGN: LCR 574, 506.11/9.

62. "Un vastísimo programa del D. Forestal," *El Nacional*, 20 February 1936; De-partamento Forestal, n.d., AGN: LCR 1090, 606.3/44.

63. Quevedo, *Espacios libres*, 18.

64. For instance, see "La Delegación Forestal y de Caza y Pesca en Michoacán," *El Universal*, 13 November 1935, and "Las ventajas de un nuevo departamento admin-istrativa," *El Universal*, 4 December 1934.

65. Emily Wakild, "Revolutionary Resource Populism: President Cárdenas and the Creation of Environmental Policies," 73–86, in Kiddle and Muñoz, *Populism*.

66. Gonzalo Vázquez Vela, "Memoria de la Secretaría de Educación Pública Sep-tiembre de 1938 a Agosto de 1939 Presentada al H. Congreso de la Unión Por El. C. Secretario Del Ramo Lic. Gonzalo Vazquez Vela," *Boletín de la Secretaría de Edu-cación Pública*, 2 (1939): 159.

67. Ibid.

68. "Parque Nacional Lagunas de Zempoala," *Protección a la Naturaleza* 3:5 (1937): 8–13.

Chapter 3. Productivity

1. Ezequiel Ezcurra, Marisa Mazari-Hiriart, Irene Pisanty, and Adrián Guillermo Aguilar, *The Basin of Mexico: Critical Environmental Issues and Sustainability* (Tokyo: United Nations University Press, 1999), 12.

2. José N. Iturriaga, *El Popocatépetl, ayer y hoy: "Don Gregorio" en las crónicas de extranjeros, desde el siglo XVI hasta la actualidad* (Mexico City: Editorial Diana, 1997), 6. Popocatépetl is almost universally referred to by that spelling. Iztaccíhuatl is also spelled with an x or an l, as in Ixtaccíhuatl and Ixtlazíhuatl. For clarity, I have standardized the spellings here as Iztaccíhuatl or Izta.

3. I borrow here from Craib's phrase "fugitive landscapes," *Cartographic Mexico*. While the land's contents and usage changes, the permanence of the volcanic profiles

provided a clear, fixed justification for their cultural significance especially to park planners, see Quevedo, "La política forestal del Gobierno Mexicano para la protección del territorio y el fomento del gran turismo," *Boletín DFCP*, 1:2 (1935): 149–152. The order of the names Popo and Izta varies, and although the decree named the park Izta-Popo, it seems that Popo-Izta is more common among residents and will be used here.

4. Mexico's first forest reserve at El Chico in Hidalgo State was declared in 1898, and it is later referred to as a national park by federal employees, although its declared status never officially changes. Desierto de los Leones in Mexico City declared in 1917 without any significant administrative support was the first place explicitly called a national park.

5. *Diario Oficial*, 8 November 1935.

6. Lorenzo R. Ochoa, 1909, AHA: AS, 3049: 41966. Entrepreneurs even proposed building funicular tramways to the volcanoes' peaks to increase tourism in the area. Helios Olvera Ach, "Anteproyecto para la construcción de un teleférico en el Parque Nacional Iztaccíhuatl-Popocatépetl," M.A. thesis, Universidad Nacional Autónoma de México, 1966.

7. Quevedo suggested banning collection in areas around the capital to prevent further erosion and soil loss. He advocated subsidies to railroads to transport firewood into the capital from distant forests. Quevedo, "La cuestión del carbón vegetal y su explotación en los bosques del Distrito Federal, que importa poner en veda," *México Forestal*, 10:11–12 (1932): 133–136.

8. Some foresters advocated oil and gas subsidies to wean the populace away from wood based fuel, Anastasio Núñez to Cárdenas, 21 February 1939, AGN: LCR 574, 506.11/9.

9. All of these activities took place in or near the park's boundary, which was drawn at 3,000 meters altitude around the volcanoes. The paper factory resided outside this boundary, as did most residents' homes, but the forest resources often came directly from inside the park.

10. Loret de Mora, "En plena crisis de papel, San Rafael deja de producir" *Novedades*, 16 August 1947.

11. Luis Ramírez de Arellano to President Manuel Ávila Camacho, 5 February 1945, AGA: Amecameca 24/1026, 8, 303–305.

12. Rodolfo Sada Paz, 14 September 1937, AGN: SARH 1437, 1/2177.

13. Lorenzo Aizpuru to Forestry Department, 12 March 1940, AGN: SARH 1428, 21/1926.

14. Presidente Municipal de Tlalmanalco to Gobernación, 26 May 1925, AGA 24/1026, 8, pp. 31–32.

15. Ramírez to Ávila Camacho, 5 February 1945.

16. Hans Arthur Meyer and Carlos Treviño Saldaña, "Los métodos para la elaboración y apilado de la leña usados en México y tablas auxiliares para la cubicación de la misma," *Boletín DFCP* 2:5 (1936): 235–247.

17. Francisco Fernández Almendaro to Oficial Mayor del Ramo, 2 July 1937, AGN: SARH 1437, 1/2177. All amounts remain in the original 1937 peso values.

18. The most common pine tree was called *ocote*, or pitch pine. Resin gatherers were referred to as *ocoteros*.

19. Juárez Flores, "Malintzin Matlalcuéyetl," 106.

20. R. Cattin and J. J. Saint-Jours, "Objeto de la explotación de un pinar: La resinación de los pinos y su madera," trans. Gilberto Serrato Abrego, *México Forestal* 1:9,10 (1923): 7–12.

21. Carlos Castro Flores, "La resinación de nuestros pinares," *Protección a la Naturaleza* 2:5 (1938): 13. Castro concluded that the American system of resination, as practiced in Durango by American companies, resulted in great damage to the trees.

22. The Río Frio district existed west of Mexico City in the municipality of Chalco and the hacienda of Zoquiapan resided partially within the boundaries of the Popo and Izta park and partially alongside the park. Francisco Almendaro to Quevedo, 29 January 1937, AGN: SARH 1437, 1/2177.

23. Rafael M. Farrera to Delegado Forestal, 16 February 1938, AGN: SARH 1437, 1/2177, tomo 1. The factory provided colophony to Colgate Palm Olive (an American firm), El Pino S.A. (a Mexican company), and Vicente Solernou (unknown). See Rafael M. Farrera to Colgate Palm Olive, 23 June 1938, AGN: SARH 1437, 1/2177, 1. Foreign contracts for resins were rare but could prove lucrative.

24. Sidronio Choperena to Department of Forestry, 5 July 1937, AGN: SARH 1437, 1/2177. Quevedo cautioned Cárdenas against giving out ejidos in the area, Quevedo to Cárdenas, 11 June 1935, AGN: LCR 232, 404.1/1698. On the forestry cooperative keeping products, see Francisco Fernández Almendaro to Ceferino Teneria "El Pilar" Gutierrez, 15 December 1937, AGN: SARH 1437, 1/2177, 1. Other projects existed for Zoquiapan through the Forestry Department, Quevedo proposed it as a possible location for the national forestry school and Silvestre Guerrero and Alfredo Bernal requested part of the hacienda be used as a leper colony (neither transpired). Agustín Leñero to Silvestre Guerrero, 11 October 1940, AGN: LCR 365, 424/24, and Alfredo Bernal to Cárdenas, 21 January 1938, AGN: LCR 365, 424/24.

25. At those prices, the minimum ton (approximately 907 kilos) price of colophony was $108 and the minimum ton price for turpentine was $226.

26. Eduardo García Díaz, "Los Grandes Daños que Producen los 'Ocoteros' en los Pinares de la República," *México Forestal* 12:3 (1933): 58–61.

27. Rodolfo Huerta González calls it a new form of production, "Transformación del paisaje: el caso de la fábrica de San Rafael, estado de México, 1890–1934," in *Tierra, agua, y bosques: Historia y medio ambiente en el México central*, ed. Alejandro Tortolero Villaseñor (Mexico City: Centre Francais d'études Mexicaines et Centraméricaines, Instituto Mora, Potrerillos Editores, Universidad de Guadalajara, 1996), 286.

28. Hans Lenz, *Historia del papel en México y cosas relacionadas, 1525–1950* (Mexico City: Miguel Ángel Porrúa, 1990). Lenz expanded Loreto-Peña Pobre in Villa Nicolás Romero and La Venta.

29. Ibid., 687–692.

30. "Industria: Nuevas Industrias," *Revista de Economía*, 31 October 1943.

31. Lenz, *Historia del papel*, 643–645.

32. Secretaría de Hacienda y Crédito Público, *El problema actual de la industria papelera en México* (Mexico City: Secretaria de Hacienda, 1936), 15–17. San Rafael also received subsidized railroad cars for paper transport.

33. Quevedo, "Informes mensuales presentados al consejo colectivo del gabinete presidencial," *Boletín DFCP* 1:2 (1935): 64–99.

34. Ibid.

35. Blanca E. Suárez Cortés, "Las fábricas de papel de San Rafael y Anexas S.A. y un viejo problema, la contaminación del río Tlalmanalco," *Boletín del Archivo Histórico del Agua* 2:6 (1996): 12–14.

36. "Obreros que reciben más de un millón de pesos por utilidades." *El Universal,* 16 March 1944; Loret de Mola, "En plena crisis de papel, San Rafael deja de producir," *Novedades,* 16 August 1947.

37. Lenz, *Historia de papel,* 686. Stephen Haber, *Industry and Underdevelopment: The Industrialization of Mexico 1890–1940* (Stanford: Stanford University Press, 1989), 96–99.

38. Quevedo to Cárdenas, 18 September 1939, AGN: LCR, 554, 501.1/56.

39. Quevedo to Cárdenas, 27 January 1938, AGN: LCR 454, 433/84.

40. Agustín Rayón to Cárdenas, 18 August 1937, AGN: LCR, 454, 433/84.

41. 12 May 1936 AGN: LCR, 454, 433/84.

42. Cárdenas, Acuerdo, 30 June 1937, *Diario Oficial.* The reform is discussed by local authorities in Amecameca in a memorandum, 12 July 1937, Archivo Histórico Municipal Amecameca, Mexico (hereafter AHMA), vol. 159, 22.

43. Carlos Pichardo to Municipal President, 12 July 1937, AHMA, vol. 159, 22. Though controversial, such a limitation on market entry is a common feature of more recent conservation arrangements elsewhere, such as extractive reserves for Brazil nuts.

44. Asunción Juárez et al. to Francisco Varela Camacho, 5 July 1937, AHMA, vol. 159, 22.

45. Alfonso Castro, AHMA, vol. 159, 22.

46. El Corresponsal, "Explotan los bosques del parque nacional," *El Universal,* Mexico City, 6 May 1939.

47. El Corresponsal, "Las reservas forestales de los volcanes se están agotando," *El Universal,* Mexico City, 9 March 1939.

48. A. S. Packard, "Ascent of the Volcano of Popocatepetl," *American Naturalist,* 20:2 (1886): 109–123.

49. O. H. Howarth, "Popocatépetl, and the Volcanoes of the Valley of Mexico," *Geographic Journal,* 8:2 (1896): 137–150; 142.

50. Paul Waitz, "La nueva actividad y el estado actual del volcán Popocatépetl," *Memoria y revista de la Sociedad Antonio Alzate* 37 (1921): 293–313.

51. Gerardo Murillo, *Sinfonías de Popocatépetl* (Mexico City: Ediciones México Moderno, 1921). An employee hoped to increase the emission of vapors by exploding twenty-eight cartridges of dynamite in the inner crater, which Murillo believed triggered the eruption. The geographer J. L. Tamayo took a more skeptical view, claiming that so little explosive could not set off such a long series of volcanic emissions, Iturriaga, *El Popocatépetl,* 10–11.

52. See collections of Compañía Mexicana Aerofoto, Fundación ICA.

53. John H. Beaman, "The Timberlines of Iztaccíhuatl and Popocatepetl, Mexico," *Ecology* 43:3 (July 1962): 377–385.

54. Alexander von Humboldt, *The Political Essay on New Spain* [Abridged], trans. John Black (Norman: University of Oklahoma Press [Alfred A. Knopf], 1988), 237.

55. William H. Beezley, *Judas at the Jockey Club and Other Episodes of Porfirian Mexico* (Lincoln: University of Nebraska Press, 1987), 35–41.

56. Howarth, "Popocatépetl," 150.

57. Jon Lee Anderson, *Che Guevara: A Revolutionary Life* (New York: Grove Press, 1997), 172.

58. Liner notes, Duke Ellington, *Latin American Suite* (Fantasy Records, 8419).

59. Carlos Fuentes, *Myself with Others: Selected Essays* (New York: Farrar, Straus & Giroux, 1981), 31.

60. Elena Poniatowska, "Los volcanes," *La Jornada*, 5 July 2005.

61. Phillip T. Terry, *Terry's Mexico: Handbook for Travellers* (London: Gay & Hancock, 1909); Conkling, *Mexico and the Mexicans* (New York: Taintor Brothers Merrill, 1883).

62. A. Melgareio, "The Greatest Volcanoes of Mexico," *National Geographic Magazine* 21:9 (1910): 741–760, 759.

63. Octavio Benavides, "Conociendo a nuestro México: El Parque Nacional "Popocatépetl-Iztaccíhuatl," *Protección a la Naturaleza* 3:5 (1939): 14–19. Attention to gendered landscape it is underexplored for Latin America in general with the exception of Franco, *Plotting Women*. Two collections regarding gender and nature in the United States provide useful analysis. See Virginia J. Scharff, ed., *Seeing Nature through Gender* (Lawrence: University of Kansas Press, 2003); and Mark Allister, ed., *Eco-Man: New Perspectives on Masculinity and Nature* (Charlottesville: University of Virginia Press, 2004).

64. "Fue brillante la excursión al Popo," *Excelsior*, 18 September 1936.

65. Benavides, "Conociendo a nuestro México," 15.

66. *Diario Oficial*, 8 November 1935.

67. Benavides, "Conociendo a nuestro México," 14–19.

68. There exist numerous versions of this tale around the theme of denied love embodied in the natural landscape. See Beatriz Donnet, *Leyendas del Popo y algo más* (Mexico City: Lectorum, 1999), 14–27; Rafael Pérez-Torres, *Movements in Chicano Poetry: Against Myths, against Margins* (Cambridge: Cambridge University Press, 1995), 191; Instituto Nacional de Antropología y Historia and CONACULTA, *El mito de dos volcanes, Popocatépetl and Iztaccíhuatl* (México: CONACULTA, 2005).

69. Donnet, *Leyendas*, 2.

70. Art depicting and interpreting the volcanoes is plentiful and merits its own study. Among the more famous are José Velasco's landscape paintings, including *El valle de México*, and Saturnino Herrán's 1910 three-panel depiction of the legend, using tormented human forms. Dr. Atl expressed his reverence for the mountains through his paintings and his physical attempts to get close to them. In *Autorretrato con volcán al fondo*, he appears with a shiny forehead, bearded and smirking, a cigarette in one hand and Popo in the background. In *Autorretrato en crater*, he appears with a pointed hat and walking stick in the snow on the edge of Popo's crater, with clouds rising in the background. Alma Lilia Roura, *Dr. Atl: paisaje de hielo y fuego* (Mexico: Círculo de Arte, 1990), 13–16; Salvador Albiñana, "Entre volcanes con el Dr. Atl," *Los dos volcanes: Artes de México* 73 (2005): 45. Edmundo O'Gorman, José Clemente Orozco, and other artists used the landscape as the backdrop for their murals or paintings. Diego Rivera painted *Paisaje Zapatista* in Paris, but the volcanic backdrop nationalized the avant-garde. Rivera's *The Great City of Tenochtitlan*, 1945, portrays both Popo and Izta. *The History of Mexico*, 1929–1935, contains a fiery Popo, and *The Mechanization of the Country*, 1926, has a vivid outline of Izta. Edmundo O'Gorman used the

volcanoes in *La ciudad de México*, 1949, and in *El crédito transforma a México*, 1965. See Desmond Rochfort, *Mexican Muralists: Orozco, Rivera, Siqueiros*. The volcanoes have not been lost on photographers either; see Hugo Brehme and Charles Waite among others.

71. Iturriaga, *Popocatépetl*, 10–11.

72. For enfranchisement see, Olcott, *Revolutionary Women*, 2. Additional important recent works on women and the revolution include, Susie Porter, *Working Women in Mexico City: Public Discourses and Material Conditions, 1879–1931* (Tucson: University of Arizona Press, 2003); Stephanie J. Smith, *Gender and the Mexican Revolution: Yucatan Women and the Realities of Patriarchy* (Chapel Hill: University of North Carolina, 2009); Stephanie Mitchell, *The Women's Revolution in Mexico, 1910–1953* (Lanham, MD: Rowman and Littlefield, 2006); Jocelyn Olcott, Mary Kay Vaughan, and Gabriela Cano, *Sex in Revolution: Gender, Politics, and Power in Modern Mexico* (Durham: Duke University Press, 2007).

73. Poniatowska, "Los volcanes."

74. Catrióna Rueda Esquibel, "Velvet Malinche: Fantasies of '"The" Aztec Princesa in the Chicana/o Sexual Imagination," in *Velvet Barrios: Popular Cultura & Chicana/o Sexualities*, ed. Alicia Gaspar de Alba, 295–307 (New York: Palgrave Macmillan, 2003), 301.

75. Despite the resurgence of forestry training, only 147 technical foresters served the whole country by 1950, and just twelve students majored in forestry at the National School of Agriculture at Chapingo. Tom Gill, *Land Hunger in Mexico* (Washington DC: Charles Lathrop Pack Forestry Foundation, 1951), 48.

Chapter 4. Property

1. Antonio Sosa to Quevedo, report on inspection of forests at San Diego Pinar near Malinche, 20 June 1939, AGN: SARH 1462, 21/3671.

2. Ibid. He also mentions his disdain for *"agrarismo"* that caused private property owners to fear an *"invasión ejidal"* and so cleared forests in order to avoid missing out when their lands were redistributed.

3. Jesús Solóranzo Pleigo, "El muérdago y otras plagas de las arboledas," *Protección a la Naturaleza* 2:12 (1938): 8–15.

4. Jacobs, *Environment, Power, Injustice*.

5. Gilbert Joseph and Daniel Nugent, *Everyday Forms of State Formation: Revolution and the Negotiation of Rule in Modern Mexico* (Durham: Duke University Press, 1994). This literature is well developed for the colonial period. R. Douglas Cope, *The Limits of Racial Domination: Plebian Society in Colonial Mexico City, 1660–1720* (Madison: University of Wisconsin Press, 1994); Cynthia Radding, *Wandering Peoples: Colonialism, Ethnic Spaces, and Ecological Frontiers in Northwestern Mexico, 1700–1850* (Durham: Duke University, 1997).

6. For an overview of changing interpretations, see Matthew Restall, *Seven Myths of the Spanish Conquest* (Oxford: Oxford University Press, 2004).

7. Camilla Townsend, *Malintzin's Choices: An Indian Woman in the Conquest of Mexico* (Albuquerque: University of New Mexico Press, 2006); Roger Bartra, "Los hijos

de la Malinche," in *La Malinche: Sus padres y sus hijos*, ed. Margo Glantz, 195–199 (Mexico City: Taurus, 2001); Susan Kellogg, "Marina, Malinche, Malintzin: Nahua Women and the Spanish Conquest," in *José Limón and La Malinche: The Dancer and the Dance*, ed. Patricia Seed, 79–94 (Austin: University of Texas Press, 2008).

8. Octavio Paz, *The Labyrinth of Solitude*, trans. Lysander Kemp (New York: Grove, 1961), 86. See also Sonia Hernández's consideration of the term *malinchista* on the U.S.-Mexico border, "Malinche in Cross-Border Historical Memory," in *José Limón and La Malinche: The Dancer and the Dance*, ed. Patricia Seed, 95–110 (Austin: University of Texas Press, 2008).

9. Paz, *Labyrinth*, 86. Anne Lanyon, *Malinche's Conquest* (Australia: Allen & Unwin, 1999), 6, 82.

10. Lanyon notes a monument in Coyoacán, to *mestizaje* that include Malinche, Cortés, and their son Martin, was created in 1982 by the town council. Residents protested and the memorial was torn down, Lanyon, *Malinche*, 205.

11. Like many topographical names, the volcano has pseudonyms, including Malintzi, Malintzin, and Matlalcuéyatl, but the park decree specifically noted the park as the mountain La Malinche or Matlalcuéyatl. For this reason, the name *La Malinche* is used to refer to the park rather than Malintzin. Declaration of Parque Nacional La Malinche o Matlalcueyatl, *Diario Oficial*, 6 October 1938.

12. Antonio H. Sosa, "El problema forestal del estado de Tlaxcala." *México Forestal* 10:11,12 (1932): 137–144, and Antonio H. Sosa, "El problema forestal del estado de Tlaxcala continuación," *México Forestal* 11:2 (1933): 35–43.

13. Mario Ramírez Rancaño, *El sistema de haciendas en Tlaxcala* (Mexico City: CONACULTA, 1990), 22.

14. Nevado de Colima's decree specified the limit at 2,500 meters, while Nevado de Toluca and Iztaccíhuatl and Popocatépetl's park boundaries rested at 3,000 meters. See the *Diario Oficial* decrees from 5 September 1936, 19 February 1937, and 8 November 1935.

15. Humberto Vidal Romero to Department of Forestry, 7 September 1938, AGN: SARH 1462, 21/3671.

16. Bernal Díaz del Castillo, *Conquest of New Spain*, trans. J. M. Cohen (New York: Penguin, 1963), 144.

17. Ramírez Rancaño, *Haciendas*, 13. Tlaxcala had eighty-eight haciendas over 1,000 hectares in 1920, which took up more than half the area of the state.

18. Sosa, "El problema forestal," 137–144.

19. Ramírez Rancaño, *Haciendas*, 47. Henderson, *Worm in the Wheat*, 35.

20. Quevedo to Juan Moreno Gallardo, 15 August 1939, AGN: SARH 1462, 21/3671.

21. San Pablo Zitlaltepec was also called Xitlaltepec, Citlaltepec, and other variations. For consistency, it will be abbreviated as Zitlaltepec and San Juan Bautista Ixtenco will be Ixtenco.

22. For example, the community of San Francisco Tetlanohcan, within the park boundaries, claimed they had retained continuous and peaceful residence in that community for more than sixty-five years. Their ancestors purchased the property in 1869 in a transaction recorded in the public register. San Francisco Tetlanohcan, 5 October 1938, AGN: SARH 1462, 21/3671.

23. Mendez names the founders that include Srs. Juan Ponce de León, Diego Gabriel, Francisco de Barba Torres Paredes, Francisco Contreras, and Antonio Gomez. Francisco B. Mendez, 6 November 1923, San Juan Bautista Ixtenco: AGA, 23/5011, 2.

24. Mendez, 6 November 1923.

25. Ramon Corral Soto to Secretary of National Agrarian Commission, 16 July 1923, AGA: San Juan Bautista Ixtenco, 23/1/5011, 2.

26. Ramon Corral Soto, 7 August 1923, AGA: San Juan Bautista Ixtenco, 25/5016, 14.

27. Mario Sucede Pozo, Memorandum, grant to San Pablo Zitlaltepec, 18 July 1923, AGA: San Pablo Zitlaltepec 25/5016, 14.

28. Ramón Corral Soto, informe, 7 August 1923, AGA: 25/5016, 14.

29. Antonio Aquino Daza and Vicente García to Cárdenas, 24 September 1938, AGN: SARH 1462, 21/3671.

30. Ibid.

31. Martín Pérez to Presidente de la Comisión Nacional Agraria, 9 September 1923, AGA: San Juan Bautista Ixtenco 23/5016, 14.

32. Charles A. Hale, "The Civil Law Tradition and Constitutionalism in Twentieth-Century Mexico: The Legacy of Emilio Rabasa," *Law and History Review* 18:2 (2000): 257–279, 270.

33. Carlos Gil, *Life in Provincial Mexico National and Regional History as Seen from Mascota, Jalisco, 1867–1972* (Los Angeles: UCLA Latin American Center, 1983).

34. José Mesa y Gutiérrez, 26 January 1924, AGA: San Juan Bautista Ixtenco 23/5016, 14.

35. Decree by Obregón, 29 November 1923, AGA: San Juan Bautista Ixtenco 23/5016, 14.

36. Antonio Palma et al. to Emilio Portes Gil, 28 March 1936, AGA: San Pablo Zitlaltepec 23/5016, 6. This petition lists ninety-three men and thirteen women.

37. Martín Pérez et al. to Felix Ramos Hernández, 5 March 1936, AGA: San Pablo Zitlaltepec 23/5016, 6.

38. Ibid.

39. Martín Pérez et al. to Cárdenas, 23 April 1936, AGA: San Pablo Zitlaltepec 23/5016, 6.

40. Aurelio Robles Castillo, Memorandum of Consulting, 29 March 1942, AGA: San Pablo Zitlaltepec 23/5016, 6. Robles finds in a new census that by 1942 only 274 capacitated recipients existed to receive certified agrarian rights.

41. There is considerable slippage between the dates of these allocations and decrees that demonstrates the slow communication that existed among bureaucratic organizations. Presidential decree, 7 June 1937, AGN: SARH 1421, 1/1472. See also Quevedo to President Cárdenas, 7 September 1937, AGN: SARH 1421, 1/1472.

42. Antonio Sosa, "Breves apuntes sobre el problema forestal en el estado de Tlaxcala," *México Forestal* 6:5–6 (1926): 54–63.

43. Sosa, "Breves apuntes," 62.

44. Sosa, "Breves apuntes," 62.

45. Cortés is the first of the forty-five signatories from these pueblos. See Residents of Coajomulco, Teacalco, Guadalupe Tlachco, San Miguel Contla, Coahuixmatla, Tlalcuapan, Tetlahohca, Xochitiotla, Tepatlaxco, Teolocholco, Axotla del Monte, San Cosme Masatecochco, San Marcos Contla, San Pablo del Monte, Santa Catarina

Ayometla, Miguel Hidalgo, San Isidrio Buensuceso, and Tenancingo to Cárdenas, 2 September 1938, AGN: SARH 1462, 21/3671.

46. Ibid.

47. Ibid.

48. Uno de Tantos, "El clamor de Malintzi," *La Prensa*, 26 September 1938.

49. Tomás Mendoza to Cárdenas, 2 December 1936, AGN: LCR 280, 404.1/5699.

50. Miguel Rivera to Antonio Sosa, 2 December 1939, AGN: SARH 1462, 21/3671.

51. Quevedo, *Relato*, 75.

52. Ángel Roldán, "Cultivo de ocote (pinus, varias especies)," *Protección a la Naturaleza*, 2:10 (1938): 9–10.

53. Román Díaz Rosas to Forestry Department, 24 January 1936, AGN: LCR 561, 502/12.

54. Quevedo to Cárdenas, 7 February 1938, AGN: LCR 554, 501/8.

55. See, for instance, Gregorio Pacheco to Tlaxcala Delegate, 31 May 1939, AGN: SARH 1462 21/3671, whose inspection report recommends allowing pasturage within the park for cattle but not goats.

56. Ramón Corral Soto, report on forest exploitation by Ixtenco and Zitlaltepec, 7 August 1923, AGA: 25/5016, 14.

57. Ricardo Ortiz R. to Director Tierras, 30 October 1931, AHA: AS, 1732, 25575.

58. Ibid.

59. Fernando Nuñez, Report on population of Zitlaltepec, 27 March 1938, AGA: San Pablo Zitlaltepec 23/5016, 6. A total of ten complaints were corrected by the survey, out of 494 ejidatarios.

60. Humberto Vidal Romero and Othón Mercado Peyró to Departamento Forestal y de Caza y Pesca, 9 September 1938, AGN: SARH 1462, 21/3671.

61. Pedro Rochin Segovia to Emiliano Mendoza, 29 December 1938, AGN: SARH 1462, 21/3671, tomo 1.

62. Unfortunately González's report does not survive, only a transcription of parts of it by his superiors. Salvador Guerrero to Governor of Tlaxcala, 4 January 1939, AGN: SARH 1462, 21/3671.

63. Román Díaz Rosas to Cárdenas, 24 January 1936, AGN: LCR 561, 502/12.

64. Sosa, "Breves apuntes," 54–63.

65. Sosa, report.

66. Quevedo to Raúl Castellano, 20 December 1938, AGN: LCR 559, 501.2, 278.

67. Acuerdo Presidencial, 28 April 1937.

68. Sosa, report.

69. Antonio Sosa to Salvador Guerrero, 4 December 1939, AGN: SARH 1462 21/3671

70. Ibid.

71. Raúl Calderón Cora to Chief of the Department of Legislative Consultation, 3 April 1940, AGN: SARH 1462 21/3671.

72. Antonio Sosa to Director General of Forests and Hunting, 15 November 1940, AGN: SARH 1462 21/3671. The park's size is changed from an angular boundary connecting communities and including most forests to a boundary line drawn directly above 3000 meters. The fortress term has been applied to parks since Yellowstone National Park, but for the most forceful critique, see Brockington, *Fortress Conservation*.

Chapter 5. Tradition

1. The other villages are San Juan, Santo Domingo, Amatlán, Ixcatepec, Gabriel Mariaca, San Andrés, and Santiago.

2. Oscar Lewis, *Life in a Mexican Village: Tepoztlán Restudied* (Urbana: University of Illinois Press, 1951), 3.

3. Pilar Sánchez Ascencio, *Antología histórica de Tepoztlán* (Acapatzingo, Morelos, Mexico: Museo y centro de documentación histórica, Exconvento de Tepoztlán, 1998), 157.

4. Oscar Lewis, *Tepoztlán: Village in Mexico* (New York: Holt, Rinehart and Winston, 1960), 44; Lewis, *Life in a Mexican Village*, 240.

5. Robert Redfield, *Tepoztlán, a Mexican Village* (Chicago: University of Chicago, 1930), 206.

6. Oscar Lewis, *Pedro Martínez: A Mexican Peasant and His Family* (New York: Random House, 1964), 266–269.

7. There is no shortage of studies of Mexican villages. John Steinbeck, *The Forgotten Village* (New York: Viking, 1941); George M. Foster, *Empire's Children: People of Tzintzuntzan* (Washington DC: Smithsonian Institute, Institute for Social Anthropology Publication No. 6, 1948), and *Tzinzuntzan: Mexican Peasants in a Changing World* (Boston: Little, Brown, 1967); Manuel Avila, *Tradition and Growth: A Study of Four Mexican Villages* (Chicago: University of Chicago Press, 1969); Michael Belshaw, *A Village Economy: Land and People of Huecorio* (New York: Columbia University Press, 1967); Paul Friedrich, *Agrarian Revolt in a Mexican Village* (Chicago: University of Chicago Press, 1970); Luis González y González, *Pueblo en vilo: Microhistoria de San José de Gracia* (Mexico City: El Colegio de México, 1972).

8. One exception is Tutino, "Revolutionary Capacity." He discusses "ecological autonomy" as communities' ability to produce subsistence crops, livestock, and basic tools, 214.

9. Wendy Waters, "Remapping Identities Road Construction and Nation Building in Postrevolutionary Mexico," in *The Eagle and the Virgin: Nation and Cultural Revolution in Mexico, 1920–1940*, ed. Mary Kay Vaughan and Stephen E. Lewis, 221–242 (Durham: Duke University Press, 2006), 226–229.

10. John Noble et al., *Lonely Planet Mexico*, 9th ed. (China: Bookmaker International, 2004), 218.

11. Emiliano Zapata's Anenencuilco might be an equivalent small community receiving a disproportionate amount of attention from scholars, foreign and domestic alike. Hart, *Bitter Harvest*; Alicia Hernández Chávez, *Anenecuilco, memória y vida de un pueblo* (Mexico City: El Colegio de México, 1991); Womack, *Zapata*; Warman, *"We Come to Object."*

12. Redfield, *Tepoztlán*, vii, 1.

13. Redfield, Field Notes Diary, n.d., University of Chicago Special Collections, Robert Redfield Papers (hereafter RRP), Box 43, Folder 1.

14. Lewis, *Life in a Mexican Village*, and *Tepoztlán: Village in Mexico*.

15. Redfield, *Tepoztlán*, 1.

16. Redfield, *Tepoztlán*, 14; Clifford Wilcox, *Robert Redfield and the Development of American Anthropology* (Lanham, MD: Lexington Books, 2004), 4–6.

17. Wilcox, *Redfield*, 14.

18. Manuel Gamio, *Forjando Patria* (Mexico City: Editorial Porrúa, [1916] 1982); David A. Brading, "Manuel Gamio and Official Indigenismo in Mexico," *Bulletin of Latin American Research* 7:1 (1988): 75–89; Gamio also shaped transnational ideas of race and development, see Casey Walsh, "Eugenic Acculturation Manuel Gamio, Migration Studies, and the Anthropology of Development in Mexico, 1910–1940," *Latin American Perspectives* 31:5 (2004): 118–145.

19. Wilcox, *Redfield*, 65–66; Susan M. Rigdon, *The Culture Facade: Art, Science, and Politics in the Work of Oscar Lewis* (Urbana–Champaign: University of Illinois Press, 1988); and on the circulation of Lewis's ideas, Karin Alejandra Rosemblatt, "Other Americas: Transnationalism, Scholarship, and the Culture of Poverty in Mexico and the United States," *Hispanic American Historical Review* 89:4 (2009): 603–641.

20. Phillip K. Bock, "Tepoztlán Reconsidered," *Journal of Latin American Lore* 6:1 (1980); Avila, *Tradition and Growth*; Daniel Ruzo, *El valle sagrado de Tepoztlán* (Mexico City: Editorial Posada, 1976); Joáquin Gallo Sarlat, *Tepoztlán vida y color* (Mexico City: Editorial Libros de México, 1977); Waters, "Remapping Identities."

21. JoAnn Martin, *Tepoztlán and the Transformation of the Mexican State the Politics of Loose Connections* (Tucson: University of Arizona Press, 2005).

22. Oscar Lewis Papers, University of Illinois, Urbana–Champaign (hereafter OLP), Series 15/2/20; Tepoztlán, Box 110.

23. Lewis, *Life in a Mexican Village*, xxii.

24. Lewis, *Life in a Mexican Village*, 238. On cooperatives, Boyer, "Contested Terrain," 32.

25. The village had maintained other industries based on its natural endowments, particularly small-scale paper production and a foundry. Neither became a community-run business or a cooperative; they were private enterprises. Juan Dubernard Chauveau, *Apuntes para la historia de Tepoztlán* (Cuernavaca, Morelos, México: Impresores de Morelos, 1983), 75, 93.

26. Margarito Florez, Francisco Terán, Leonardo Camaño, Placido Rojas denounce Demetrio Moreno, 19 July 1929, Instituto Nacional Antropologia e Historia: Biblioteca Exconvento Tepoztlán, Archivo Histórico de Tepoztlán, Ramo Penal 1929, Expediente 12.

27. Calixto Betanzos and Abundio Ramírez to Oficial Mayor de la Comisión Nacional Agraria, 22 September 1932, AGA: 24/3131, 11.

28. Starting as a small group opposing forest destruction, the faction organized into the Unión de Campesinos Tepoztecos in 1922 and then joined the Confederación Revolucionario de Obreros Mexicanos. They were then dubbed "Bolshevikis" by their political opponents. Lewis, *Life in a Mexican Village*, 236, calls them "Bolshevikis," and Lomnitz calls them the "bolcheviques." Claudio Lomnitz, *Evolución de una sociedad rural* (Mexico City: Fondo de Cultura Económica, 1982).

29. Lewis, *Life in a Mexican Village*, 236.

30. For more specific details about the community divisions and the centrality of the charcoal debate, see Lewis, *Life in a Mexican Village*, 163–165, and Lomnitz, *Evolución*, 159–176. Also, OLP, Series 15/2/20 Tepoztlán, Box 111.

31. Lewis, *Life in a Mexican Village*, 237. Carnaval proved a repeated forum for Cristero tensions, Valentín López González, *El Morelos posrevolucionario, 1919–1930 Fuentes documentales del estado de Morelos* (Cuernavaca, Morelos, Mexico: Cuadernos Históricos Morelenses, 2002), 25.

32. Lewis, *Pedro Martínez*, 122.

33. Lomnitz, *Evolución*, 105.

34. Lomnitz, *Evolución*, 100.

35. OLP, Series 15/2/20; Pedro Martínez, Box 47.

36. Forestry cooperatives became a component of Cardenista forest policy, although they developed more extensively in the 1940s and 1950s. Boyer, "Contested Terrain," 28.

37. Lewis, *Life in a Mexican Village*, 239.

38. Lomnitz, *Evolución*, 105 and 172–178.

39. The Bolshevikis became the Fraternales and remained in support of conservation.

40. I encountered no evidence of federal interference with either the murder of Juan Hidalgo or the final collapse of the cooperative. Neither anthropologists nor federal records mention the possibility of federal involvement in Hidalgo's assassination.

41. Lewis, *Pedro Martínez*, 130.

42. Rafael Villornil and Vicente Ruiz to Galicia, 22 January 1953, AGN: SARH 1467, 1/4307.

43. Tlacotenco residents to Roberto Galvan López and Galicia, 6 August 1953, AGN: SARH 1467, 1/4307.

44. See denunciations of the municipal president of Tepoztlán for cutting twenty-five trees in 1939; complaints about the need to cut down diseased trees in 1943; investigations into Francisco Medina, Hipólito Vargas, Porfirio Vargas, Eufrosino Vázquez, and others in September 1945; complaints by the municipal president, Luis Masias Arrellano, in September 1948; accusations against Joaquín Cortés, September 1949; and others in AGN: SARH 1467, 1/4307.

45. Mariano Rojas, "Excursión escolar a la Villa de Tepoztlán el día 18 Nov de 1922," *El Tepozteco: Publicación Mensual de Religión, Ciencias, Literatura, Lingüística Mexicana y Variedades* (15 December 1922) 2:29. Acervos: Archivo Histórico del INAH (hereafter AH-INAH) 4a. Serie, 76 Doc 5 FJ 135.

46. Rojas, "Excursión."

47. Lewis, *Life in a Mexican Village*, 38; Redfield, *Tepoztlán*, 217.

48. Jesús Conde Rodríguez, *Tepoztlán*, 1920, AH-INAH 4a. Serie, 76.

49. RRP, Correspondence, April 1927. Much of Redfield's correspondence describes personal concerns, including lack of finances, illness, and even dog bites and reveals a deep reliance on Conde's assistance for most logistical support.

50. "Los manantiales de La Fundición son objeto de la visita del C. Presidente," *Morelos Nuevo*, 4:495, 26 February 1933.

51. Ángel Zúñiga Navarrete, *Las tierras y montañas de Tepoztlán, Morelos* (Mexico City: Ángel Zúñiga Navarrete, 1995), 56.

52. Antonio H. Sosa, "Parque Nacional de 'El Tepozteco,'" *El Nacional*, Mexico City, 22 January 1938, 5 February 1938; and "El Parque Nacional de 'El Tepozteco,'" *Protección a la Naturaleza* 2:1 (1937): 2–13.

53. On *indigenismo*, see Alan Knight, "Racism, Revolution, and *Indigenismo*: Mexico, 1910–1940," in *The Idea of Race in Latin America, 1870–1940*, ed. Richard Graham (Austin: University of Texas Press, 1990); Dawson, *Indian and Nation*; Stephen Lewis, *The Ambivalent Revolution: Forging State and Nation in Chiapas, 1910–1945* (Albuquerque: University of New Mexico Press, 2005).

54. Sosa to Quevedo, n.d., AGN: SARH, 1467, 1/4307.

55. Roberto Quirós Martínez, "Los parques nacionales y el espíritu forestal," *El Nacional*, 12 February 1939.

56. Lewis, *Pedro Martínez*, 156.

57. Zúñiga Navarrete, *Las tierras y montañas*, 39.

58. Chauveau, *Apuntes*, 124.

59. Vázquez Vela, "Memoria"; José Reygadas Vértiz, 9 August 1932, SEP, Departamento de Bellas Artes, Dirección de Monumentos Artísticos, Arqueológicos e Históricos, caja 44.

60. Sosa, "Parque Nacional," 2–13.

61. See appendix A.

62. Gilberto Serrato A. Translation and commentary on J. Berlioz, "Protección de la Naturaleza," *México Forestal* 10:1 (1932): 1–4.

63. Two authoritative works on nature, representation, and race in Latin America are Mary Louise Pratt, *Imperial Eyes: Travel Writing and Transculturation* (London: Routledge, 1992), and Deborah Poole, *Vision, Race, Modernity: A Visual Economy of the Andean World* (Princeton: Princeton University Press, 1997). The paintings of José María Velasco and the maps of Antonio García Cubas are examples of nineteenth-century Mexican nationals representing their national landscapes. See Craib, *Cartographic Mexico*; Justino Fernández, *Arte moderno y contemporáneo de México, José María Velasco* (Toluca, México: Monografías de Arte, 1976); and Alfonso Sánchez Arteche, *Velasco íntimo y legendario* (Toluca, México: Instituto Mexiquense de Cultura, 1992).

64. Jean Meyer, *The Cristero Rebellion: The Mexican People between Church and State 1926–1929* (Cambridge: Cambridge University Press, 1976).

65. Paul Vanderwood, *The Power of God against the Guns of Government: Religious Upheaval in Mexico at the Turn of the Nineteenth Century* (Stanford: Stanford University Press, 1998); *Juan Soldado: Rapist, Murderer, Martyr, Saint* (Durham: Duke University, 2004); Marjorie Becker, *Setting the Virgin on Fire: Lázaro Cárdenas, Michoacán Peasants, and the Redemption of the Mexican Revolution* (Berkeley: University of California Press, 1995); Edward Wright-Rios, *Revolutions in Mexican Catholicism: Reform and Revelation in Oaxaca, 1887–1934* (Durham: Duke University Press, 2009); Bantjes, *Jesus Walked*; Fallaw, *Cárdenas Compromised*.

66. The declaration of parks in historic or sacred spaces was not unique to Mexico. In 1937, Argentina declared a national park "Criollo 'Ricardo Güiraldes'" to honor a literary master and preserve his gaucho way of life. The park had a colonial museum, a wooden watchtower, and a hacienda with livestock, 100 km northwest of Buenos Aires. See Enrique Udaondo, "Algunos Parques de América: El Parque Criollo 'Ricardo Güiraldes,'" *Boletín de la Unión Panamericana*, December 1938. Palmares, the largest and most famous runaway slave community in Brazil, was declared a national park in 1974, see John Burdick, "Brazil's Black Consciousness Movement," *NACLA: Report on the Americas* 25:4 (1992): 23–27. A Caribbean plantation was established as a national park in 1970s, see Karen Fog Olwig and Kenneth Olwig, "Underdevelopment and the Development of 'Natural' Park Ideology," *Antipode* 11:2 (1979): 16–25.

67. Antonio Sosa, "Cincuentenario de la Enseñanza," *El Universal*, 27 December 1960.

68. Franco López to Cárdenas, 31 October 1937, AGN: LCR 561, 502/12. Cárdenas did not attend.

69. Quevedo, "Alocución del Jefe del Departamento Forestal y de Caza y Pesca, ingeniero Miguel A. de Quevedo, al iniciarse las primeras clases en el Instituto de Enseñanza Forestal y de Caza y Pesca, el 6 de mayo de 1936," *Boletín DFCP* 2:4 (1936): 211–14.

70. Antonio H. Sosa, "La influencia de Francia en el desarrollo forestal de México," *México Forestal* 16:9–10 (1936): 73–75.

71. For regulatory activities in Los Remedios, see Rodolfo Sada Paz to Presidente Municipal, San Bartolo Naucalpan, Mex., 28 July 1937, AGN: SARH 1437, 21/2100; E. Flores to Departamento Forestal y de Caza y Pesca, 15 August 1939, AGN: SARH 1412, 1/1202, 1.

72. Epigmenio Guzmán, Bibiano Ayala, Eliseo Villamar, Juan Ayala, Bonficacion N. Bello, and Miguel Barragán to President Manuel Ávila Camacho, 1 April 1945, AGA: Tepoztlán, Morelos, 24/3131, 11. The document also contains a list of thirty-five additional supporters, several of them women.

73. Roberto Alba Galindo to Director General de Protección y Repoblación Forestales, 23 May 1960, AGN: SARH 1467, 1/4307.

74. Ricardo Cortés C., Agustín Flores P., and Marcos Bello Lara to Director de Protección y Repoblación Forestales, 24 November 1963, AGN: SARH 1467, 1/4307.

75. Rosas, *Tepoztlán*, 16–17.

76. Sam Dillon, "Golf Course Inflames Mexican Town," *New York Times*, 6 September 1995. In a similar episode also related to land and resource autonomy, 100 villagers occupied the mansion of Guillermo de Jesús Occelli, the brother-in-law of the former president Carlos Salinas de Gortari. Although Occilli claimed he had legitimate title, the campesinos claimed the mansion was constructed on village lands. Anthony DePalma, "Income Gap in Mexico Grows, and So Do Protests," *New York Times*, 20 July 1996.

77. Jorge Munguía Espitia and Margarita Castellanos Ribot, "Informe sobre la opinión de la población de Tepoztlán en torno al conflicto suscitado a raíz del proyecto de construcción del club de golf El Tepozteco" (Mexico City: Universidad Autónomo de México, Xochimilco, n.d.), 7.

78. Rosas, *Tepoztlán*, 19–20.

79. Dillon, "Golf Course."

80. Magda Bogin, "Skirmishes from Mexico's Golf War," *New York Times*, 8 October 1995. Bogin identifies herself as a Tepoztlán resident, living there on and off for thirty years.

81. Maria Rosas, *Tepoztlán: Crónica de desacatos y resistencia* (Mexico City: ERA, 1997), 146.

82. *Diario Oficial*, 22 January 1937.

83. Guha, "Radical American Environmentalism," 72; David V. Carruthers, ed., *Environmental Justice in Latin America: Problems, Promise and Practice* (Cambridge, MA: MIT Press, 2008); Giovanna Di Chiro, "Beyond Ecoliberal 'Common Futures' Environmental Justice, Toxic Touring, and a Transcommunal Politics of Place," in *Race, Nature, and the Politics of Difference*, ed. Donald S. Moore, Jake Kosek, and Anand Pandian, 204–232 (Durham: Duke University Press, 2003); Luke W. Cole and Sheila R. Foster, eds., *From the Ground Up: Environmental Racism and the Rise of the Environmental Justice Movement* (New York: New York University Press, 2001).

Conclusion

1. Firso Espinosa, Guadalupe Rosas, and Salomé Romero to Cárdenas, 14 March 1939, AGN: LCR 561, 502/12.

2. Theirs was not the only complaint. The engineer Ernesto Sánchez Paulin accused the Forestry Department of fraud, mismanagement, and inconsistently levying the forestry tax. "Hace una aclaración el Ing. de Quevedo," *El Universal*, 14 March 1939, and "Escandalosos mangoneos en caza y pesca," *La Prensa*, 11 March 1939. Others claimed that Quevedo could not be considered a true revolutionary because he had not risked his life for the country. Román Díaz Rosas to Cárdenas, 26 January 1936, AGN: LCR 561, 502/12. Similar complaints had been publicized about Quevedo's predecessor Gumaro García de la Cadena, when the Forestry Department resided in the Secretary of Agriculture. "Hay gran descontento entre elementos campesinos contra un funcionario de caza y pesca," *El Nacional*, 4 June 1931, and "Acusación al director del Depto. Forestal," *La Prensa*, 1 October 1934.

3. Along with the Forestry Department, Cárdenas reduced the size and authority of the Departamento Autónoma de Prensa y Publicidad and the Departamento de Educación Fisica.

4. Santiago, *Ecology of Oil*, 352.

5. Sergio Barojas A., 31 January 1940, AGN: SARH 1425 1/1609. For a captivating discussion of changes in the countryside in the mid-twentieth century, see Angus Wright, *Death of Ramón González: The Modern Agricultural Dilemma* (Austin: University of Texas Press, 1990).

6. Increased urbanization did not result in only poor people encroaching on forests. In 1980, several wealthy urbanites wanted to build "Swiss chalets" in the woods of Ajusco National Park, and residents of the area protested. Alfonso Garcia, "Enfrenta a comuncros y fraccionadores la posesión de la tierra en el Ajusco," *Novedades*, 13 July 1980.

7. Simon, *Endangered Mexico*, 87.

8. Oscar Lewis, *Five Families: Mexican Case Studies in the Culture of Poverty* (New York: Basic Books, [1963] 1975), and *The Children of Sánchez: Autobiography of a Mexican Family* (New York: Vintage Books [1969] 1979).

9. Carlos Fuentes, *Where the Air Is Clear* (New York: Farrar, Straus & Giroux, 1960).

10. Emily Young, "Local People and Conservation in Mexico's El Vizcaino Biosphere Reserve," *Geographical Review* 89:3 (1999), 364–390; Breunig, "Conservation in Context."

11. Simon, *Endangered Mexico*, 236; Terborgh, *Requiem for Nature*, 184.

12. Dean, "The Tasks of Latin American Environmental History," 6. More recent literature suggests otherwise for Brazil; see Pádua, *Um sopro de destruição*; Franco and Drummond, *Wilderness*.

13. Global conservation efforts now include a large portfolio of protected areas in developing countries, including parks designed with justice in mind. Extractive reserves, protected areas with sustainable use, and biosphere reserves have designs akin to what Mexican foresters contemplated in the 1930s. An important study would consider the social origins of these different designations as well as their effectiveness at protecting nature and sustaining rural livelihoods.

14. On U.S. environmentalism, see Nash, *Wilderness and the American Mind*; Hays, *Conservation*; Riley E. Dunlap and Angela G. Mertig, *American Environmentalism: The U.S. Environmental Movement, 1970–1990* (London: Taylor & Francis, 1992); Robert Gottlieb, *Forcing the Spring: The Transformation of the American Environmental Movement* (Washington DC: Island Press, 1994); and Adam Rome, "Give Earth a Chance: The Environmental Movement and the Sixties, *Journal of American History* 90:2 (2003), 525–554.

15. Guha, *Environmentalism*, and "Radical American Environmentalism." Guha's work pushed American environmentalism to look at the bigger picture of resource use in ways that rippled through new critiques of environmentalism. For these reverberations, see Paul Sutter, "When Environmental Traditions Collide: Ramachandra Guha's *The Unquiet Woods* and U.S. Environmental History," *Environmental History* 14 (2009): 543–550.

16. See the numerous popular works, including the Ken Burns's documentary *The National Parks: America's Best Idea* (PBS, 2009), and Kim Heacox, *An American Idea: The Making of the National Parks* (Washington DC: National Geographic Society, 2001).

17. Runte, *National Parks*, 44–45.

18. The field of conservation biology focuses on variability among living organisms and concerns over large-scale extinctions and habitat decline. It differs from related disciplines by its transparent aims for "the protection and perpetuation of the Earth's biological diversity," Curt Meine, Michael Soulé, Reed F. Noss, "A Mission Driven Discipline," 631. See also, Edward O. Wilson, *Biophilia* (Cambridge, MA: Harvard University Press, 1984); Thomas Lovejoy, "The Obligations of a Biologist" *Conservation Biology* 3:4 (1989); Peter Brussard, "The Current Status of Conservation Biology" *Bulletin of the Ecological Society of America*, 66:1 (1985): 9–11; Michael E. Soulé, ed., *Conservation Biology: The Science of Scarcity and Diversity*; Society for Conservation Biology, http://www.conbio.org/AboutUs/.

19. Enrique Beltrán, "Use and Conservation: Two Conflicting Principles," in *First World Conference on National Parks*, ed. Alexander B. Adams, 35–43 (Washington DC: National Park Service, 1962), 37. For more on Beltrán, see Simonian, *Defending the Land*, 132–140.

20. Beltrán, "Use and Conservation," 39.

21. Hugh Elliott, ed., *Second World Conference on National Parks* (Switzerland: IUCN, 1974).

22. International Technical Conference on Nature Protection, Lake Success. Martin Holdgate, *The Green Web* (London: Earthscan, 1999), 52–66.

23. *United Nations List of National Parks and Equivalent Reserves* (Brussels: Hayez, 1971).

24. For general critiques, see Dowie, *Conservation Refugees*, and Anderson and Berglund, *Ethnographies of Conservation*.

25. Public Law 88–577 (16 U.S. C. 1131–1136), 88th Congress, Second Session 3, September 1964. http://www.wilderness.net/index.cfm?fuse=NWPS&sec=legisAct.

26. Nash, *Wilderness and the American Mind*, 222.

27. Harmon, "Cultural Diversity."

28. Anja Nygren, "Nature as Contested Terrain: Conflicts over Wilderness Protection and Local Livelihoods in Río San Juan, Nicaragua," in Anderson and Berglund, *Ethnographies of Conservation*, 33–49; 47. That 14 percent did not is also a significant

detail; the lack of a wilderness ideal does not necessarily correlate to a lack of wilderness in remote areas.

29. Guha, "Radical American Environmentalism"; William Cronon, "Trouble with Wilderness"; J. Baird Callicott and Michael P. Nelson, eds., *The Great New Wilderness Debate* (Athens: University of Georgia Press, 1998).

30. For masterful histories of fire, see Stephen J. Pyne's volumes on the cycle of fire, including *World Fire: The Culture of Fire on Earth* (Seattle: University of Washington Press, 1995), and *Fire in America: A Cultural History of Wildland and Rural Fire* (Seattle: University of Washington Press, 1997). William Denevan, "The Pristine Myth: The Landscape of the Americas in 1492," *Annals of the American Association of Geographers* 82:3 (1992): 369–385; Dowie cites an unnamed 1997 study by Krishna Ghimire and Michel Pimbert that found "the biological diversity of the Serengeti grasslands was being enhanced by the grazing and migration practices of the Maasai, which tend to mimic the grazing habits of local wildlife," in *Conservation Refugees*, 134.

31. Homero Aridjis, of Mexico's *Grupo de los cien*, remarks that no Spanish word for "wilderness" exists.

32. Gómez-Pompa and Kaus, "Taming the Wilderness Myth," 275.

33. The term "megadiverse" is also used. Antony Challenger, *Utilización y conservación de los ecosistemas terrestres de México. Pasado, presente, y futuro*, 34.

34. The important exception for Latin America is Costa Rica, which has promoted much conservation in the past several decades. Interestingly for historicizing conservation, Costa Rica was not the first place to begin conservation projects but instead the nation's timing coincided with this new scientific framework.

35. John Terborgh and Carel Van Schaik, "Why the World Needs Parks," in *Making Parks Work: Strategies for Preserving Tropical Nature*, ed. John Terborgh, Carel van Schaik, Lisa Davenport, and Madhu Rao (Washington DC: Island Press, 2002), 4.

36. Surveys of park wildlife starting in 1929 served as the first in-depth scientific studies in support of natural resource management. Richard West Sellars, "The Rise and Decline of Ecological Attitudes, of Ecological Attitudes in National Park Management, 1929–1940, Part I" *George Wright Forum* 10:1 (1993): 55. Terborgh attributes this fortunate effect to the mixed and stable system of land tenure in the United States, *Requiem for Nature*, 158. Scientific understandings of the need for large habitats began to be recognized after the publication of Robert H. MacArthur and Edward O. Wilson, *The Theory of Island Biogeography* (Princeton: Princeton University Press, 1967). In the 1980s, further studies, including Lovejoy's islands in the Amazon and the reintroduction of wolves to Yellowstone, solidified scientific thinking. Of course, people who worked with animals had long recognized the benefits of large open spaces.

37. Sellars, "Rise and Decline," 58.

38. Nash, *Wilderness and the American Mind*, 113.

39. Judith Meyer, "Re-packing the Yellowstone Model: Historical Geography and the Transnational Transfer of an Ideal," paper presented at "Civilizing Nature: Toward a Global Perspective of National Parks" conference, German Historical Institute, June 2008.

40. Candace Slater, ed., *In Search of the Rain Forest* (Durham: Duke University Press, 2003).

41. I do not dispute the value of tropical nature as a reservoir of species diversity and source of biological security, nor do I critique its position as a priority given the

scarce resources available to promote conservation worldwide. Conservationists themselves give much attention to these difficult decisions. See, for example, T. M. Brooks et al., "Global Biodiversity Conservation Priorities," *Science* 313 (7 July 2006): 58–61.

42. David Barton Bray, Leticia Merino-Pérez, and Deborah Barry, eds., *The Community Forests of Mexico: Managing for Sustainable Landscapes* (Austin: University of Texas Press, 2005), 8. Dan Klooster and Shrinidhi Ambinakudige claim that Mexico is second only to Papua New Guinea, "The Global Significance of Mexican Community Forests," in Bray, Merino-Pérez, and Barry, *Community Forests* (305–334), 307.

43. Judith Shapiro, *Mao's War on Nature: Politics and the Environment in Revolutionary China* (New York: Cambridge University Press, 2001); Sergio Díaz-Briquets and Jorge F. Pérez-López, *Conquering Nature: The Environmental Legacy of Socialism in Cuba* (Pittsburgh: University of Pittsburgh Press, 2000).

44. Quoted in Dowie, *Conservation Refugees*, ix.

Bibliography

Archival Collections

AGA	Archivo General Agrario
AGN	Archivo General de la Nación
AHA	Archivo Histórico del Agua
AH-INAH	Archivo Histórico del Instituto Nacional Antropología e Historia Acervos, Biblioteca, Mapoteca
AHMA	Archivo Histórico Municipal Amecameca
Exconvento	Archivo Histórico del Tepoztlán, Instituto Nacional Antropología e Historia: Biblioteca Exconvento Tepoztlán
LCR	Presidente Lázaro Cárdenas del Río
OLP	Oscar Lewis Papers, University of Illinois Urbana–Champaign
RRP	University of Chicago Special Collections, Robert Redfield Papers
SARH	Secretaría de Agricultura y Recursos Hidráulicos
SEP	Secretaría de Educación Pública

Periodicals: Mexico City

Boletín de Departamento Forestal y de Caza y Pesca (Boletín DFCP)
Boletín de la Secretaria de Educación Pública
Diario Oficial
El Excélsior
Memoria y revista de la Sociedad Antonio Alzate
México Forestal

El Nacional
La Naturaleza
La Prensa
Protección a la Naturaleza
El Universal

Secondary Sources

Aboites, Luis. *El agua de la nación: Una historia política de México (1888–1946)*. Mexico City: Centro Investigaciones y Estudios Superiores Antropología Social, 1998.

Agrawal, Arun. *Environmentality: Technologies of Government and the Making of Subjects*. Durham: Duke University Press, 2005.

Aguilar Camín, Héctor, and Lorenzo Meyer. *In the Shadows of the Mexican Revolution: Contemporary Mexican History, 1910–1989*, trans. Luis Alberto Fierro. Austin: University of Texas Press, 1993.

Alanís Enciso, Fernando Saúl. *El gobierno del General Lázaro Cárdenas, 1934–1940: Una visión revisionista*. Mexico City: Colegio de San Luis, 2000.

Alanís Patiño, Emilio. "Síntesis del Ciclo de Conferencias sobre 'Los Problemas Agrícolas de México,'" *Los Problemas Agrícolas de México* 1:2 (1934): 669–739.

Albiñana, Salvador. "Entre volcanes con el Dr. Atl," *Los dos volcanes: Artes de México* 73 (2005).

Allister, Mark, ed. *Eco-Man: New Perspectives on Masculinity and Nature*. Charlottesville: University of Virginia Press, 2004.

Amend, Stephan, and Thora Amend, eds. *Espacios sin habitantes? Parques nacionales de América del Sur*. Caracas, Venezuela, and Gland, Switzerland: UICN and Nueva Sociedad, 1992.

Anderson, David G., and Eeva K. Berglund. *Ethnographies of Conservation: Environmentalism and the Distribution of Privilege*. London: Berghahn Books, 2003.

Anderson, Jon Lee. *Che Guevara: A Revolutionary Life*. New York: Grove Press, 1997.

Avila, Manuel. *Tradition and Growth: A Study of Four Mexican Villages*. Chicago: University of Chicago Press, 1969.

Bancroft, Hubert H. *A Popular History of the Mexican People*. London: Trubner, 1888.

Bantjes, Adrian. *As If Jesus Walked on Earth: Cardenismo, Sonora, and the Mexican Revolution*. Wilmington, DE: Scholarly Resources Books, 1998.

Bartra, Roger. "Los hijos de la Malinche," in *La Malinche: Sus padres y sus Hijos*, ed. Margo Glantz, 195–199. Mexico City: Taurus, 2001.

———. "Paradise Subverted: The Invention of Mexican Character," in *Primitivism and Identity in Latin America: Essays on Art, Literature, and Culture*, ed. Erik Camayd-Freixas and José Eduardo González, trans. Christopher J. Hall, 3–22. Tucson: University of Arizona Press, 2000.

Bassols Batalla, Ángel. *Recursos naturales: Climas, agua, suelos, teoria y uso*. Mexico City: Editorial Nuestro Tiempo, 1967.

Beaman, John H. "The Timberlines of Iztaccíhuatl and Popocatépetl, Mexico." *Ecology* 43:3 (1962): 377–385.

Becker, Marjorie. *Setting the Virgin on Fire: Lázaro Cárdenas, Michoacán Peasants, and the Redemption of the Mexican Revolution.* Berkeley: University of California Press, 1995.

Beezley, William H. *Judas at the Jockey Club and Other Episodes of Porfirian Mexico.* Lincoln: University of Nebraska Press, 1987.

Beezley, William H., Cheryl English Martin, and William E. French. *Rituals of Rule, Rituals of Resistance: Public Celebrations and Popular Culture in Mexico.* Wilmington, DE: Scholarly Resources, 1994.

Belshaw, Michael. *A Village Economy: Land and People of Huecorio.* New York: Columbia University Press, 1967.

Beltrán, Enrique. "Use and Conservation: Two Conflicting Principles," in *First World Conference on National Parks*, ed. Alexander B. Adams, 35–43. Washington, DC: National Park Service, 1962.

Benjamin, Thomas. *La Revolución: Mexico's Great Revolution as Memory, Myth, and History.* Austin: University of Texas Press, 2000.

Berger, Dina. *The Development of Mexico's Tourism Industry: Pyramids by Day, Martinis by Night.* New York: Palgrave Macmillan, 2006.

Binneman, Theodore, and Melanie Niemi. "'Let the Line Be Drawn Now': Wilderness, Conservation, and the Exclusion of Aboriginal People from Banff National Park in Canada." *Environmental History* 11 (2006): 724–750.

Bock, Phillip K. "Tepoztlán Reconsidered." *Journal of Latin American Lore* 6:1 (1980): 129–150.

Bonfil Batalla, Guillermo. "Nuestro patrimonio cultural: Un laberinto de significados," in *El Patrimonio Nacional de México I: Biblioteca Mexicana*, ed. Enrique Florescano, 28–56. Mexico City: Consejo Nacional Para la Cultura y las Artes, Fondo de Cultura Económica, 1997.

Bosques, Gilberto. *The National Revolutionary Party of Mexico and the Six-Year Plan.* Mexico City: National Revolutionary Party, 1937.

Boyer, Christopher R. *Becoming Campesinos: Politics, Identity, and Agrarian Struggle in Postrevolutionary Michoacán, 1920–1935.* Stanford: Stanford University, 2003.

———. "Contested Terrain: Forestry Regimes and Community Responses in Northeastern Michoacán, 1940–2000," in *The Community Forests of Mexico: Managing for Sustainable Landscapes*, ed. David Barton Bray, Leticia Merino-Pérez, and Deborah Barry, 27–48. Austin: University of Texas Press, 2005.

———. "Revolución y paternalismo ecológico: Miguel Ángel de Quevedo y la política forestal, 1926–1940." *Historia Mexicana* 57:1 (2007): 91–138.

Boyer Christopher R., and Emily Wakild. "Social Landscaping Forests of Mexico: An Environmental Interpretation of Cardenismo, 1934–1940." *Hispanic American Historical Review* (forthcoming).

Brading, David A. "Manuel Gamio and Official Indigenismo in Mexico." *Bulletin of Latin American Research* 7:1 (1988): 75–89.

Bray, David Barton, Leticia Merino-Pérez, and Deborah Barry, eds. *The Community Forests of Mexico: Managing for Sustainable Landscapes.* Austin: University of Texas Press, 2005.

Breunig, Lydia A. "Conservation in Context: Establishing Natural Protected Areas during Mexico's Neoliberal Reformation." PhD diss. University of Arizona, 2006.

Brockington, Dan. *Fortress Conservation: The Preservation of the Mkomazi Game Preserve.* Bloomington: Indiana University Press, 2002.

Brooks, T. M., et al. "Global Biodiversity Conservation Priorities." *Science* 313 (2006): 58–61.

Brussard, Peter. "The Current Status of Conservation Biology." *Bulletin of the Ecological Society of America* 66:1 (1985): 9–11.

Burdick, John. "Brazil's Black Consciousness Movement." *NACLA: Report on the Americas* 25:4 (1992): 23–27.

Burns, Ken. *The National Parks: America's Best Idea.* PBS, 2009.

Büssing, Arndt, ed. *Mistletoe: The Genus Viscum.* Amsterdam: Harwood Academic, 2000.

Calder, Malcolm, and Meter Bernhardt, eds. *The Biology of Mistletoes.* Sydney, Australia: Academic Press, 1983.

Calderón de la Barca, Frances. *Life in Mexico.* London: Everyman's Library, 1970.

Caldicott, J. Baird, and Michael P. Nelson. *The Great New Wilderness Debate.* Athens: University of Georgia Press, 1998.

Cárdenas, Lázaro. *Apuntes.* Vol. 1. Mexico City: Universidad Nacional Autónoma de México, Dirección General de Publicaciones, 1972.

Carey, Mark. "Latin American Environmental History: Current Trends, Interdisciplinary Insights, and Future Directions." *Environmental History* 14:2 (2009): 221–252.

Carruthers, David V., ed. *Environmental Justice in Latin America: Problems, Promise and Practice.* Cambridge, MA: MIT Press, 2008.

Carruthers, Jane. *Kruger National Park: A Social and Political History.* Pietermaritzburg, South Africa: University of Natal Press, 1995.

Castro Herrera, Guillermo. "The Environmental Crisis and the Tasks of History in Latin America." *Environment and History* 3:1 (1997): 1–18.

Challenger, Anthony. *Utilización y conservación de los ecosistemas terrestres de México: Pasado, presente, y futuro.* Mexico City: CONABIO, UNAM, 1998.

Cockcroft, James D. *Intellectual Precursors of the Mexican Revolution, 1900–1913.* Austin: University of Texas Press, 1968.

Cole, Luke W., and Sheila R. Foster. *From the Ground Up: Environmental Racism and the Rise of the Environmental Justice Movement.* New York: New York University Press, 2001.

Conkling, Howard. *Mexico and the Mexicans.* New York: Taintor Brothers Merrill, 1883.

Cope, R. Douglas. *The Limits of Racial Domination: Plebian Society in Colonial Mexico City, 1660–1720.* Madison: University of Wisconsin Press, 1994.

Cothran, Dan A. "Budgetary Secrecy and Policy Strategy: Mexico under Cárdenas." *Estudios Mexicanos/Mexican Studies* 2:1 (Winter 1986): 35–58.

Craib, Raymond. *Cartographic Mexico: A History of State Fixations and Fugitive Landscapes.* Durham: Duke University Press, 2004.

Craig, Ann L. *The First Agraristas: An Oral History of Mexican Agrarian Reform.* Berkeley: University of California Press, 1983.

Cronon, William. "The Trouble with Wilderness; or, Getting Back to the Wrong Nature," in *Uncommon Ground: Rethinking the Human Place in Nature*, ed. William Cronon, 69–90. New York: W. W. Norton, 1995.

Crowe, Beryl L. "The Tragedy of the Commons Revisited," in *Managing the Commons*, ed. Garrett Hardin and John Baden, 56–72 San Francisco: W. H. Freeman, 1977.

Davis, Diana K. *Resurrecting the Granaries of Rome: Environmental History and French Colonial Expansion in North Africa*. Athens: Ohio University Press, 2007.

Dawson, Alexander. *Indian and Nation in Revolutionary Mexico*. Tucson: University of Arizona Press, 2004.

Dean, Warren. "The Tasks of Latin American Environmental History," in *Changing Tropical Forests: Historical Perspectives on Today's Challenges in Central and South America*, ed. Harold K. Steen and Richard P. Tucker, 5–15. Durham: Forest History Society, 1992.

DeJanvry, Alain. *The Agrarian Question and Reformism in Latin America*. Baltimore: Johns Hopkins University Press, 1981.

Denevan, William. "The Pristine Myth: The Landscape of the Americas in 1492." *Annals of the American Association of Geographers* 82:3 (1992): 369–385.

Díaz-Briquets, Sergio, and Jorge F. Pérez-López. *Conquering Nature: The Environmental Legacy of Socialism in Cuba*. Pittsburgh: University of Pittsburgh Press, 2000.

Díaz del Castillo, Bernal. *Conquest of New Spain*. Trans. J. M. Cohen. New York: Penguin, 1963.

Di Chiro, Giovanna. "Beyond Ecoliberal 'Common Futures': Environmental Justice, Toxic Touring, and a Transcommunal Politics of Place," in *Race, Nature, and the Politics of Difference*, ed. Donald S. Moore, Jake Kosek, and Anand Pandian, 204–232. Durham: Duke University Press, 2003.

Donnet, Beatriz. *Leyendas del Popo y algo más*. Mexico City: Lectorum, 1999.

Dorner, Peter. *Latin American Land Reform in Theory and Practice*. Madison: University of Wisconsin Press, 1992.

Dowie, Mark. *Conservation Refugees: The Hundred-Year Conflict between Global Conservation and Native Peoples*. Cambridge, MA: MIT Press, 2009.

Drummond, José Augusto. *Devastação e preservação ambiental: Os parques nacionais do Estado do Rio de Janeiro*. Rio de Janeiro: Editora da Universidade Federal Fluminense, 1997.

———. "The Garden in the Machine: Rio de Janeiro's Tijuca Forest." *Environmental History* 1:1 (1996): 83–104.

Dubernard Chauveau, Juan. *Apuntes para la historia de Tepoztlán*. Cuernavaca, Morelos, Mexico City: Impresores de Morelos, 1983.

Dudley, Nigel. *Guidelines for Applying Protected Area Management Categories*. Gland, Switzerland: IUCN, 2008.

Dunlap, Riley E., and Angela G. Mertig. *American Environmentalism: The U.S. Environmental Movement, 1970–1990*. London: Taylor & Francis, 1992.

Dwyer, John. *Agrarian Dispute: The Expropriation of American-Owned Rural Land in Postrevolutionary Mexico*. Durham: Duke University Press, 2008.

Elliott, Hugh. *Second World Conference on National Parks*. Switzerland: IUCN, 1974.

Escobar, José U. *Las tribus de exploradores mexicanos*. Mexico City: SEP, 1929.

Evans, Sterling. *The Green Republic: A Conservation History of Costa Rica*. Austin: University of Texas Press, 1999.

———. Historiografía Verde: Estado de la historia sobre la conservación de la naturaleza en América Latina," in *Naturaleza en declive: Miradas a la historia ambiental de América Latina y el Caribe*, ed. Reinaldo Funes Monzote, 81–96. Valencia, Spain: Centro Francisco Tomás y Valiente UNED Alzira-Valencia/Fundación Instituto de Historia Social, 2008.

Ezcurra, Ezequiel, Marisa Mazari-Hiriart, Irene Pisanty, and Adrián Guillermo Aguilar. *The Basin of Mexico: Critical Environmental Issues and Sustainability.* Tokyo: United Nations University Press, 1999.

Fallaw, Ben. *Cárdenas Compromised: The Failure of Reform in Postrevolutionary Yucatán.* Durham: Duke University Press, 2004.

Fernández, Justino. *Arte moderno y contemporáneo de México: José María Velasco.* Toluca, Mexico City: Monografías de Arte, 1976.

Florescano, Enrique. "El patrimonio nacional: Valores, usos, estudio y difusión," in *El Patrimonio Nacional de México I: Biblioteca Mexicana*, ed. Enrique Florescano, 15–27. Mexico City: CONACULTA, Fondo de Cultura Económica, 1997.

Ford, Caroline. "Reforestation, Landscape Conservation, and the Anxieties of Empire in French Colonial Algeria." *American Historical Review* 113 (2008): 341–362.

Foresta, Ronald. *America's National Parks and Their Keepers.* Washington, DC: Resources for the Future and Johns Hopkins Press, 1984.

Foster, George M. *Empire's Children: People of Tzintzuntzan.* Institute for Social Anthropology Publication No. 6. Washington, DC: Smithsonian Institution, 1948.

———. *Tzinzuntzan: Mexican Peasants in a Changing World.* Boston: Little, Brown, 1967.

Franco, Jean. *Plotting Women: Gender and Representation in Mexico.* New York: Columbia University Press, 1989.

Franco, José Luiz de Andrade, and José Augusto Drummond. "Wilderness and the Brazilian Mind (I): Nation and Nature in Brazil from the 1920s to the 1940s." *Environmental History* 13:4 (2008): 724–750.

———. "Wilderness and the Brazilian Mind (II): The First Brazilian Conference on Nature Protection (Rio de Janeiro, 1934)." *Environmental History* 14:1 (2009): 82–102.

Franz, Carl. *People's Guide to Mexico: Wherever You Go . . . There You Are.* 11th ed. Santa Fe: John Muir, [1972] 1998.

Friedrich, Paul. *Agrarian Revolt in a Mexican Village.* Chicago: University of Chicago Press, 1970.

Fuentes, Carlos. *Myself with Others: Selected Essays.* New York: Farrar, Straus & Giroux, 1981.

———. *Where the Air Is Clear.* New York: Farrar, Straus & Giroux, 1960.

Gadgil, Madhav, and Ramachandra Guha. *The Use and Abuse of Nature.* New Delhi: Oxford University Press, 2000.

Gallo Sarlat, Joáquin. *Tepoztlán vida y color.* Mexico City: Editorial Libros de México, 1977.

Gamio, Manuel. *Forjando patria.* Mexico City: Editorial Porrúa, [1916] 1982.

Gamiz, Abel. *Geografía Nacional de México.* Mexico City: Compañía Nacional Editora Aguilas, S.A., 1926.

García Canclini, Néstor. "El patrimonio cultural de México y la construcción imaginaria de lo nacional," in *El Patrimonio Nacional de México I: Biblioteca Mexicana*, ed. Enrique Florescano, 15–27. Mexico City: CONACULTA, Fondo de Cultura Económica, 1997.

García Martínez, ed. Bernardo. "Regiones y paisajes de la geografía mexicana," in *Historia general de México*, 25–91. Mexico City: Colegio de México, Centro Estudios Históricos, 2000.

Gil, Carlos. *Life in Provincial Mexico: National and Regional History as Seen from Mascota, Jalisco, 1867–1972*. Los Angeles: UCLA Latin American Center, 1983.

Gill, Tom. *Land Hunger in Mexico*. Washington, DC: Charles Lathrop Pack Forestry Foundation, 1951.

Gilly, Adolfo. *La revolución interrumpida*. Mexico City: Ediciones El Caballito, 1971.

———. *El Cárdenismo: Una utopía Mexicana*. Mexico City: Cal y Arena, 1994.

Gledhill, John. *Casi Nada: A Study of Agrarian Reform in the Homeland of Cardenismo*. Austin: Institute for Meso-American Studies, 1991.

Gómez-Pompa, Arturo, and Andrea Kaus. "From Pre-Hispanic to Future Conservation Alternatives: Lessons from Mexico." *Proceedings of the National Academy of Sciences of the United States of America*. 96:11 (1999): 5982–5986.

———. "Taming the Wilderness Myth." *BioScience* 42:4 (1992): 271–279.

González, Ambrosio, and Víctor Manuel Sánchez L. *Los parques nacionales de México: Situación actual y problemas*. Mexico City: Instituto Mexicano de Recursos Naturales Renovables, 1961.

González, Rodolfo Huerta. "Transformación del paisaje: El caso de la fábrica de San Rafael, estado de México, 1890–1934," in *Tierra, agua, y bosques: Historia y medio ambiente en el México central*, ed. Alejandro Tortolero Villaseñor, 283–315. Mexico City: Centre Français d'études Mexicaines et Centraméricaines, Instituto Mora, Potrerillos Editores, Universidad de Guadalajara, 1996.

González Navarro, Moisés. "La obra social de Lázaro Cárdenas." *Historia Mexicana* 34:2 (1984): 353–374.

———. "Las ideas raciales de los científicos, 1890–1910." *Historia Mexicana* 37:4 (1988): 565–583.

González y González, Luis. *Pueblo en vilo: Microhistoria de San José de Gracia*. Mexico City: El Colegio de México, 1972.

Gottlieb, Robert. *Forcing the Spring: The Transformation of the American Environmental Movement*. Washington, DC: Island Press, 1994.

Gudiño, María Rosa, and Guillermo Palacios. "Peticiones de tierras y estrategias discursivas campesinos: Procesos, contenidos y problemas metodológicos," in *Estudios campesinos en el Archivo General Agrario*, ed. Antonio Escobar Ohmstede et al. 75–118. Mexico City: Centro de Investigaciones y Estudios Superiores en Antropología Social, 1998.

Guha, Ramachandra. *Environmentalism: A Global History*. New York: Longman: 1999.

———. "Radical American Environmentalism and Wilderness Preservation: A Third World Critique." *Environmental Ethics* 11 (1989): 71–83.

Haber, Stephen. *Industry and Underdevelopment: The Industrialization of Mexico, 1890–1940*. Stanford: Stanford University Press, 1989.

Haber, Stephen, Armando Razo, and Noel Maurer. *The Politics of Property Rights: Political Instability, Credible Commitments, and Economic Growth in Mexico, 1876–1929*. Cambridge: Cambridge University Press, 2003.

Haenn, Nora. *Fields of Power, Forests of Discontent: Culture, Conservation, and the State in Mexico*. Tucson: University of Arizona Press, 2005.

Hale, Charles A. "The Civil Law Tradition and Constitutionalism in Twentieth-Century Mexico: The Legacy of Emilio Rabasa." *Law and History Review* 18: 2 (2000): 257–279.

Hamilton, Nora. "Mexico: The Limits of State Autonomy." *Latin American Perspectives* 2:2 (1975): 81–108.

Harmon, David. "Cultural Diversity, Human Subsistence, and the National Park Ideal." *Environmental Ethics* 9 (1987): 147–158.

Hardin, Garrett. "The Tragedy of the Commons." *Science* 162 (1968): 1243–1248.

Hart, John M. *Revolutionary Mexico: The Coming and Process of the Mexican Revolution.* Berkeley: University of California Press, 1987.

Hart, Paul. *Bitter Harvest: The Social Transformation of Morelos, Mexico and the Origins of the Zapatista Rebellion, 1840–1910.* Albuquerque: University of New Mexico Press, 2007.

Hays, Samuel. *Conservation and the Gospel of Efficiency: The Progressive Conservation Movement, 1890–1920.* Cambridge, MA: Harvard University Press, 1959.

Heacox, Kim. *An American Idea: The Making of the National Parks.* Washington, DC: National Geographic Society, 2001.

Hecht, Susana, and Alexander Cockburn. *The Fate of the Forest: Developers, Destroyers, and Defenders of the Amazon.* New York: Harper Perennial, 1990.

Henderson, Timothy. *The Worm in the Wheat: Rosalie Evans and Agrarian Struggle in the Puebla-Tlaxcala Valley of Mexico, 1906–1927.* Durham: Duke University, 1998.

Hernández, Sonia. "Malinche in Cross-Border Historical Memory," in *José Limón and La Malinche: The Dancer and the Dance*, ed. Patricia Seed, 95–110. Austin: University of Texas Press, 2008.

Hernández Chávez, Alicia. *Anenecuilco: Memória y vida de un pueblo.* Mexico City: El Colegio de México, 1991.

Herzog, Jesús Silva. *El agrarismo mexicano y la reforma agraria: Exposición y crítica.* Mexico City: Fondo de Cultura Económica, 1964.

Holdgate, Martin. *The Green Web.* London: Earthscan, 1999.

Holdridge, Leslie R. "Determination of World Plant Formations from Simple Climatic Data." *Science* 105:2727 (1947): 367–368.

Honey, Martha. *Ecotourism and Sustainable Development: Who Owns Paradise?* Washington, DC: Island Press, 1999.

Howarth, O. H. "Popocatepetl, and the Volcanoes of the Valley of Mexico." *Geographic Journal* 8:2 (1896): 137–150.

Humboldt, Alexander von. *The Political Essay on New Spain.* Abridged ed. Trans. John Black. Norman: University of Oklahoma Press [Alfred A. Knopf], 1988.

Instituto Nacional de Antropología y Historia and CONACULTA. *El mito de dos volcanes: Popocatépetl and Iztaccíhuatl.* Mexico City: CONACULTA, 2005.

Instituto Nacional para la Educación de Adultos. *Ecología del Estado de Tlaxcala: Región Malinche.* Mexico City: Secretaría de la Educación Pública, 1995.

International Union for Conservation of Nature. *First World Conference on National Parks.* Washington, DC: National Park Service, 1962.

Iturriaga, José N. *El Popocatépetl, ayer y hoy: "Don Gregorio" en las crónicas de extranjeros, desde el siglo XVI hasta la actualidad.* Mexico City: Editorial Diana, 1997.

Jacobs, Nancy J. *Environment, Power, and Injustice: A South African History.* Cambridge: Cambridge University Press, 2003.

Jacoby, Karl. *Crimes against Nature: Squatters, Poachers, Thieves and the Hidden History of American Conservation.* Berkeley: University of California Press, 2001.

Joseph, Gilbert, and Daniel Nugent, eds. *Everyday Forms of State Formation: Revolution and the Negotiation of Rule in Modern Mexico.* Durham: Duke University, 1994.

Juárez Flores, José Juan. "Malintzin Matlalcuéyetl: Bosques, alumbrado público y conflicto social en la desarticulación de un etorno ecológico (Puebla-Tlaxcala, 1760–1870)." MA thesis, Universidad Autónoma Metropolitana, Iztapalapa, January 2005.

Judd, Richard W. *Common Lands, Common People: The Origins of Conservation in Northern New England.* Cambridge: Harvard University Press, 1997.

Kellogg, Susan. "Marina, Malinche, Malintzin: Nahua Women and the Spanish Conquest," in *José Limón and La Malinche: The Dancer and the Dance,* ed. Patricia Seed, 79–94. Austin: University of Texas Press, 2008.

Kiddle, Amelia M., and María L. O. Muñoz, *Populism in Twentieth Century Mexico: The Presidencies of Lázaro Cárdenas and Luis Echeverría.* Tucson: University of Arizona Press, 2010.

Klooster, Dan. "Campesinos and Mexican Forestry Policy during the Twentieth Century." *Latin American Research Review* 38:2 (2003): 94–126.

Knight, Alan. "Cardenismo: Juggernaut or Jalopy?" *Journal of Latin American Studies* 26:1 (1994): 73–107.

———. "Land and Society in Revolutionary Mexico: The Destruction of the Great Haciendas." *Mexican Studies/Estudios Mexicanos* 7:1 (1991): 73–104.

———. *The Mexican Revolution.* 2 vols. Cambridge: Cambridge University Press, 1986.

———. "Racism, Revolution, and *Indigenismo*: Mexico, 1910–1940," in *The Idea of Race in Latin America, 1870–1940,* ed. Richard Graham, 71–114. Austin: University of Texas Press, 1990.

Knox, Thomas W. *The Boy Travellers in Mexico.* New York: Harper & Brothers, 1890.

Konrad, Herman. "Tropical Forest Policy and Practice during the Mexican Porfiriato, 1876–1910," in *Changing Tropical Forests: Historical Perspectives on Today's Challenges in Central and South America,* ed. Harold K. Steen and Richard P. Tucker, 123–143. Durham: Forest History Society, 1992.

Kourí, Emilio. "Interpreting the Expropriation of Indian Pueblo Lands in Porfiran Mexico: The Unexamined Legacies of Andres Molina Enriquez." *Hispanic American Historical Review* 82:1 (2002) 69–117.

Kramer, R. C., Carol van Schaik, and J. Johnson, eds. *Last Stand: Protected Areas and the Defense of Tropical Biodiversity.* Oxford: Oxford University Press, 1997.

Krech, Shepard, III. *The Ecological Indian: Myth and History.* New York: W. W. Norton, 1999.

Lanyon, Anne. *Malinche's Conquest.* St. Leonards, Australia: Allen & Unwin, 1999.

Leach, Melissa, and James Fairhead. "Challenging Neo-Malthusian Deforestation Analyses in West Africa's Dynamic Forest Landscapes." *Population and Development Review* 26:1 (2000): 17–43.

Lenz, Hans. *Historia del papel en México y cosas relacionadas, 1525–1950.* Mexico City: Miguel Ángel Porrúa, 1990.

Lewis, James G. *The Forest Service and the Greatest Good: A Centennial History.* Durham: Forest History Society, 2005.

Lewis, Oscar. *The Children of Sánchez: Autobiography of a Mexican Family*. New York: Vintage Books, [1969] 1979.

——. *Five Families: Mexican Case Studies in the Culture of Poverty*. New York: Basic Books, [1963] 1975.

——. *Life in a Mexican Village: Tepoztlán Restudied*. Urbana: University of Illinois Press, 1951.

——. *Pedro Martínez: A Mexican Peasant and His Family*. New York: Random House, 1964.

——. *Tepoztlán: Village in Mexico*. New York: Holt, Rinehart and Winston, 1960.

Lewis, Stephen. *The Ambivalent Revolution: Forging State and Nation in Chiapas, 1910–1945*. Albuquerque: University of New Mexico Press, 2005.

Lomnitz, Claudio. *Evolución de una sociedad rural*. Mexico City: Fondo de Cultura Económica, 1982.

López González, Valentín. *El Morelos posrevolucionario, 1919–1930: Fuentes documentales del estado de Morelos*. Cuernavaca, Morelos, Mexico City: Cuadernos Históricos Morelenses, 2002.

Lovejoy, Thomas. "The Obligations of a Biologist." *Conservation Biology* 3:4 (1989): 329–330.

MacArthur, Robert H., and Edward O. Wilson. *The Theory of Island Biogeography*. Princeton: Princeton University Press, 1967.

Markiewicz, Dana. *The Mexican Revolution and the Limits of Agrarian Reform, 1915–1946*. Boulder, CO: Lynne Reinner, 1993.

Martin, JoAnn. *Tepoztlán and the Transformation of the Mexican State: The Politics of Loose Connections*. Tucson: University of Arizona Press, 2005.

Martinez-Alier, Joan. "Ecology and the Poor: A Neglected Dimension of Latin American History." *Journal of Latin American Studies* 23 (1991): 621–639.

Mathews, Andrew S. "Unlikely Alliances: Encounters between State Science, Nature Spirits, and Indigenous Industrial Forestry in Mexico, 1926–2008." *Current Anthropology* 50:1 (2009): 75–101.

Meine, Curt, Michael Soulé, and Reed F. Noss. "A Mission Driven Discipline: The Growth of Conservation Biology." *Conservation Biology* 20:3 (2006): 331–351.

Melgareio, A. "The Greatest Volcanoes of Mexico." *National Geographic Magazine* 21:9 (1910): 741–760.

Meyer, Jean. *The Cristero Rebellion: The Mexican People between Church and State 1926–1929*. Cambridge: Cambridge University Press, 1976.

Meyer, Judith. "Re-packing Yellowstone: The American National Park in Global Perspective." Paper presented at the conference Civilizing Nature: National Parks in Transnational Historical Perspective, German Historical Institute, June 2008.

Meyers, William K. *Forge of Progress, Crucible of Revolt: Origins of the Mexican Revolution in La Comarca Lagunera, 1880–1911*. Albuquerque: University of New Mexico Press, 1994.

Mitchell, Stephanie. *The Women's Revolution in Mexico, 1910–1953*. Lanham, MD: Rowman and Littlefield, 2006.

Molina Enriquez, Andrés. *Los grandes problemas nacionales*. Mexico City, Imprenta de A. Carranza e hijos, 1909.

Monsivais, Carlos. "'Just over That Hill': Notes on Centralism and Regional Cultures," in *Mexico's Regions: Comparative History and Development*, ed. Eric Van Young, 207–229. La Jolla: University of California, San Diego, 1992.

Moya López, Laura Angélica. *La nación como organismo: México, su evolución social, 1900–1902*. Mexico City: Universidad Autónoma Metropolitana Azcapotzalco, 2003.

Muir, John. *Our National Parks*. Boston: Houghton Mifflin and Company, 1901.

Munguía Espitia, Jorge, and Margarita Castellanos Ribot. "Informe sobre la opinión de la población de Tepoztlán en torno al conflicto suscitado a raíz del proyecto de construcción del club de golf 'El Tepozteco.'" Xochimilco, Mexico: Universidad Autónoma Metropolitana, n.d.

Nash, Roderick. *Wilderness and the American Mind*. New Haven: Yale University Press, 1967.

Neumann, Roderick. *Imposing Wilderness: Struggles over Livelihood and Nature Preservation in Africa*. Berkeley: University of California Press, 1998.

———. "Nature-State-Territory: Toward a Critical Theorization of Conservation Enclosures," in *Liberation Ecologies: Environment, Development, Social Movements*, ed. Richard Peet and Michael Watts, 195–217. New York: Routledge, 2004.

Niemeyer, E. V., Jr. *Revolution at Querétaro: The Mexican Constitutional Convention of 1916–1917*. Austin: University of Texas Press, 1974.

Noble, John, et al. *Lonely Planet Mexico*, 9th ed. China: Bookmaker International, 2004.

Nugent, Daniel. *Spent Cartridges of Revolution: An Anthropological History of Namiquipa, Chihuahua*. Chicago: University of Chicago Press, 1993.

Olcott, Jocelyn. *Revolutionary Women in Postrevolutionary Mexico*. Durham: Duke University Press, 2005.

Olcott, Jocelyn, Mary Kay Vaughn, and Gabriela Cano. *Sex in Revolution: Gender, Politics, and Power in Modern Mexico*. Durham: Duke University Press, 2007.

Olvera Ach, Helios. "Anteproyecto para la construcción de un teleférico en el Parque Nacional Ixtaccihuatl-Popocatépetl." MA thesis, Universidad Nacional Autónoma de México, 1966.

Olwig, Karen Fog, and Kenneth Olwig. "Underdevelopment and the Development of 'Natural' Park Ideology." *Antipode* 11:2 (1979): 16–25.

O'Malley, Ilene V. *The Myth of the Revolution: Hero Cults and the Institutionalization of the Mexican State, 1920–1940*. New York: Greenwood Press, 1986.

Orlove, Benjamin S. *Lines in the Water: Nature and Culture at Lake Titicaca*. Berkeley: University of California Press, 2002.

Ortiz Monasterio, Fernando. *Tierra profanada: Historia ambiental de México*. Mexico City: INAH and Secretaría de Desarrollo Urbano y Ecología, 1987.

Ostrom, Elinor. "Collective Action and the Tragedy of the Commons," in *Managing the Commons*, ed. Garrett Hardin and John Baden, 173–181. San Francisco: W. H. Freeman, 1977.

Packard, A. S. "Ascent of the Volcano of Popocatepetl." *American Naturalist* 20:2 (1886): 109–123.

Padua, José. *Um sopro de destruição: pensamento político e crítica ambiental no brasil excravista (1786–1888)*. Rio de Janeiro: Jorge Zahar, 2002.

Palacios, Guillermo. *La pluma y el arado: Los intelectuales pedagogos y la construcción sociocultural del "problema campesino" en México, 1932–1934*. Mexico City: El Colegio de México Centro de Investigación y Docencia Económicas, 1999.

Pareyon Axpeitia, Armando R. *Cárdenas ante el mundo: Defensor de la república espanola, eitiopia, finlandia, africa, luchas populares de asia*. Mexico City: La Prensa, 1971.

Partido Nacional Revolucionario. *Memoria, Segunda Convención Nacional del Partido Nacional Revolucionario.* Mexico City: PNR, 1934.

———. *Plan Sexenal del P.N.R.* Mexico City: 1934.

Paz, Octavio. *The Labyrinth of Solitude.* Trans. Lysander Kemp. New York: Grove, 1961.

Peluso, Nancy Lee. *Rich Forests, Poor People: Resource Control and Resistance in Java.* Berkeley: University of California Press, 1992.

Pérez Bertruy, Ramona Isabel. "La constitución de paseos y jardines públicos modernos en la ciudad de México durante el Porfiriato: Una experiencia social," in *Los espacios públicos de la ciudad siglos XVII y XIX,* ed. Carlos Aguirre Anaya, Marcela Cávalas, and María Amparo Pos, 314–334. Mexico City: Casa Juan Pablos, 2002.

———. "Parques y jardines públicos de la Ciudad de México, 1881–1911." PhD diss., Colegio de México, 2003.

Pérez-Torres, Rafael. *Movements in Chicano Poetry: Against Myths, against Margins.* Cambridge: Cambridge University Press, 1995.

Perfecto, Ivette, John Vandermeer, and Angus Wright. *Nature's Matrix: Linking Agriculture, Conservation, and Food Sovereignty.* London: Earthscan, 2009.

Perló Cohen, Manuel. *El paradigma porfiriano: Historia del desague del Valle de México.* Mexico City: Instituto de Investigaciones Sociales, Miguel Ángel Porrúa, 1999.

Pinchot, Gifford. *Breaking New Ground.* Washington, DC: Island Press, 1998.

Porter, Susie. *Working Women in Mexico City: Public Discourses and Material Conditions, 1879–1931.* Tucson: University of Arizona Press, 2003.

Poole, Deborah. *Vision, Race, Modernity: A Visual Economy of the Andean World.* Princeton: Princeton University Press, 1997.

Prado, Julio. *El apóstol del árbol.* Vol. 1. Mexico City: Emilio Pardo e Hijos, Legión de Divulgación Cultural "Hijos del estado de Michoacán," 1936.

Pratt, Mary Louise. *Imperial Eyes: Travel Writing and Transculturation.* London: Routledge, 1992.

Pyne, Stephen J. *Fire in America: A Cultural History of Wildland and Rural Fire.* Seattle: University of Washington Press, 1997.

———. *World Fire: The Culture of Fire on Earth.* Seattle: University of Washington Press, 1995.

Quevedo, Miguel Ángel de. "Espacios libres y reservas forestales de las ciudades: Su adaptación á jardines, parques y lugares de juego, aplicación á la Ciudad de México." Mexico City: Gomar y Busson, 1911.

———. "Labor activo del Departamento Forestal de México." *Boletín de la Unión Panamericana,* Washington, DC, 1939.

———. *Relato de mi vida.* Mexico City: n.p., 1942.

Raat, William D. "Ideas and Society in Don Porfirio's Mexico." *Americas* 30:1 (1973): 32–53.

Radding, Cynthia. *Wandering Peoples: Colonialism, Ethnic Spaces, and Ecological Frontiers in Northwestern Mexico, 1700–1850.* Durham: Duke University, 1997.

Radkau, Joachim. *Nature and Power: A Global History of the Environment.* Trans. Thomas Dunlap. Cambridge: Cambridge University Press, 2008.

Ramírez Rancaño, Mario. *El sistema de haciendas en Tlaxcala.* Mexico City: CONACULTA, 1990.

Redfield, Robert. *Tepoztlán, a Mexican Village: A Study of Folk Life*. Chicago: University of Chicago Press, 1930.

Restall, Matthew. *Seven Myths of the Spanish Conquest*. Oxford: Oxford University Press, 2004.

Restrepo, Iván, and Salamón Eckstein. *La agricultura colectiva en México: La experiencia de La Laguna*. Mexico City: Siglo XXI, 1971.

Rigdon, Susan M. *The Culture Facade: Art, Science, and Politics in the Work of Oscar Lewis*. Urbana-Champaign: University of Illinois Press, 1988.

Rochfort, Desmond. *Mexican Muralists: Orozco, Rivera, Siqueiros*. San Francisco: Chronicle Books, 1993.

Rodfeldt, David. *Atencingo: The Politics of Agrarian Struggle in a Mexican Ejido*. Stanford: Stanford University Press, 1973.

Rome, Adam. "Give Earth a Chance: The Environmental Movement and the Sixties." *Journal of American History* 90:2 (2003): 535–554.

Rosas, María. *Tepoztlán: Crónica de desacatos y resistencia*. Mexico City: ERA, 1997.

Roura, Alma Lilia. *Dr. Atl: Paisaje de hielo y fuego*. Mexico City: Círculo de Arte, 1990.

Rueda Esquibel, Catrióna. "Velvet Malinche: Fantasies of 'The' Aztec Princesa in the Chicana/o Sexual Imagination," in *Velvet Barrios: Popular Cultura & Chicana/o Sexualities*, ed. Alicia Gaspar de Alba, 295–307. New York: Palgrave Macmillan, 2003.

Ruedas de la Serna, Jorge. *Los orígenes de la visión paradisiaca de la naturaleza Mexicana*. Mexico City: Universidad Nacional Autónoma de México, Colección Posgrado, 1987.

Ruiz Velasco, Felipe. "Bosques y manantiales del estado de Morelos y apéndice sintético sobre su potencialidad agrícola e industrial," in *Fuentes Geográficas y Estadísticas del Estado de Morelos*, ed. Valentín López González, 11–37. Cuernavaca, Morelos, Mexico City: Cuadernos Históricos Morelenses, [1925] 2004.

Runte, Alfred. *National Parks: The American Experience*. Lincoln: University of Nebraska Press, 1979.

Ruzo, Daniel. *El valle sagrado de Tepoztlán*. Mexico City: Editorial Posada, 1976.

Sánchez Arteche, Alfonso. *Velasco íntimo y legendario*. Toluca, Mexico City: Instituto Mexiquense de Cultura, 1992.

Sánchez Ascencio, Pilar. *Antología Histórica de Tepoztlán*. Acapatzingo, Morelos, Mexico: Museo y centro de documentación histórica, Ex-convento de Tepoztlán, 1998.

Sanderson, Susan W. *Land Reform in Mexico, 1910–1980*. Orlando, FL: Academic Press, 1984.

Santiago, Myrna I. *The Ecology of Oil: Environment, Labor, and the Mexican Revolution, 1900–1938*. Cambridge: Cambridge University Press, 2006.

Sax, Joseph. *Mountains without Handrails: Reflections on the National Parks*. Ann Arbor: University of Michigan Press, 1980.

Scharff, Virginia J., ed. *Seeing Nature through Gender*. Lawrence: University of Kansas Press, 2003.

Schrepfer, Susan R. *Nature's Altars: Mountains, Gender, and American Environmentalism*. Lawrence: University Press of Kansas, 2005.

Schwartz, Katrina Z. S. *Nature and National Identity after Communism: Globalizing the Ethnoscape*. Pittsburgh: University of Pittsburgh Press, 2006.

Scott, James C. *Seeing Like a State: How Certain Schemes to Improve the Human Condition Have Failed*. New Haven: Yale University Press, 1998.

Secretaría de Agricultura y Fomento. *Ley forestal y su reglamento*. Mexico City: Talleres Gráficos de la Secretaría de Agricultura y Fomento, 1930.

Secretaría de Hacienda y Crédito Público. *El Problema Actual de la Industria Papelera en México*. Mexico City: Secretaría de Hacienda, 1936.

Sellars, Richard West. "The Rise and Decline of Ecological Attitudes in National Park Management, 1929–1940, Part I." *George Wright Forum* 10:1 (1993):55–76.

Shapiro, Judith. *Mao's War on Nature: Politics and the Environment in Revolutionary China*. New York: Cambridge University Press, 2001.

Shelhas, John. "The USA National Parks in International Perspective: Have We Learned the Wrong Lesson?" *Environmental Conservation* 28 (2001): 300–304.

Sherman, John. "Reassessing Cardenismo: The Mexican Right and the Failure of a Revolutionary Regime, 1934–1940." *The Americas* 54:3 (1998): 357–378.

Simon, Joel. *Endangered Mexico: An Environment on the Edge*. San Francisco: Sierra Club Books, 1997.

Simonian, Lane. *Defending the Land of the Jaguar: A History of Conservation in Mexico*. Austin: University of Texas Press, 1995.

Sinkin, Richard N. *The Mexican Reform 1855–1876: A Study in Liberal Nation-Building*. Austin: University of Texas Press, 1979.

Slater, Candace, ed. *In Search of the Rain Forest*. Durham: Duke University Press, 2003.

Smith, Stephanie J. *Gender and the Mexican Revolution: Yucatan Women and the Realities of Patriarchy*. Chapel Hill: University of North Carolina Press, 2009.

Smith, T. Lynn, ed. *Agrarian Reform in Latin America*. New York: Alfred A. Knopf, 1965.

Soulé, Michael E., ed. *Conservation Biology: The Science of Scarcity and Diversity*. Sunderland, MA: Sinauer Associates, 1986.

Spence, Mark. *Dispossessing the Wilderness: Indian Removal and the Making of the National Parks*. New York: Oxford University Press, 1999.

Steinbeck, John. *The Forgotten Village*. New York: Viking, 1941.

Suárez Cortés, Blanca E. "Las fábricas de papel de San Rafael y Anexas S.A. y un viejo problema: La contaminación del río Tlalmanalco." *Boletín del Archivo Histórico del Agua* 2:6 (1996): 12–14.

Sutter, Paul S. "When Environmental Traditions Collide: Ramachandra Guha's *The Unquiet Woods* and U.S. Environmental History." *Environmental History* 14 (2009): 543–550.

Tannenbaum, Frank. *The Mexican Agrarian Revolution*. New York: Macmillan, 1929.

Terborgh, John. *Requiem for Nature*. Washington, DC: Island Press, 1999.

Terborgh, John, and Carel Van Schaik. "Why the World Needs Parks," in *Making Parks Work: Strategies for Preserving Tropical Nature*, ed. John Terborgh, Carel van Schaik, Lisa Davenport, and Madhu Rao, 3–14. Washington, DC: Island Press, 2002.

Terry, T. Philip. *Terry's Mexico: Handbook for Travellers*. London: Gay & Hancock, 1909.

Thiesenhusen, William. *Broken Promises: Agrarian Reform and the Latin American Campesino*. Boulder, CO: Westview Press, 1995.

Toledo, Víctor Manuel. "Modernidad y ecología: La nueva crisis planetaria," in *Sociedad y medio ambiente en México*, ed. Gustavo López Castro. Mexico City: El Colegio de Michoacán, 1997.

——. *Naturaleza, producción, cultura: Ensayos de ecología política.* Mexico City: Universidad Veracruzana, 1989.

Tortolero Villaseñor, Alejandro, ed. *Entre lagos y volcanes: Chalco, Amecameca: Pasado y presente.* Vol. 1. Mexico City: El Colegio Mexiquense, 1993.

——. *Notarios y agricultores: Crecimiento y atraso en el campo mexicano, 1780–1920.* Mexico City: Universidad Autónoma Metropolitana, Iztapalapa, Siglo XXI editores, 2008.

——. *Tierra, agua, y bosques: Historia y medio ambiente en el México central.* Mexico City: Centre Français d'études Mexicaines et Centraméricaines, Instituto Mora, Potrerillos Editores, Universidad de Guadalajara, 1996.

Townsend, Camilla. *Malintzin's Choices: An Indian Woman in the Conquest of Mexico.* Albuquerque: University of New Mexico Press, 2006.

Tutino, John. *From Insurrection to Revolution in Mexico: Social Bases of Agrarian Violence, 1750–1940.* Princeton: Princeton University Press, 1989.

——. "The Revolutionary Capacity of Rural Communities: Ecological Autonomy and Its Demise," in *Cycles of Conflict, Centuries of Change: Crisis, Reform, and Revolution in Mexico,* ed. Elisa Servín, Leticia Reina, and John Tutino, 211–268. Durham: Duke University Press, 2007.

Udaondo, Enrique. "Algunos Parques de América: El Parque Criollo 'Ricardo Güiraldes.'" *Boletín de la Unión Panamericana,* 1938.

Ugalde Gómez, Nadia, Américo Sánchez Hernández, María Estela Duarte, and Gerardo Estrada. *Alameda: Visión histórica y estética de la Alameda de la Ciudad de México.* Mexico City: Américo Arte Editores Landucci; Instituto Nacional de Bellas Artes, 2001.

Vanderwood, Paul. *The Power of God against the Guns of Government: Religious Upheaval in Mexico at the Turn of the Nineteenth Century.* Stanford: Stanford University Press, 1998.

——. *Juan Soldado: Rapist, Murderer, Martyr, Saint.* Durham: Duke University, 2004.

van Heijnsbergen, P. *International Legal Protection of Wild Fauna and Flora.* Amsterdam: IOS Press, 1997.

Vaughan, Mary Kay. *Cultural Politics of Revolution: Teachers, Peasants, and Schools in Mexico, 1930–1940.* Tucson: University of Arizona Press, 1997.

Vos, Jan de. *Oro verde: La conquista de la Selva Lancondona por los madereros tabasquenos, 1822–1949.* Mexico City: Fondo Cultura Económica, 1988.

Wakild, Emily. "Border Chasm: International Boundary Parks and Mexican Conservation, 1935–1945." *Environmental History* 14:3 (2009): 453–475.

——. "'It Is to Preserve Life, to Work for the Trees': The Steward of Mexican Forests, Miguel Ángel de Quevedo, 1862–1948." *Forest History Today* (Spring/Fall 2006): 4–14.

——. "Naturalizing Modernity: Urban Parks, Public Gardens, and Drainage Projects in Porfirian Mexico City." *Estudios Mexicanos/Mexican Studies,* 23:1 (2007): 101–123.

Walsh, Casey. "Eugenic Acculturation: Manuel Gamio, Migration Studies, and the Anthropology of Development in Mexico, 1910–1940." *Latin American Perspectives,* 31:5 (2004): 118–145.

Warman, Arturo. *"We Come to Object": The Peasants of Morelos and the National State.* Trans. Stephen K. Ault. Baltimore: Johns Hopkins University Press, 1980.

Warren, Louis. *The Hunters Game: Poachers and Conservationists in Twentieth-Century America*. New Haven: Yale University Press, 1997.

Waters, Wendy. "Remapping Identities: Road Construction and Nation Building in Postrevolutionary Mexico," in *The Eagle and the Virgin: Nation and Cultural Revolution in Mexico, 1920–1940*, ed. Mary Kay Vaughan and Stephen E. Lewis, 221–242. Durham: Duke University Press, 2006.

Weiner, Douglas R. *A Little Corner of Freedom: Russian Nature Protection from Stalin to Gorbachev*. Pittsburgh: University of Pittsburgh Press, 1999.

——. *Models of Nature: Ecology, Conservation, and Cultural Revolution in Soviet Russia*. Pittsburgh: University of Pittsburgh Press, 1989.

Weisman, Alan. *Gaviotas: A Village to Reinvent the World*. White River Junction, VT: Chelsea Green, 1998.

West, Patrick C., and Steven R. Brechin, eds. *Resident Peoples and National Parks: Social Dilemmas and Strategies in International Conservation*. Tucson: University of Arizona Press, 1991.

Wilcox, Clifford. *Robert Redfield and the Development of American Anthropology*. Lanham, MD: Lexington Books, 2004.

Wilkie, Raymond. *San Miguel: A Mexican Collective Ejido*. Stanford: Stanford University Press, 1971.

Wilson, Edward O. *Biophilia*. Cambridge, MA: Harvard University Press, 1984.

Womack, John. *Zapata and the Mexican Revolution*. New York: Knopf, 1969.

Worster, Donald. *Nature's Economy: A History of Ecological Ideas*. Cambridge: Cambridge University Press, [1977] 1994.

Wright, Angus. *The Death of Ramón González: The Modern Agricultural Dilemma*. Austin: University of Texas Press, 1990.

Wright-Rios, Edward. *Revolutions in Mexican Catholicism: Reform and Revelation in Oaxaca, 1887–1934*. Durham: Duke University Press, 2009.

Young, Emily. "Local People and Conservation in Mexico's El Vizcaino Biosphere Reserve." *Geographical Review* 89:3 (1999): 364–390.

Zerner, Charles, ed. *People, Plants, and Justice: The Politics of Nature Conservation*. New York: Columbia University Press, 2000.

Zolov, Eric. *Refried Elvis: The Rise of Mexican Counterculture*. Berkeley: University of California Press, 1999.

Zúñiga Navarrete, Ángel. *Las tierras y montañas de Tepoztlán, Morelos*. Mexico City: Ángel Zúñiga Navarrete, 1995.

Illustration Credits

Mexican national parks, ca. 1942. Courtesy of the Archivo General de la Nación, Fondo Secretaría de Agricultura e Recursos Hidráulicos, box 1425, file 1/1609, vol. 2.

Popocatépetl and Iztaccíhuatl from the north. Reproduced with permission from the Fundación ICA.

National Parks in the Valley of Mexico, ca. 1940. Map by Mapping Specialists.

Walking along the road to Desierto de los Leones, 1925. Reproduced with permission of the Fototeca Nacional de Instituto Nacional de Antropología e Historia; © 372204 CONACULTA.INAH.SINAFO.FN.MÉXICO

The nursery at Viveros de Coyoacán, ca. 1920. Reproduced with permission of the Fototeca Nacional de Instituto Nacional de Antropología e Historia; © 121333 CONACULTA.INAH.SINAFO.FN.MÉXICO

A lake in Lagunas de Zempoala National Park. Reproduced with permission of the Fototeca Nacional de Instituto Nacional de Antropología e Historia; © 372581 CONACULTA.INAH.SINAFO.FN.MÉXICO

An excursion to the lake at the future Lagunas de Zempoala National Park in 1935. Reproduced with permission of the Fototeca Nacional de Instituto Nacional de Antropología e Historia; © 373136 CONACULTA.INAH.SINAFO.FN.MÉXICO

Popocatépetl and Iztaccíhuatl, with Amecameca in the foreground. Reproduced with permission from the Fundación ICA.

Popocatépetl, forests, the San Rafael paper factory, and fields, ca. 1910. Reproduced with permission of the Fototeca Nacional de Instituto Nacional de Antropología e Historia; © 459733 CONACULTA.INAH.SINAFO.FN.MÉXICO

Climbers on Popocatépetl, with Iztaccíhuatl in the background. Charles B. Waite photograph reproduced with permission of the Fototeca Nacional de Instituto Nacional de Antropología e Historia; © 464984 CONACULTA.INAH.SINAFO.FN.MÉXICO

Reproductions of Helgura figure types in a Mexico City marketplace in 2010. Author's collection.

A schematic map of land reform allocations near La Malinche National Park, ca. 1965. Note the national park labels in parcels at the top left and bottom right. The larger park extension is not pictured. The Bold border line in the center is that between the states of Tlaxcala and Puebla. Courtesy of the Archivo General Agrario of the Registro Agrario Nacional.

President Cárdenas with villagers on the pyramid in Tepoztlán, 1935. Courtesy of Fototeca Histórica del Museo Ex-convento de Tepoztlán, Instituto Nacional de Antropología e Historia.

President Cárdenas with villagers on the roof of a former convent in Tepoztlán. Pyramid is within the ridgeline above them. Courtesy of Fototeca Histórica del Museo Ex-convento de Tepoztlán, Instituto Nacional de Antropología e Historia.

The roof of the former convent in Tepoztlán, 1930. Hugo Brehme photo. Reproduced with permission of the Fototeca Nacional de Instituto Nacional de Antropología e Historia; © 373157 CONACULTA.INAH.SINAFO.FN.MÉXICO

On the road through the pass between Popocatépetl and Iztaccíhuatl. Hugo Brehme photograph reproduced with permission of the Fototeca Nacional de Instituto Nacional de Antropología e Historia; © 372715 CONACULTA.INAH.SINAFO.FN.MÉXICO

Index

Note: Page numbers in italics indicate illustrations.

About the Author

Emily Wakild is an assistant professor of history at Wake Forest University. She earned her Ph.D. from the University of Arizona in May 2007. She specializes in the history of Mexico and modern Latin America, with a focus on social change, revolution, and the environment. She has been awarded grants from Fulbright-Hays and the National Endowment for the Humanities for this work. Wakild has published several journal articles, including "Naturalizing Modernity: Urban Parks, Public Gardens, and Drainage Projects in Porfirian Mexico City," in *Estudios Mexicanos/ Mexican Studies*, 2007, and "Border Chasm: International Boundary Parks and Mexican Conservation, 1935–1945," in *Environmental History* in 2009. Her next project will be a comparative history of modern conservation in Latin America.

Emily teaches courses on all periods of Latin American and environmental history as well as a freshman seminar on issues in international development and a research seminar drawing on anthropological theories and field notes. With a biologist, she leads a summer study abroad program on nature conservation in Peru. Prior to graduate school, she spent three years teaching middle school through the Teach for America program in deep South Texas.

→ drug topics
→ Stratfor
→ Cell
→ final paper topics
→ review classes / Martin Leats
→ Cristero Rebellion

CPSIA information can be obtained at www.ICGtesting.com
Printed in the USA
LVOW080007110213

319488LV00002B/4/P

9 780816 529575